THE FLAGSTAFF "DIG"

"Artifacts have been recovered throughout the shaft; of the 58 predictions tested so far, 55 have been proven correct. *If the predictions continue to prove accurate, not only our concepts about the first men in the Americas but all our concepts about human cultural and biological evolution will have to be drastically revised.* The revolutionary picture of the past that the Flagstaff Dig reveals does not deal with simplistic evolution or with Gifts from Space Gods—it deals with 100,000-year-old evidence of a lost human race of which this site was only an outpost!"

from the *Introduction*

To a lovely Gal —
Audi
Wright

PSYCHIC ARCHAEOLOGY

TIME MACHINE TO THE PAST

JEFFREY GOODMAN

BERKLEY BOOKS, NEW YORK

PSYCHIC ARCHAEOLOGY

A Berkley Book / published by arrangement with
Archaeological Research Associates, Inc.

PRINTING HISTORY
Berkley edition / July 1978
Second printing / October 1980

For information address: Archaeological Research Associates, Inc.,
3737 North Country Club Road
#219 S, Tucson, Arizona 85719.

ISBN: 0-425-05000-9

A BERKLEY BOOK® TM 757,375

PRINTED IN THE UNITED STATES OF AMERICA

This book is dedicated to my mother,
Irene S. Goodman

Acknowledgments

Thanks to D. Scott Rogo for his editorial assistance. And thanks to my wife Phyllis and children Joy and Robin for their unlimited patience and help on all fronts, and also to the following who have given me substantial encouragement, help and/or support: Richard Ambler, Tony Arlotta, Polly Baker, Jim Baraff, Frank Baranowski, Mike Brewer, Bob Calhoun, Kathy Campbell, Charles Thomas Cayce, Hugh Lynn Cayce, Bob Diggs, Don Dove, Fran Farely, Art Gilliam, Richard Heavly, Paul Henshaw, Charles Hoffman, Glen Huling, Beverly Jaegers, William Kautz, John and Cheryl Kettenhoffen, Sol Lewis and Friend, Joseph Long, Mark, Paul Martin, John and Betty Nissen, Tom Perry, Chuck Peterson, William Rathje, Peter Riddle, Cecil Rogers, Phil Schaeffer, Dennis Stanford, Dave Stanowski, Brad Steiger, Harry Stenerman, and Jane Underwood. Very special thanks to Aron and Doris Abrahamsen, Donna and Elbert Burgett, Bob and Marilyn Christian, Thomas Jaeger, Jaine Smith, and John White. And finally thanks to the many, many others who dug at the site, supplied supplemental psychic information, or just listened.

Contents

Foreword

In the early fifties the University of Michigan campus was diverted from its usual preoccupations by an unusual news story. A history professor admitted that he had been consulting a spiritualist. The séances, he claimed, helped him to uncover new facts about the Napoleonic era. We all enjoyed the thought of a psychic historian, but nobody seemed surprised, much less outraged, when he was quietly dismissed.

Energy and enthusiasm were up for pure research. Successful young Ph.D.'s in white lab coats could apply for, and sometimes win, grants with more research money than their professors had known in their entire careers. The ancient walls guarding privileged academic fiefdoms fell, or, more often, were simply overrun by new programs. In those days an ESP psychologist might hope for seminar privileges only if he came armored with a Ph.D. and tenure. A remarkable hint of what lay ahead came from the Harvard botanist Richard Schultes, who shared his experiences of Upper Amazon tribes and their hallucinogenic drugs. Nevertheless, for most of us there was more than enough adventure in conventional science to ignore a far-out ethnobotanist who had actually tried exotic tropical drugs with the natives.

But in the sixties conventional science had grown monumental; it was showing signs of bloat. The spirit of adventure had waned. My own middle-age slump, I rationalized. Nevertheless, I felt that the old missionary excitement seemed harder to detect among undergraduates. Then, increasingly, the old, and some new, mysteries—the new parasciences—intruded. One of the best researchers in atmospheric physics at Arizona threw himself into the investigation of UFO sightings. More unsettling reports came over the ivy wall; acupuncture, psychokinesis, and psychic surgery, to name a few.

Now, in the late seventies, the uproar among parascientists

outside the stockade of orthodoxy simply can't be ignored. For me, a more tolerant attitude came partly through the unpredictable and undeniable new experiences on a well-guided acid trip. In my novitiate during the fifties I would have dismissed Psychic Archaeology, as I did the psychic historian, with no more than a chuckle. Now, with William James, I know from experience. Logic by itself is a trap. The unknown should be dealt with patiently and with humility.

In October, 1975, Jeff Goodman took me to his site at Flagstaff. He knew that I advocate a version of new-world prehistory which ties the extinction of mammoths, mastodons, and other large mammals to the first human invasion of America. In my chronology this happened a good deal later than the age Jeff would attribute to his site at Flagstaff, as it is my belief that there was no one in North America before twelve thousand years ago. This doesn't mean I'm right; it does mean I'm automatically, and perhaps blindly, skeptical to claims such as Jeff's.

On our ride to Flagstaff, Jeff convinced me that Psychic Archaeology has some theory going for it. Prehistorians estimate conservatively that a huge population—forty million human ancestors—preceded us in an Ice Age world, before the rise of agriculture. The life of the wandering hunters of the Paleolithic must of necessity have sharpened the senses. Sight, smell, hearing, taste, and touch were all functioning differently, and I suspect much more acutely, for the Neanderthals from the way they do for us. If my purpose were to search for a sensitive medium for ESP research or dowsing, or for Jeff's brand of psychic geology and archaeology, I'd seek out a Neanderthaler. I'd look for someone who combined acute awareness out of doors with limited speech. Lacking complicated speech patterns or intense cognitive skill, the Neanderthals may well have enjoyed tremendous psychic power. Such an awareness—the ability perhaps to know the location of animals, other tribes, and enemies, and to know what was on and in the ground—would command tremendous selective advantage in the last million years. Then, and much earlier, were the human senses formed. How much have we lost, living indoors, in the last few centuries?

At Flagstaff, I was impressed with Jeff's field technique, willing to believe his geological-age interpretation, and dubious mainly about his supposed artifacts. Were they indeed man-made and not the result of weathering? I'm not an archaeologist, and if those who diagnose tools *all* agree that Jeff has the real thing, then I must yield. I believe that the Flagstaff site is not better or worse than most of the early-early-man sites given by MacNeish in the May-June, 1976, issue of *American Scientist*. That Aran, Jeff's medium, could locate a good potential site is certainly newsworthy. At the very least, Jeff's Flagstaff site deserves an attempt at replication.

It's still speculative. No one has captured a UFO or taught us when to expect a sighting. Western medicine can't account for acupuncture, and perhaps it works well as an anesthetic only for those with high pain thresholds. The psychic surgeons of the Philippines have not been subjected to an experimental design to prove "scientifically" their healing powers. No specimens have been obtained of Bigfoot or of the Loch Ness Monster. No spacecraft landing sites have been found near the mysterious monumental prehistoric designs at Nasca, in Peru. Opportunists are cashing in on our credulity. There is much chaff to winnow. The risk of failure and rejection is great. Nevertheless, I think the chance of surprise is quite good. Jeff Goodman's stimulating move into Psychic Archaeology deserves our serious attention.

DR. PAUL S. MARTIN
Professor and Chief Scientist,
Laboratory of Paleoenvironmental Studies,
Department of Geosciences, University of Arizona

Introduction

> The whole history of scientific advancement is full of scientists investigating phenomena the Establishment did not believe were there.
>
> ——*Margaret Mead to the American Association for the Advancement of Science*

Psychic Archaeology demonstrates the everyday truth of psychic phenomena. I always knew that eventually a few dedicated scientists would provide unimpeachable proof of psychic phenomena. This was years before my own head-on collision with the world of the paranormal. Several years ago my interest in archaeology led me on an Alice in Wonderland journey into the realm of the psychic, a journey that changed my entire outlook on life and reality. On this journey *many times over* I came face-to-face with the work of scientists which constituted unimpeachable proof of the reality of psychic phenomena—work not confined to dreary labs and over technical journals, but exciting work done in towering mountains, shimmering deserts, and steaming jungles around the world. For archaeology is the search for man's past, work involving the discovery and understanding of tangible relics from long ago.

My journey began as a graduate archaeological student studying remains of people and cultures from the distant past. Where did the first men in North and South America live, I wondered, and where did they come from? At the time, I wanted to discover an entirely new site that would shed light on this perplexing issue. I felt that the famed Dr. Louis Leakey was right when he guessed of much, much earlier dates for the first appearance of man in the Americas. During my special studies, *I have indeed been fortunate to discover such a crucial site in the mountains outside Flagstaff, Arizona*. But in making this discovery there was no gnashing of teeth and no endless hours of exploration. The discovery itself was relatively easy. I simply asked a man who many claimed had psychic powers to tell me where I could find such a new site. To the dismay of the academic establishment, the discovery was based on nothing more than the carefully documented tape recordings sent to me by this psychic aeronautical engineer from Oregon, Aron Abrahamson, and my own psychic dreams.

The digging so far consists of a 28-foot-deep exploratory shaft. Not only was the psychic amazingly accurate in locating a new deep site which had no surface indications to recommend it—a site most archaeology professors said couldn't possibly exist—but the psychic was also amazingly accurate in the geological, chronological, and archaeological details he predicted we would encounter in our diggings. Crude stone tools have been recovered throughout the shaft as predicted; changes in geology have occurred at the exact depths predicted and radiocarbon dating proves the very early dates predicted. Of the fifty-eight specific predictions tested so far, fifty-one have proven correct. That is 87 percent accuracy. But just as important as statistics, at this new site we have already discovered what could be the oldest clear-cut evidence of man in the Americas—over 100,000 years old. At the very least, we have to credit psychic power with the discovery of a significant new early man site. Critics and professors may scoff at psychic sources, but they can't scorn the discovery itself. Simply stated, at Flagstaff psychic methods put meat on the archaeologist's table!

The full story of this discovery will be related in later chapters, but I must say now that if Aron's further predictions continue to prove accurate at this site, not only will our concepts about the first men in the Americas have to be changed, but also all our concepts about man's biological and cultural evolution will have to be drastically revised. The revolutionary and exciting picture of the past that Aron has painted does not deal with simplistic and orderly evolution, nor does it deal with Gifts from Space Gods. It deals with long-buried gifts from a lost human race of which this site was an outpost. We are presented an incredible story which is already being substantiated by artifacts and promises the discovery of human bones from a race academicians don't even believe ever existed.

After my first round of excavations at Flagstaff, I discovered that I was not the first archaeologist to rely successfully on psychic information. I learned the story of the Glastonbury scripts and how presumably dead monks can speak. Just before Frederick Bligh Bond became director of excavations at the ruined Glastonbury Abbey in England in 1907, he established a dialogue with the allegedly long-dead inhabitants of this historic British site through the automatic writings of a gifted psychic named John Bartlett. By following their directions, he was able to reconstruct the intricate features of a shrine which at the time lay in total ruin. Bond also received a very personal and touching account of medieval life. Bligh Bond's pioneering work makes him the father of psychic archaeology.

Next I learned of the case of Stefan Ossowiecki, an amazing Polish wizard. A professor in the prehistory department of the University of Warsaw experimented with this famous Polish psychic who was able to recall scenes from the ages when Neanderthal and Cro-Magnon Man inhabited Europe. As he was handed stone spearpoints, bone fishhooks and ceramic figurines from the university's collection, scenes of the past unfolded before his eyes like a motion picture panorama.

I also learned of the Akashic Records and the story of the Sleeping Prophet. Edgar Cayce was an American clairvoyant who, after entering a sleeplike trance induced by self-hypnosis, said he was able to read the Akashic Records. Cayce was able to predict and detail accurately a number of key archaeological discoveries decades before they were actually made. He spoke not only about past peoples, but also of civilizations which have not yet been uncovered. The Flagstaff site may have some bearing here! Through Cayce's readings we can sail along with the first ocean travelers, walk the Holy Land with Jesus, and confront the enigma of Atlantis.

Ossowiecki, Cayce, Bond. These men can be ridiculed or forgotten by some. They can be viewed as believe-it-or-not curios. But the truth is that all research on psychic frontiers must be dedicated to their memory.

As I came to learn of the historical precedents for psychic

archaeology, I was also surprised to discover that other archaeologists are also using psychics in their work. I came to learn of the quest of the president of the Canadian Archaeological Association, Dr. Norman Everson, head of the archaeology department of the University of Toronto, who has been successfully using the advice of psychics in his excavations of Iroquois settlements. Other Canadian archaeologists have also begun to use several psychics who have employed everything from map dowsing to psychometry to assist in locating ruins and buried artifacts. Indeed, I discovered that psychic archaeology is presently being conducted everywhere from South America to Russia. Archaeology today is in the throes of a revolution where ESP is replacing the spade as archaeology's primary tool.

Man has always had a curious fascination about his own past. Where did man come from? Why is he here? These are questions which each of us has pondered. Archaeologists, both amateur and professional, have been crawling around, digging up, and exploring the earth's surface in the hope that some vestiges of the past can be unearthed. Ruins and artifacts are the only clues we have about human evolution from primitive culture to modern technological society. But even when archaeologists have been lucky enough to find these remnants of bygone peoples, the discoveries haven't told us very much. All too often all that has survived is "garbage," the broken pots and pans of their world. Archaeologists have had to reconstruct the life-styles of ancient peoples by relying on the meagerest of clues, while the most important questions seem securely locked away: What were these people trying to accomplish with their lives? Why did their cultures evolve the way they did? What daily activities and exploits concerned them?

But now the door to the past *can* be unlocked! The keys to a fabulous time machine are dangling in front of the archaeologist like a carrot before a mule; for, just like mules, archaeologists will have to overcome stubbornness, fear, and prejudice to grasp these keys. By using this time machine we can secure for ourselves a front seat at the court of the pharaohs. We can watch their ancient ceremonies being performed; we can hear the chants of their priests, and watch the smoke of burning incense as it curls into the air.

How is this all possible? Where is this time machine?

Man's intuition can provide the answers to his desire to learn the mysteries of the past. Deep within the mind is a faculty—extrasensory perception, or ESP—which can be used to explore the ancient mysteries. Using gifted psychics to aid in our archaeological exploration can be as fruitful as if we really did have a tool like H. G. Wells's *Time Machine*. Today we face mountainous evidence that certain gifted people have a psychic porthole to the past which allows them access to information about ancient people; the way they lived and the way they died. Now their beliefs and attitudes appear as well preserved as their pots and stone tools. If a psychic were to touch a piece of rock from the Yucatán, he might be enveloped by visions of or impressions about the Mayans. Touching volcanic ash from Italy could catapult him to the lip of Mount Vesuvius as it rained death on a sleeping Pompeii. All we need do is sit back and listen . . . and learn.

The discovery that psychics can serve archaeology has startling implications for science in general. Where does this psychic information come from? What is its source? The ultimate answer will jolt religious leaders, psychologists, and even the man on the street. Some scholars have proposed that this information comes from spirits of the dead. Others believe that the psychics are activating memories of their own past lives in these cultures. Or, as the noted psychoanalyst C. G. Jung believed, there may be some collective unconscious memory within man's mind into which we can dip to learn of our own past. Even Eastern religion teaches us that there is an Akashic record, some nebulous cosmic reservoir, to use William James's phrase, in which all the thoughts and actions of man have been recorded since even before man began making physical records of his life. Finally we have to ask ourselves: How adequate are our concepts of time and space? Can they accommodate *psychical* reality as well as physical reality? What is the true nature of man and what are his highest potentials?

Today we are watching a revolution taking place. This is the emergence of psychic archaeology. All over the world archaeologists and researchers are beginning to rely on psychic information for clues about where to dig, what they can expect to find, and what the answers to remaining questions are.

In this book, after learning how psychics are helping us to

solve the mysteries of the ancients, we will also learn more about the psychic force, or psi-faculty itself, whose potential is unlimited. We are seeing science give birth to a new way of studying the past; in the centuries ahead, man may view our methods and discoveries today as the infancy of the universe's greatest science.

PART I

The Founders

Here are the stories of three men who first penetrated the veil of time and returned with relics. Their journeys have been scientifically confirmed. They helped establish the basic premises and the great potential of psychic archaeology.

Chapter 1

Dead Monks Speak—

Bligh Bond and His Quest at Glastonbury

Man has always sought to unlock the secrets of the past with all the tools available to him. Psychic archaeology was first used in 1907, when a mild-mannered ecclestiastic architect named Frederick Bligh Bond consulted a psychic friend as an attempt to understand the past. Bond had long been interested in the ancient Abbey of Glastonbury, a lost citadel that he hoped to excavate.

Until Bond recruited his psychic aide, virtually nothing was known of its design or floor plan. The abbey was only the last in a long succession of shrines built on the same location. In fact, the first rituals celebrated at Glastonbury took place before Christianity. There is also evidence that the Celts had built a temple on this island site. According to most historical accounts, Glastonbury became the first Christian church in England when a chapel for St. Mary was built there in A.D. 166. The history of Glastonbury is saturated with colorful and moving tales. Legend has it that Joseph of Arimathea introduced Christianity to Britain by bringing the blood of Jesus to Glastonbury. In another version, Glastonbury was the location of the Isle of Avalon described in the tales of King Arthur. It is even claimed that Arthur himself was buried in the sacred ground of Glastonbury and a plaque is there today commemorating the alleged site.

Despite these intriguing legends, we have only a few scattered details about the abbey before the eighth century. It was then that King Ine of Wessex built the first portion of the abbey. In 1184 the abbey and its subsidiary buildings were ravaged by fire but were rebuilt by King Henry II and thereafter had an almost unbroken history of both physical and spiritual expansion. It prospered as did no other abbey in

England; it was a western Rome. Its religious and social importance is no better illustrated than by the fact that three kings—Edmund, Edgar, and Edmund Ironside—chose to be buried there. Thousands of pilgrims came each year, and since the monks manufactured everything from gloves to clocks, the abbey became a trade center as well. Glastonbury became enormously wealthy and was continually expanded and refurbished. Eventually the original abbey grew into a town within itself consisting of one hundred buildings that housed five hundred monks and two thousand workmen. It consisted of a church with jeweled altars, neighboring workshops, vineyards, fields, a library and even a university. Glastonbury Abbey was a brilliant beacon piercing the medieval darkness.

Despite being one of the last Catholic churches suppressed under Henry VIII's dissolution decree, Glastonbury Abbey's end in 1539 was sudden and merciless. When the new Protestant regime took control of England, every building at the abbey was pulled down except the abbot's kitchen. The stones of its buildings were carted away, almost as conscious desecration, to pave roads and build barns and farmhouses. Of course, the treasure from its altars disappeared. By 1600 A.D. all that was left to mark the site of what had been the most important church in England was nothing more than a few ruined walls and its foundations. In 1907 the ruined Abbey of Glastonbury was bought by the Church of England from a private party and the deed placed with the Archbishop of Canterbury. The Somerset Archaeological and Historical Society was empowered to oversee any excavation attempts. The likely choice as chief excavator was Frederick Bligh Bond, one of the most respected and able church architects of his day.

Bond was born on June 30, 1854, in Kent County, England. His father, the Reverend Hooky Bond, was headmaster of Marlborough Royal Free Grammar School and later of Bath College. Frederick was his mother's favorite among seven brothers and sisters. He was clever, but moody and "different" from the other children. Even at an early age he felt alienated from the world and turned to imaginary or unseen spirits and supernatural presences, fantasies more exciting and inviting than the doldrums of his real life. Bond has provided us with these clues in his own memoirs:

> I could not enter into the normal pleasures of childhood. Always ailing and sickly, I shrank from contact with the robust personalities of my young associates, preferring a dream life in which imagination afforded me always a strange solace and a sense of companionship . . . that seemed to transcend the limitations of my conscious being . . . but about the age of fourteen the glory faded and I was shot out unreconciled into a world I neither understood nor took any interest in. I shall not attempt to describe a suffering which can never be put into words. I had known heaven, I now knew hell. Small wonder that the state between seemed to me dull, futile, and meaningless. But there came soon the first revelation of a way of escape . . . in the form of a knowledge of the spiritualistic literature of the day. The book which made the earliest mark with me was Mrs. Crowe's *Night Side of Nature*, which I practically knew by heart when I was fourteen or so.

Written in 1848, Katherine Crowe's book had all the spice of a Gothic thriller; yet it was one of the first sincere attempts to compile a wide range of psychic material for serious consideration. Organized science did not take note for many decades, but Bond did; it was only natural to amalgamate his psychic and ecclesiastic interests.

Bond's fascination with the paranormal was set aside when he threw himself into his architectural studies after high school. With two established architects as his mentors, Sir A. Bloomfield and Charles Hansen (who specialized in Gothic architecture), Bond learned quickly. He easily passed the examination of the Royal Institute of British Architects and was thereupon admitted as a Fellow (F.R.I.B.A.). He became Hansen's full partner, specializing in Gothic architecture and the restoration of old churches. Eventually he set up his own practice as an ecclesiastic architect and for some time was the diocesan architect. As Bond was called upon more and more to restore medieval churches, his personal interest in the life and architecture of those times underwent a transformation. His articles began to appear in a number of publications. Seven years of research into medieval woodwork culminated in a massive two-volume study, *Roofscreens and Rooflofts*, that was published in 1909 and established him as one of England's foremost authorities on medieval church architecture. Also about this time, Bond became a member of the Somerset Archaeological and Historical Society. His importance in ecclesiastical and archaeological quarters grew steadily as a plethora of articles, correspondence, notes, and debates flowed from his pen and were published in the society's *Proceedings*. As a result, Bond became increasingly in demand as a lecturer for various church, antiquarian and historical groups.

With these impressive credentials, it is easy to see why Bond was the obvious choice to supervise excavations at Glastonbury. Bond's interest in the abbey did not begin with his selection to excavate there, however; his curiosity had been aroused sometime earlier.

It all started on the afternoon of November 17, 1907 when Bond decided to carry out a psychic experiment with his friend Captain John Bartlett. This was a rather unusual pastime for two proper Victorian gentlemen, but Bartlett was an amateur psychic of sorts who was able to produce automatic writing: that is, he let his hand write without consciously willing what it should write. Although Bartlett had dabbled with automatic writing, he had never tried systematically to develop or discipline the ability. So the November 17 experiment began half-playfully. Imagine the staid, bespectacled, gaunt-looking Bond in his study with tongue in cheek as he rested his fingers on the back of Bartlett's hand. Within Bartlett's firm grasp was a pencil poised over a sheet of foolscap. Bond asked the first question, addressing it to no "specific entity".

"Can you tell us anything about Glastonbury Abbey?"

Bartlett's outstretched hand scribbled an erratic reply: "All knowledge is eternal and is available to mental sympathy. I was not in sympathy with monks. I cannot find a monk yet."

Two plans of the abbey were drawn as Bartlett's hand struggled with the force moving it. Both resembled blindfold tracings. The first plan showed the main features of the abbey, and written over the sketch was the name Gulielmus Monachus (William the Monk). The second diagram sketched the great enclosure of the abbey church in detail.

The first drawing puzzled Bond: It showed a chapel at the east of the abbey which didn't seem correct. The position of the chapel was not in accordance with architectural practices of the time it was supposedly built. With a mixture of scorn and true curiosity, he asked for a more careful drawing of the east end of the abbey. Again a rectangular chapel was drawn on the east end; as in the earlier diagram, the chapel was drawn double, as if to emphasize it. Whoever was communicating to Bond wrote in an almost indecipherable script beneath the sketch.

"Please repeat, we cannot read this," Bond urged impatiently. The writing continued.

Bond requested that the length of the chapel be given again and, growing more and more excited, asked the name of the abbot who built the chapel.

The answer, in Latin, was that a very large chapel named after King Edgar existed at the east end of the abbey. This had been built by Abbot Beere and was added to, along with other building projects, by Abbot Whiting, in whose reign it was also destroyed.

This information seemed hopelessly muddled. No existing data about the abbey showed any sort of major eastern extension or chapel as was so emphatically drawn by Bartlett. These psychic sketches showed a very different plan for Glastonbury than the one which scholars presumed had existed. The logical conclusion was that these drawings were products of Bond's and Bartlett's subconscious fantasies. The two men shook hands and returned to more acceptable pursuits.

In 1908, almost a year later, Bond was appointed director of excavations for the old ruined abbey. As he began his work in the summer of 1909, it gradually became apparent to him that the drawings he had received previously were uncannily accurate. Contrary to all expectations, on the east end of the abbey, Bond unearthed a large chapel—the Edgar Chapel. Even the measurements given by or through Bartlett were correct! Bond was only too well aware of the controversy in which he would be embroiled if he publicly announced that his discoveries had been guided and predicted by psychic advice. The only clue Bond gave for the success of the digging in what appeared to be barren ground was presented in his first excavation report:

"I had formed the opinion," he wrote, "that some work of a more extensive and important nature was to be looked for, and in the winter of 1907 this feeling had become a strong conviction."

As Bond's biographer, Dr. William Kenawell, has written in *The Quest at Glastonbury* , these cryptic words no doubt were an allusion to Bartlett's automatic writing. After all, Bond was in a difficult position. The Church of England owned Glastonbury, and Bond's appointment had come from the bishop. Was he supposed to tell the ecclesiastic authorities that his success was due to messages received from dead monks? Despite this dilemma, in the years that followed Bond went on to conduct his excavations using just this source for clues and directions—directions given him by intelligences who claimed to be the monks who had built and lived at the abbey. They called themselves the Company of Avalon, the Watchers from the Other Side.

Not until 1918 did Bond publish the full story of his psychic probes and discoveries at Glastonbury. He called it *The Gate of Remembrance*. With its publication, the abbey walls reverberated: budgets were cut, a co-director was appointed, new committees were convened to inundate Bond with red tape, and an attempt was made to ease him out completely. Then in 1922, Joseph Armatage Robinson, the dean of Welles, dismissed Bond and put an end to the excavations. Landmarks were obliterated and trenches filled. It seemed some people wished Glastonbury had never existed.

Eventually Bond tried to get the Society of Antiquaries, the Royal Archaeological Institute, and the Society for Psychical Research interested in forming a joint committee to persuade the abbey trustees to allow him to resume excavations. The plan died before it was even born; the trustees banned Bond from the abbey grounds. The only glimmer of hope came one day in 1937. A group of American friends were interested in financing excavations at Glastonbury, following Bond's suggestions. They wanted to test his statements concerning buried treasure, the Holy Grail, and the location of a church thought to have been built by Joseph of Aramathea. The group, by not hinting of any link with Bond and his methods, cajoled the trustees into granting permission to excavate. Funds were put up for the work. But Bond demolished the deal. His impatience and eccentricity got the better of him, and word soon leaked out that he was coming back to dig at Glastonbury. The trustees reneged, and the plan was shelved. So, although his life was studded by discovery and psychic triumph, it was also a tragedy. Bond died of a heart attack on March 8, 1945.

In 1952 the same American group was able to reach an accord with the Glastonbury trustees, who graciously accepted the funds that were offered. After ten more years of intermittent excavations, the ancient parts of the abbey that Bond had spoken about still remained unexplored. Dr. Radleigh Radford, who was in charge of the excavations, did report the finding of at least one pyramid foundation and perhaps a second, but for some reason was unable to explore them fully. So Glastonbury remains much as Bond left it.

This story has climaxed only in recent years. The noted architect, Keith Critchtlow, has independently confirmed Bond's findings and hopes that the climate is now finally favorable to permit archaeologists, the church, and others to recognize and continue the work of this pioneer, for, ironically, while Bond succeeded in his psychic work at Glastonbury, he also failed at it.

Today, with psychic archaeology still scorned, it is worth considering the reasons why Bond failed. One area which might have contributed to this sorry state of affairs was Bond's personal life. Bond was prone to unnecessary worry, and he was constantly defending and attacking, believing that plots were brewing all around him to deprive him of his just credit and rewards. His fears were partially justified, but his paranoia eroded his character. He became eccentric—a person with whom it was very difficult to deal. Despite his *own* character flaws, Bond had another problem to contend with—his estranged and mentally disturbed wife, who never passed up an opportunity to character-assassinate the husband who was legally separated but not divorced from her. She made it her life's nefarious work to persecute him, both personally and legally. She accused him of molesting their daughter and subjecting the girl to various "occult" practices. Bond had to defend himself against these and many other charges continually. Although he was successful, the constant harangues caused him difficulty within his community. Also, he did not have the social connections to make his work easier. So while he was engaged in mental fisticuffs with the church and academia, he was battling his wife as well in a rearguard action.

The format and tone of his reports also contributed to Bond's eventual failure to make a mark on archaeology. He was caught in the ticklish position of when, who, and how much to tell about the *real* reason for his successful work at

Glastonbury. If he provoked church authorities, he would not only place his directorship in jeopardy, but could ruin his entire career, for Bond was also the diocesan architect and specialized in church reconstruction. These institutions provided his bread and butter. He once said, "Archaeological research has been hidebound, and it must be admitted with some reason, for as a comparatively young science it has had to protect itself against many a foolish fantasy launched by a half-instructed or overenthusiastic devotee."

Bond placed all his archaeological cards on the table before making his incredible psychic story public. So far just his official excavation reports were in print. Except for a small circle of friends including Captain Bartlett; Sir William Barrett, a founder of the Society for Psychical Research; and Everard Feilding, the secretary of the society, few knew the story behind the Glastonbury excavations until ten years after Bond had made his first startling discovery under the guidance of the "Company." Even in 1918, in *The Gate of Remembrance*, Captain Bartlett's identity was disguised as "John Alleyne," a name Bond probably borrowed from one inscribed on a fifteenth-century tomb found in the Abbey precincts. To validate his book, Bond included in it a letter from Everard Feilding:

". . . There is no question that the writing about the Edgar Chapel preceded the discovery of it by many months. I was present at . . . the beginning of——'s [Bartlett's] automatism . . . and that was before you ever started your work at Glastonbury and before you were even appointed to the work."

But some critics were still suspicious even in the light of this validation because of the long delay between the excavations and the book's publication. Skeptics also pointed an accusing finger at the fact that dialogue from some of the sittings had been deleted in the published version, and that the accounts of other sittings were missing from the book entirely.

It is true that only twenty-five of the fifty "Glastonbury" sittings held during the critical period prior to and during the excavations were included. Bond stated that this was done in order to spare the reader from having to wade through information not germane to the abbey and to edit writings which were either illegible or which made no sense. Even so, the exact sequence of the sittings and excavations is confusing at times. Yet there are clear sections of the book in which Bond compares portions of the script to the existing data about Glastonbury as well as the excavation results. In addition, one section is devoted to unfinished excavations where the scripts suggest future discoveries. Bond stated clearly what he expected to find on further digs, and no clearer statement of any research expectations and results anywhere can be found in archaeological literature today.

Of course one could also charge that Bond cooked up the whole story. Could he have invented the whole thing post hoc, to give spice and flavor to the story of his discoveries? Those tempted to believe this should consider first, the sheer magnitude of the many sittings and even the many internal consistencies that they contain; second, the "tip-offs" published while critical excavations were directly underway; third, the originally absurd thesis regarding the hitherto-unknown Edgar Chapel; fourth, the sum of what Bond stood to lose by endorsing these controversial methods; and finally, the influence of the Company on Bond's purely academic publications—he even quoted a portion of scripts before the queen during her royal visit to Glastonbury in 1909. In his eighth excavation report dated 1915, Bond almost revealed his secret by alluding to Bartlett by name (before he disguised him as John Alleyne), so the story could not be totally post hoc. Bond reported:

> This may seem a fitting place for the acknowledgment of Capt. J.A. Bartlett's services to the writer in the several years of his work at the Abbey. It was an old friendship and a community of interest which led to this association and the sympathy of ideas sometimes almost telepathic in its nature—which existed between the writer and his friend—undoubtedly laid the foundation of much of the success which all along so fortunately attended the work. An association of this nature is apt to produce a subconscious activity which in combination with purely intellectual work, may sometimes yield exceptional results. More might be said on this subject and possibly may in its due time and place.

Perhaps things would have gone more smoothly for Bond had he taken noted archaeological professionals into his confidence at the beginning of his work. Or he could have had transcripts of the sittings notarized and left in a sealed, dated envelope with some outside source. This would have added needed confirmation to the genuineness of the scripts. But then, such particulars never impress skeptics anyway.

Gematria is yet another factor which might have contributed to Bond's downfall. Gematria is the theory that ancient buildings carried within their measurements esoteric codes which revealed the secret knowledge of the builders. The best example of it is the Great Pyramid of Giza in Egypt where the physical dimensions can be directly correlated to mathematical constants and planetary measurements. Bond was a student of this theory and paid great attention to making detailed measurements of the abbey. This somewhat unorthodox practice became a bone of contention between Bond, the Society of Antiquaries, and the church. To this day, archaeologists do not put much credence in the theory. Bond showed bad gamesmanship when he lectured on this subject before an audience that included the newly elected president of the Somerset Archaeological and Historical Society conservative Joseph Armatage Robinson, an Anglican priest and the dean of Welles. The debate went on to incredible lengths as Bond's opponents attempted to discredit him. After he was dismissed, stones at Glastonbury were actually moved to alter the measurements!

The most likely cause of the fiasco, however, was the social-religious implication of Bond's work. As Kenawell prudently asks, "What learned society would not look askance at one of their members who would announce that his work was under the direction through automatic writing of those who once inhabited that very site?" Bond's psychic methods went far beyond the traditions of both archaeology and religion. What was the Church to do? By acknowledging the legitimacy of the extraordinary excavation results, it would in the same breath be acknowledging the Company of Avalon. The church would be drawing itself into the tricky issue of spiritualism and the survival of the soul after death. Survival after death is an issue that the established church could confront in theology and dogma, but not in practical application! How was the bishop supposed to react to a message from the long-dead sixteenth century archbishop regarding religious philosophy? These were heretical issues even before Bond uncovered Glastonbury, the sensitivity of which is reflected in the fact that the bookshop at Glastonbury

Abbey is not permitted to sell any of Bond's many books even to this day. This ban extends beyond his psychic books to his orthodox archaeological handbook on Glastonbury.

So when we ask what went wrong at Glastonbury, we have several possible answers. While Bond had conceived of, applied, and demonstrated a new approach to archaeology, one with immense potential, he failed on one tragic front. While he presented archaeology with a new structure, or paradigm, he failed to overturn the old way of doing things—the conventional "safe" way. Bond failed to get his new paradigm accepted and consequently had to be dismissed along with his "dangerous" ideas.

Of course, nothing can obscure the fact that John Bartlett's psychic help was instrumental in Bond's resurrection of the abbey. The discovery of both the Edgar Chapel and the western towers had been predicted in advance. They were not due to the sheer luck or random reasoning that usually characterizes archaeology. Digging quickly provided the evidence needed to check the accuracy of the information being relayed through Bartlett. And the Edgar Chapel was not the only discovery made as a result of the phantom monks' communications. For example, on April 20, 1908, several months before he began his first excavation season, Bond had received a message from a monk writing under the name Johannes Bryant and was told, "ye shall find proof of ye goodly towers at ye west end." This fact was easily substantiated. Bond dug in the area indicated and uncovered the towers as promised. He felt strongly enough about these results to say in his first excavation report:

". . . it may be said that they [the results] strongly support the theory that the isles were terminated with two massive towers . . . flanking the great west gable of this nave."

The monk's message had been accurate. Bond gave the exact measurements and details of the newly discovered western towers in his fifth excavation report.

How much Bond discovered *solely* on the basis of Bartlett's guidance is hard to determine. One cannot always be certain from his reports whether many of the pertinent psychic messages came before or after key excavations began. For example, on September 1, 1910, Bond received detailed information about what was called the monks' kitchen. In his fourth official report, dated 1911, Bond reports on the excavation but omits to tell the exact date when this work first commenced. There are further complications as well. Because of budgetary problems and the First World War, much of the information Bond received psychically was never followed up; his eventual removal as director of excavations ended any further attempts to substantiate Bartlett's writings.

It is only after discovery that the *real* work of an archaeologist begins. With only a few remnants or artifacts as his "primitive tools," the archaeologist must accurately reconstruct entire buildings and monuments. If a building foundation has been located, the archaeologist might try to recreate the architecture of the building and determine how and for what purpose the structure was used. Here again the cogency of Bond's reliance on psychic help paid multiple dividends. The Company of Avalon not only told him where to dig but also supplied him with key information about the original designs and purposes of the ruined buildings. As Bond tried to reconstruct the Glastonbury of old, they patiently guided him, supplying him with details, dimensions, and even colors. In one sitting they described an altar, how it was used, and gave other information that could never have been brought to light using any of "normal" archaeology's mundane tools.

> We wold make ye see it—square and as it were square buttresses with canopies and imagry. Full forty feet in height, somewhat level in ye toppe like a screene, and in ye midst a faire canopy of guilded stone in width four feet and full of fifteen feet in height and in front an ymage of Our Lady in gold and scarlet robes holding in her hands the Christ and a scepter of power. On either side two doors with steppys leading down to the path for processions behind ye altare. *Can ye not see it?* Black stone and images, and guilding in the hollow places under the ornaments. On ye south side as we deem it ye will find most of ye pieces—all black stone with much guilding and ye effigies of ye Kinge and ye Queen with ye Lyons in black stone—nay rather ye Lyons were in light stone like ye bases of ye tombes.
>
> And ye grete east window in pannels like unto ye sides of ye choir and very faire, with a balcony. Ye balcony was underneath ye window and from yt did lead the way to ye altare back where was an ymage of Saint

Mary of great value and very olde which was saved from the fire long since.

Ego sum Johannes qui exmemoria rei dico-nauminisco dixi annorum 1492. ["I am Johannes who speaks from memory of the matter. The time of which I spoke would be 1492, as I remember it."]

A gold and crimson roof was described in another session, and later Bond indeed found what he described as "architectural moldings with members painted in red and black and retaining traces of gold" just where the monks said he would.

There were many, many instances when the Company of Avalon was of invaluable aid as Bond began reconstructing minute and ornate architectural details so common to the medieval construction of the period.

It really makes little difference whether or not he really was communicating with deceased spirits or some element of Bartlett's or even his own mind which had clairvoyant access to the past. The fact remains that Bond was able miraculously to reconstruct a number of buildings and bring Glastonbury back from the twilight of legend to the appreciation of twentieth-century man. Over the years he reconstructed the refectory, the monks' dormitory, the cloisters, the chapter house, a glass and pottery kiln, the Great North Porch of the abbey, the monks' kitchen, Peter Lightfoot's clock in the bell tower, the western towers, and five chapels (the Chapel of the Holy Sepulcher, St. Dunstan's Chapel, St. Michael's Chapel, the Edgar Chapel and what may be the Loretto Chapel). Needless to say, a large number of invaluable artifacts, medallions, potsherds, fragments of stained glass windows, and gilded wood were recovered in the process.

At one of the excavation trenches, Bond chanced upon a curious entombment. Along an old ruined building wall he exhumed a skeleton, an elderly man, 6′3″ in height. There was no coffin housing the bones, but instead the skull rested within an ornate stone cradle. Between the legs were the broken skull and bones of yet another body. Another archaeologist would have been unable to interpret this odd find. As with the fate of so many other unique artifacts in archaeology and anthropology, this grave site would have been ignored as merely an anomaly. Instead of taking the easy route of simply ignoring it, Bond consulted the Company of

Avalon. Through their counsel the Watchers' story behind the grave unfolded:

> "Radulphus Cansollarius who slew Eawulf in fair fight did nevertheless suffer by his foeman's seaxes, which broke his bones assunder. He, dying, after many years desired that they who loved him should bury him without the church where he was wont to feed the birds in his chair. The sun did shine there as he loved it for his blood was cold. It is strange yet wee know it is true. The head of Eawulf *fell* and so laye betwixt his feet, and thus have ye found it."

On reinspecting the bones Bond found that the right forearm of the large skeleton (of Radulphus) was fractured, just as if he suffered a blow from a foe's ax. A fractured forearm is not concrete evidence for such an elaborate historical reconstruction, but later the scripts offered Bond additional information—information which forces us to place much more stock in the Watchers' story. Bond was given names, exact dates, details concerning the circumstances of the confrontation between Radulphus and Eawulf, one a Norman the other a Saxon. When Bond started digging into historical documents in order to verify these facts, a slender but lengthening line of confirmation came to light. Radulphus is mentioned in several historical texts. He served Turston, the first Norman abbot, who had a great hatred for the Saxons and was responsible for the slaughter of Saxon monks by mercenaries. Further, on referring to the *Anglo-Saxon Chronicles* (a series of early English histories dating back to the ninth century) it was found that indeed there was an Eawulf buried at Glastonbury Abbey.

Despite Bond's unusual belief that he could communicate with a group of dead monks, what kind of archaeologist was he in his more normal work? How was he regarded by others in the field? Was he a talented amateur or bumbling professional? An incompetent amateur or bona fide professional? Perhaps the best evaluation of Bond's nine excavation reports and supplements was made by Dr. Raleigh Radford, director of excavations at Glastonbury and one of England's best-known archaeologists, Dr. Radford has written:

"The interim reports which he published in the Somerset Archaeological Society are factual and precise and show that he [Bond] was working scientifically with a technique as advanced as any at the time. . . . In brief, I would say that . . . the errors in the . . . reports were such as inevitably come to light when earlier work is reexamined in the light of fuller knowledge and advanced techniques."

Bond's credentials appear to be in good order.

Dr. Radford's comments also pose another interesting question: How much more could Bond have given us if he had access to tree-ring dating, radiocarbon dating, thermoluminescence dating on pottery, and pollen analysis? Bond clearly fulfilled the main goals of his discipline: discovery, excavation and evaluation. Almost all that we know today of the physical structure of Glastonbury Abbey we know because of him. In his books Bond went beyond recreating the material world of an historic religious community. He used his artifactual discoveries and reconstruction as mere stepping stones. Pushing aside the shadows of the past revealed only by inanimate relics, he brought the past to life. He opened a psychic and spiritual door to the world of Glastonbury Abbey from the perspective of those who lived there centuries ago.

Between 1907 and 1922, which included the years during which Bond excavated, there were at least one hundred sittings in which over two dozen "personalities" manifested themselves. Communications from the Company were received as late as 1934 while Bond was living in the United States. Four other independent automatists were subsequently used in addition to Captain Bartlett, but they were ignorant of the communications and results procured through him. Nonetheless, concordant information coming from the same intelligences which had written through Bartlett was obtained. This "cross-reference" check (trying to receive the same or complementary information through two or more different mediums) seems to rule out the theory that the Company was purely a product of Bartlett's imagination. (During the early séances Bond would often read aloud from one of the lighter popular books of the day to keep Bartlett distracted or from becoming bored. But it does not rule out some form of telepathic leakage from Bond.)

The most consistent character over the thirty years of Bond's psychic investigations was Johannes the Monk. His communications often carried with them a distinctly literary flavor. Bond used them to write a number of books about the

Company. In addition to *The Gate of Remembrance* (1918), Bond wrote *The Company of Avalon* (1924), *The Gospel of Phillip the Deacon* (1932), *The Secret of Immortality* (1934), *The Mystery of Glastonbury* (1938), and also issued several privately printed tracts called *Glastonbury Scripts*. These consisted of "The Return of Johannes," "Memories of the Monks of Avalon," "St. Hugh of Avalon," "A Life of Ailnoth, Last Saxon Abbot of Glastonbury," "The Vision of the Holy Grail," "The Rose Miraculous," "The Full Story of St. Hugh of Avalon," "The Finding of the First Church at Glaston," and "King Arthur and the Quest for the Holy Grail." Communications during the 1930's were published in the *Journal of the American Society for Psychical Research* (for a time retitled *Psychic Research*) for which Bond served as editor for a few years. These communications ranged over the entire history of Glastonbury, but any hints that one might extract from them to explore historical Glastonbury have never been followed up. One must mention that a historical search for evidence of a "Johannes the Monk" by the British scholar G.W. Lambert failed to uncover any clear evidence of his existence.

Nonetheless, the scripts became even more impressive when we examine their use of language. As Bond points out there "is a curious patchwork of low Latin, Middle English of mixed periods, and modern English of varied style and diction." When Latin was used, the outcome was very much what one might expect to have resulted from the colloquial jargon the community members must have used. There is simply no uniformity in the language.

"Why do they want to use Latin? . . . Why can't they talk in English? . . . It is difficult to talk in Latin tongue," one denizen complained.

Another countered, "Awfold ye Saxon hath tried but hee knows not ye tongue."

These are just the difficulties with language that one would expect to occur when talking to the inhabitants of long ago. Throughout the communications there is a tendency to revert to old forms of spelling, the phrasing appears to be even more consistently old-fashioned, and lastly and humorously, there were vocabulary problems. "What is meant by lap mason?" "Lapidor . . . stonemason," comes the answer.

This all adds up to a certain consistent humanness in the sittings. There are errors of juxtaposition in the dialogue where one word is inadvertently substituted for another as so often occurs in our conversations. Mistakes were readily admitted since the communicators never claimed ominiscience about Glastonbury. Sometimes they moaned that there were things that they couldn't describe to Bond, just as someone would have difficulty in describing a "sunset and the shadows on the mere." Neither were they beyond castigating Bond when he interpreted poorly what they were writing. As fatigue and boredom set in, juxtapositions and mistakes became more noticeable; errors occurred most frequently at the end of long sittings. Usually Bond was forewarned when the writings began to weaken or become less clear. The communicator would impart, "I . . . must gain strength," or "Johannes now far away: far and that the force is weake."

The Company was an enigma in its own right. It consisted, according to Bartlett's scripts, of over two dozen different personalities ranging from abbots to Benedictine monks, from knights to the residents of the nearby town. There was Abbot Beere, the builder of Edgar Chapel; Ambrosius Cellarius, the storeroom steward, who relates a tale about the alehouse; Peter Lightfoot, the clock maker; John Camel, purse bearer to Abbot Beere; Ricardus De Tanton, Abbot Beere's artist; Johan Parsons, the cowherd; Huerwith the Dane, a warrior; Johannes Lory, Master Mason of ye Guilde of St. Andrews, who gives the circumstances behind an unusual gargoyle which he said he carved and which was eventually found on one of the towers. These colorful if not downright garrulous characters represent only a few of the personages who sprang to life during Bond's experiments with Bartlett.

Not only did the members of the Company come from different walks of life, but also from different periods of time in Glastonbury's long history. They didn't simply talk. They drew additional plans, sketches of architectural details and ornamental lions were made, and one of the monks offered a self-portrait through Bartlett's busy pencil. One by one, the members of the Company came forward to captivate Bond with from the past. It must have seemed like a fairy tale—as though one of Sir Walter Scott's novels had come to life. It was Bond though who brought the scripts back to firm reality as he proceeded with formal excavation to determine the accuracy of the information. Apparently the Company was in sympathy with Bond, for on more than one occasion they told him, "We worked in our day. Ye must work in yours." Or "Ye must use your own intelligence."

Through the scripts Bond received answers to such questions as why so much building, rebuilding and subsidiary building was done; the philosophy behind the work; why the monks continued to build even when their future at the hands of the Protestant regime was precarious. These are questions which no other archaeologist could have answered. "John Camel" relates in an almost cosmic chant: "Chappells a many!—everywhere! Why should roysterers and evil men have it to spend? So we builded much. Chapels everywhere nay need of them."

In another moment "Peter Lightfoot," the clock maker, gave the reason for specific modifications made at the Abbey. There was no discernible logic for some of them, nor hints about them in the literature on Glastonbury. Yet through Lightfoot we know that there was no *objective* reason for the modifications. Rather, there was a very personal and human reason—jealousy:

> Then when they were building at Welles we were jealous of our howse and certain masons coming on holiday across the causeway which led straight across the marsh, did tell us we were lacking. They sedde our howse was over smalle for our community and the choir thereof was not long enow for our processions and for the brethren to sitte at the service of the church—for we were three hundred and forty-seven in number. And moreover, the towre was too lowe for beauty. And Welles, being new and faire with carven stone, our Abbot was moved to beautify our howse. Soe he that was at enmity with Jocelyn, made friends that day, and the Bishop with a faire company came on a white palfry and did dine with us. And so our choir enlonged and afterwards the towre was beautifyed with certain panelling, and this although our coffers were much in need because the body of the church was newly yfinished by very faire art.

As "Abbott Beere" told Bond, while he built the Edgar Chapel for the fairly orthodox reason of paying homage to a saintly king who was associated with the abbey, he erected the Loretto Chapel to honor a vow he had made while on embassy to visit the new pope:

> Know ye not that we were borne downe by rude men in foreign parts and the mule which bore me fell, for I was a grete and heavy man. And being like to fall down a steepe place or be tramped by ye mule, I called on Oure Lady and shee heard me, soe that my cloke catching on a thorne I was prevented, and then said I, 'Lo, when I returne I will build a chapel to Our Lady of Loretto, and soe instant was I in [my vowe] that the brethern were grieved, for yt was arranged in Chapitre that wee shold build a Chapel to oure Edgare before I went in ye shippe. Therefore builded I hym first, for it was a public vowe; but mine owne vowe I fulfilled afterer, and soe all was well—yt is given.

The abbot claimed that he built the Loretto Chapel in a new style, one he brought back with relish from Italy. Beere even named the Italian architect he used. To examine, expose, or validate this claim, one merely has to make a comparison between the architecture of the Loretto Chapel and chapels built in Italy by the same architect. Unfortunately, Bond was never able to trace this obvious clue completely, although he did find "a few fragments of plain molded work of Italian character" in the debris uncovered in the general area where Beere said he built the Loretto Chapel. Tantalizing, yes; evidential, no. Despite this, the description and details offered about the chapel by Beere are internally consistent with Italian architectural design. Eventually Bond excavated what many experts consider to be the actual foundations of the Loretto Chapel.

This is an important lesson. Orthodox archaeology can utilize and then verify psychic clues. By comparing our "psychic reconstruction" to a purely archaeological one, we can check a psychic's accuracy. Psychic information can be extremely accurate—so accurate, in fact, that we might even accept unverifiable information about buildings, peoples, and places as trustworthy if it is internally consistent with information that has been properly verified.

Of course, not all of the information Bond received related to buildings or even important issues. He was presented with the very trivia which catapults the past into a living presence, as the members of the Company dreamily recalled events from their lives. One monk recalled how another brought shame to his house by drinking too much ale on the day of the king's visit:

"He fell full sore and lay as one dead and the King was right merry. 'See,' he said, 'how heavy lies the good ale on this poor roysterer' . . . and even now the scent of good ale hangs 'round the flores."

Another monk, Johannes, talked about his portliness:

"Soe I remember those stayres for my fatness, but it availed me not. Tho' my Father Prior recommended it off. Alas, I waxed more fat.

"Not that my belly was my god, I wot not! But I was cheery and troubled not, save for services and ecclesia, for better loved I the lanes and woods where walked I much—with weariness because of my weight.

"So said I, "It is the Lord's will. Somme he made fat and somme be lean" and this I said to they that jibed, that the Gates of Heaven are made full wide for all sorts, so that none created should stick within the portall. This I said, for they vexed me with their quips.

"I would remind me of many things. Half do I remember yet the lytell things only. The greate ones (stick) even as I, myself, stuck in the portall by reason of their trick.

"I was ever soe of merry heart, when like to melt in tears. So was I made. It was not my fault. Light of thought, saved the thoughts I could not speak, and the light jests camme to me. Glad soule! Had I but turned my soule to the things that were greate, I should not be now a child among the toys. But I was never meant to be a Monk. They placed me here in Choro, when I would have drawn a sword."

Sometimes the Company seemed deliberately to entice Bond with some arcane mention of Arthur's legendary tomb, underground passageways leading to the Holy Grail, or talk of the wizard Merlin. Even though these tidbits were "the stuff of which legends are made," Bond never had time to follow them up. He, who was so easily enamored of the mystical, might easily have forsaken the tedium of his painstaking reconstruction to pursue these messages in detail. And, in fact, on more than one occasion he was seen in the presence of dowsers, employing them to help locate these hidden passageways. In his eighth excavation report, Bond does discuss three tunnels he had located but which he had found sealed up. Clues to the actual existence of King Arthur's grave did not come from Bond, though. This came in 1962 when Dr. Radford excavated at Glastonbury and discovered some artifacts including a cross with Arthur's name on it. All Radford could say was that "some prominent person was indeed buried there in the right period."

Johannes Bryant—curator of Edgar Chapel, mason, sculptor, and gentle soul—was one of the most frequent and animated characters who communicated with Bond during the thirteen years of the Glastonbury excavations. A fellow monk gave the following portrait of Johannes as a lover of nature:

". . . he ever loved the woods and the pleasant places which lie without our house. It was good, for he learnt in the temple of Nature much that he would never hear in Choro. His harte was of the country and he hearde it calling with out the walls and the Abbot winked at it for he knew full well that it was good for him. He went a-fishing, did Johannes, and tarried oft in lanes to listen to the birds and to watch the shadows lengthening over all the woods of Mere.

"He loved them well, and many times no fish had he for that he had forgot them . . . but we cared not, for he came with talk and pleasant converse, as nut-brown ale and it was well.

"And because he was of Nature his soul was pure and he is of the Company that doth watch and wait for the Glories to be renewed."

Johannes, speaking for himself, confessed that he still blushes to this day over an incident which occurred when he was ferrying a young lady across a river. This story is one of those moments where humor is injected into the all-too-serious tone of the scripts:

"I have a sin—of all innocence I must confess.

"The Hussey kissed my hot cheek before I could say "Stop" or say a prayer to St. Anthony. It's true I rubbed it off with the tail of my habit—but the memory remained and there is an unholy gladness that I could not rid myself of.

"I did penance by mopping the Refectory floor on bended knees, yet glad was I for the kiss and am to this day. Lord have mercy on mine o'er tainted soul."

The trivial flavor of this delightful tale might alone convince some that Johannes was not a product of Bartlett's own mind. It was also he who gave Bond much of the specific excavation information about the Edgar Chapel and other abbey structures. Because he proved to be so accurate in these verifiable details, his words concerning the ebb of life at the monastery take on extra meaning. One of his greatest gifts was the insight he gave into the exaltation of the medieval religious service:

"We have sat in the grate gallery under the west window and watched the pylgrims when the sun went downe. It was in truth a brave sight, and one to move the soul of one there. The orgayne that did stande in the gallery did answer hym that spake on the great screene and men were amazed not knowing which did answer which. Then did ye bellows blowe and ye . . . man who beat with his hands upon the manual did strike yet harder, and all did shout Te Deum, so that all ye town heard the noise of the shouting, and ye little orgaynes in ye chapels did join in the triumph. Then ye belles did ring and we thought hyt must have gone to ye gates of Heaven."

Similarly, Abbot Beere offered insight into medieval religious thought.

"Can you give us an idea of the state of the opinion and the religious establishments of your day—of the view and ideals current?" Bond inquired.

The abbot answered, "Nay held I with superstitions. Ever I was for ye people and ye better understanding of ye Mysteries. It was mete that it be so and not kept in the hearts of the religious only. More would ye what more I did has seemed best for the old times were changing and men loved the glory of our ceremonial. They were angered at the deceit that kept their fathers humble and meek. Through the eye, the glory of our services might make them wish for noble things, but I knew and he, my friend, knew they were no longer to be fooled with trickery. All was changing in my day and the wars made for greater knowledge. The English were asleep no more. Nay ever to be Dixi."

Another important element, the scripts is that, as indicated, when information was repeated by the same or different personalities within the Company, it was usually found to be internally consistent. Whether Bond was told about "Wall slantwise at ye cornere" or about "Walls at an angle," or when specific measurements were given, or even if he were told just to look by a certain "clump of grass," all this information was found to have alluded to the same location. Often identical information was given to Bond years apart.

For example, data about the Loretto Chapel was given in two installments four years apart. The scripts would also continue just where they had stopped even after a break of several hours. On other days though, the intelligences couldn't get through, or the channel was not clear, or Bond and Bartlett could only pressure out a "few cramped and uncertain words." If the connection was good but the information vague or required clarification, Bond simply had to ask for the message to be repeated. It usually was—and promptly. This demand had to be made often because the writings were hard to decipher. One by one the Company came through and signed off. The handwriting changed accordingly as the personalities changed. Sometimes they cut in on one another, and it was not clear just who was communicating.

The evidence that the Company was composed of independent psychic entities rests on more impressive evidence than the dynamics of their interchanges. Further evidence can be documented from the purely archaeological details contained in their messages. Many of the construction details made good architectural sense. Architectural similarities mentioned between the abbeys of Glastonbury and Welles can be easily compared. But the major appeal the scripts have for us is their wealth of details, which can be checked and verified against historical situations. In fact, the information did shed new light on historical controversies and filled in gaps in England's past. On one occasion, midway through the excavations, a Colonel Long found some ancient documents among his family heirlooms which seemed to relate to Glastonbury. The documents verified the accuracy of some of the measurements given by the Company.

Obviously somebody or something very real was "out there" helping Bond—an intelligence that seemed to have a good grasp of the intricate details pertaining to the architecture and the history of Glastonbury Abbey. And an intelligence which revealed all the idiosyncracies of being human. Bond confronted not only the ancient world of Glastonbury, but also the existing memories and microcosm of the Company. It is almost as if they had been waiting for eons of time; waiting for just the right person to come along to whom they could impart their woes, share their joys, and reveal their tales of Glastonbury. Bond was the ideal channel. He was a sensitive man who, since his youth, had sought communion with the unseen world. Between Bond and the Company was an open channel of mutual interests and motivations. Was it by chance that both were devoted to the same great goal, the reconstruction of Glastonbury?

These thoughts are suggested by the communicators themselves. In one sitting several of the Watchers said that they knew ". . . that ye also love what he [Johannes] has loved and so he strives to give you glimpses of his dreams." When Bond became director of excavations, what more could they ask? As the scripts indicated, Bond merely needed to be "waxe in our hands." The mutual interests shared by Bond and the Company also included the theory of Gematria, and the Company referred to this theme many times:

"As we have said, our Abbey was a message in ye stones. In ye foundations and ye distance be a mystery—the mystery of our Faith which ye have forgotten and ye also in ye latter days.

"All ye measures were marked in ye slabs in Mary's Chappel and ye have destroyed them."

". . . in ye floor of ye Mary's Chappel was ye Zodiac, that all might see and understand the Mystery."

During another session they wrote, "As great books were we, and our work was in stone, in a language handed down for you to read which we had forgotten and so fell." And in yet another sitting Abbot Beere tells how he sought, "A better understanding of ye mysteries."

It was Bond's concern for such esoteric measurements that first aroused the ire of the Society of Antiquaries and which hastened the collapse of the excavations. For instance, Bond noted how one particular large scale plan had been useful "in locating the position of walls destroyed and lost." When discussing the destroyed engraved geometric lines on the floor of St. Mary's Chapel which the Company claimed were messages in stone, Bond went so far as to quote the writings of William of Malmsbury, the famous twelfth-century scholar who commented after visiting the abbey, "In the pavement may be seen on every side, stones designedly inlaid in triangles and squares and figured in lead under which, if I believe, some sacred engima to be contained. I do no injustice to religion."

How does one evaluate all these details and complexities? The simplest interpretation is that the Company was just what they said they were: the surviving intelligences of many individuals who once inhabited the site. From the way they identify themselves in the scripts, it seems that some of them were "earthbound," forever chained to the site through their intense devotion to their beloved abbey. Other communicators seem independent, free, acting gratuitously to help Bond and the others. Some of these "earthbound," entities indicate that they exist in a dreamlike world, while others seem to be in an acutely analytical and composed state of mind and existence. For the most part, they constantly proclaim that they speak from their memories of the times or occasionally from "present" dreams about those memories. Sometimes an entity was not able to answer an historical question since it concerned an era in which he did not live. This situation would be quickly rectified for another member would come forth to tell "that which [another member] cannot." At other times we are told how they had to search for pertinent information, "More we will serche in the great army of passed things—they are so hard to find."

Since some of the communications came from different epochs, descriptions of the abbey were sometimes based on the original structures and sometimes on the alterations. Despite this, it also seems possible that some members of the Company— the Watchers—had been surveying Glastonbury for a long time since in the scripts they would show knowledge about historical literature bearing on Glastonbury. They would even volunteer information to Bond about his latest discoveries—before he had queried about them through Bartlett. The Company were not only communicators of Glastonbury, but the guardians as well.

Despite the spiritistic tone of the scripts, the Company indicated a more impersonal source of the writing. Once they told Bond that Johannes, ". . . lives yet in the Universal Memory and speaks and acts through every channel in which the Universal Life flows. Yet when he is himself he speaks well as he was wont in the rude times that are as yesterday."

Are the scripts alluding to something akin to Jung's collective unconscious or James's cosmic reservoir? This "Universal Memory" seems to be a collective memory bank of Glastonbury greater than any of the individuals with whom Bond communicated; a consciousness which surpasses our notion of past and present.

The Company of Avalon was no simple intelligence. There are two major likely alternatives. First, that it was a mixture of earthbound spirits and free spirits, knowledgeable ones and ignorant ones. Their reminiscences were both factual memories and idealized dreams. To Bond, the Company was an unseen yet structured world whose inhabitants had broken through the shadows of time to befriend him.

The second alternative is that Frederick Bligh Bond was an exorcist's nightmare or a psychiatrist's magnum opus, from whose mind sprang two dozen secondary personalities. Either way, we have to admit that he did pioneer and successfully implement an entirely new model for studying the past. His courage and determination in bridging the gap between the scientific world and the psychic world can only be admired.

But let us also remember that no matter how exhilarating Bond's adventures were, he remained a scientist. His motto was "Prove all things and hold fast to that which is good." He constantly emphasized that the scripts were not to be accepted with credulity, but only as a guide to verifiable facts. One of the chapters in *The Gate of Remembrance* is given the remarkable title, "Psychological Methods Applied to Archaeological Research." In this chapter Bond specifically outlined the same intuitive approach that is employed by researchers today. He appreciated the need for the psychic channel to switch off the logical machinery of the brain in order to submerge into the intuitive insights of the mind. He recognized that the very thoughts of the researcher could interact with the intelligence behind his "source" and appreciated the possibility that the information he was so carefully indexing might merely be a psychic wish-fulfillment. He was concerned with the physical state of the participants in his psychic odyssey and with the best ways to develop the intuitive source.

Bond's legacy to us also includes enough information to allow archaeologists today to make further discoveries about Glastonbury Abbey. This may placate those who still harbor doubts about Bond and the scripts. The detailed information given about the unique Loretto Chapel is still unchecked. One could verify some of the information about the monks' kitchen simply. A pollen analysis would quickly reveal if a mint garden and a stable were covered over by later buildings in the area, as claimed in the scripts. For those with open minds, Bond has left a number of challenges, some of which we are just now confronting.

In conclusion, Bond's biographer, William Kenawell, describes Bond as "a person who renounced time to himself for twenty-five years in the face of contrary conditions and overwhelming odds." A man who "possessed such clarity of insight and penetrating analysis as to be ranked among the truly great minds of the day." Today psychic archaeology is a rapidly advancing new discipline. But Bond deserves recognition as the first progenitor, if not father, of this new study. While others before Bond may have acted upon psychic impulses, it was Bond who undertook the first systematic study and application of psychic technique to archaeology. Sixty years ago he was exploring a world which we today are just rediscovering. Now more of us stand at the threshold of the gate of remembrance.

Chapter 2

The Polish Wizard

> What determines the soundness of a hypothesis is not the way it is arrived at (it may have been suggested by a dream or a hallucination), but the way it stands up when confronted with relevant observational data.
>
> —*Karl Hempel, Aspects of Scientific Explanation*

In Poland, on October 22, 1941, at the apartment of the famous psychic, Stefan Ossowiecki, six distinguished guests arrived to test his psychic powers. Two of the men present sat with pen and pads in hand, waiting to jot down anything the seer might have to say during the next several minutes. One of them was Dr. Stanislaw Poniatowski, professor of ethnology at the University of Warsaw.

At 5:45 P.M. the test began. The experimenters handed Ossowiecki a projectile-point from the museum's archaeological collection. The artifact, unbeknownst to Ossowiecki, came from the Magdalenian culture, a culture which flourished in parts of Europe over 15,000 years ago and which was the most advanced of the Paleolithic period. Twenty minutes went by as Ossowiecki felt the object, rolled it in his hand. Finally he spoke:

"I see very well . . . I'm arriving at this place . . . very many hills . . . many woods around . . . It's Belgium, France, somewhere there . . . This object . . . it is part of a spear . . . a spear used by people who were on this land. I see houses—a sort of settlement. Round houses. Haven't seen such before.

"One very close to the other . . . I approach these houses, wooden logs all around branches between . . . covered with gray, greenish clay mixed with leaves. Height of the houses: one, one and one half, two meters . . . two and one half at the most . . . In the middle, at the top of the house there is a hole . . . here, I'll draw it . . . house up to three meters high because the door is one and one half meters low. Now I see them: the people. Color of their faces, body, rather brownish and quite dark. Hair black. Rather small. Small statures. Enormous legs (feet), large hands. Low forehead (short). Sort of like this—[with his hands Ossowiecki showed a salient brow protruding above the eyes]—Eyes deeply set, large nose. I know these people from previous visions but these here have a nicer expression—dressed in skins. The time is sort of—''

The tension of the scene was interrupted as a chambermaid entered the room unexpectedly. A telephone caller, she apologized. Ossowiecki was annoyed, but after a few minutes returned to his psychic reverie:

''Oh, here we are again . . . this stone in the middle of the hut.''

''What is there inside?'' asked Professor Poniatowski.

''The walls are covered with animal hides,'' continued the seer, ''dark skins and a long snakeskin above the door . . . There is a stone on the left and right side, a hole in each, and the hole is filled with grease oil. I can see the grease and something black burning in it.''

''Can you draw the inside of the hut?'' Poniatowski asked with increasing impatience.

Ossowiecki commenced to draw and give even more details of the interior as well. The professor asked him for the diameter of the hut and the psychic was quick to respond:

''Five meters . . . exactly circular . . . these [pointing at smaller stones in one of his drawings] are stones in which they are sitting. Here I see a bunch of arrows. A skin with holes is hanging and arrows stuck into the holes [Ossowiecki made another drawing] hanging on the wall . . . The object I am holding in my hand is in this fur skin which this young man is wearing. He is sitting here and he is talking to one who is standing. Women on one side, men on the other. Women have triangles painted on their cheeks a bright red color. Large luscious lips, beautiful lips, teeth. The men have typical canines. The floor is not made of earth but all covered with hairy skins . . . I'd find living in a hut like this very comfortable. The women are doing something. There are three of them. They have bare pointed breasts. Very nice breasts, awfully large hips, rather large feet, all toes spread out. Toes are alive, moving constantly. There is a fire burning inside, sort of a kitchen stove . . . It's a pity they are leaving now. Lots of people . . . Now I understand . . ."

Ossowiecki continued with his impressions and remarked that one of the women left the hut with a wooden bowl of paint and smeared white marks on everybody's nose and forehead. They were preparing for a funeral:

"Now I am coming to this moment: They are all going down the road . . . And they are carrying a dead body . . . They are leaving and carrying on thin staffs of wood an old man (the deceased) with curly gray hair, beard, covered with a skin, very thin. All the people bow very low, hands on the ground. Some lie down . . . The men are carrying, behind there is an old woman walking, they are supporting her. They walk down the road . . . Down the hill . . . There is a great fire burning down there. And people jumping around the fire, shrieking . . . The women are holding hands, heads hanging down. All the men have spears at their sides, I mean sort of arrows, lances . . . I arrive near this place . . . There is an enormous stone in the middle with a hollow and a fire burning. Black smoke and they are putting the corpse into the fire on the wooden poles. Everybody is shrieking, dancing. They make a circle. One, two, three circles. Holding their heads [he showed how they were holding hands, crossed behind the heads of their neighbors in the circle]. The family is near the stone. The corpse is burning. Everybody is jumping, it burns fast. The fire decreases . . . Now it's finished. There are two men approaching wearing long leather coats, gathering ashes and putting them into a round urn made of clay . . . My God, what a small urn. Ashes in one urn and bones in another . . . I cannot understand . . . Everybody's quiet, all fall down, then rise. They carry these two urns. All the procession follows down there. People are waiting and a tomb is ready—a sort of grotto—This was an old man, a patriarch of the tribe . . . There are already two, three other bodies buried. They place the decorating around the urn—some red and yellow pebbles . . . now everyone is gone; only the family remains."

At this point the professor asked Ossowiecki if he would draw the tomb. Ossowiecki made a sketch of the interior of the tomb and then quickly answered the professor's questions about it. In particular, he noted that in the middle of the tomb lay a stone with a drawing of the sun on it:

"Now they are all walking—women, children, dogs. Dogs have small ears, short noses, eyes distant from one another, reddish hair, very short, elastic legs. Two dogs."

Professor Poniatowski interrupted to ask what time of day it was:

"It is in the morning, about nine, ten, eleven o'clock. Quite warm, lots of sun. They disperse themselves on all sides. I see my man. This woman is walking; many women have hairpins made of bone. Hair is artificially arranged."

Again Poniatowski interrupted, "What are the men wearing?"

"The one who is carrying the leading object [showing with his hands that he had suspenders] this across his back and a leather belt around his hips. One arrow in the belt, the one I am holding in my hand. I don't see any bows. The man on the road rubs away the white color from his nose. Others do the same . . . There is a large place . . . plaza . . . earth removed, covered with clay. They have their meetings here. They have all dispersed, dogs running with children. The man has remained with another one and sits in front of the house . . . I'm tired."

The experiment was over. It was 7:05 P.M.

Ossowiecki had described scenes and activities of a bygone era as though he were there watching them. If the Polish seer's psychic vision was accurate, he was viewing scenes that took place over 15,000 years ago, scenes no other living man had ever shared. While Bligh Bond took the psychic time tunnel back to medieval times, Ossowiecki bypassed him by thousands of years. This psychic time machine was no longer a pencil and paper, but a living, breathing, human body.

Just what sort of man was Stefan Ossowiecki? Stefan was born in 1877 of Polish parents in Moscow. His father was a chemist, and as a teen-ager, Stefan attended the Petersburg Technological Institute and also trained as a chemist. He became aware of his paranormal abilities while still in his teens when he discovered he could move small objects by willpower alone. (This is called PK—psychokinesis.) Clairvoyant ability soon followed and one of his most developed talents was the power to see objects inside closed containers.

Ossowiecki soon learned that if he concentrated on his ESP his PK abilities would diminish—and vice versa. Eventually he decided to concentrate on developing his ESP abilities and during the height of his fame his PK faculty was held in abeyance.

When Stefan was twenty-one he met an elderly self-styled clairvoyant named Vorobej who claimed that he had spent most of his life studying in the East. Ossowiecki once reminisced "This old man had great influence on my psyche, and it was he who showed me how to exercise and develop my ability." Vorobej, who lived in a small wooden house in the suburbs, spent all his time in bed dressed in a black monklike robe. In contrast, Ossowiecki did not look like an ascetic at all. He was a tall, powerfully built man who was quite stout at the peak of his fame. He looked rather like any businessman you might see on the street.

In 1917 when he was forty years old, Ossowiecki was imprisoned for six months by the Bolsheviks, and after his release went to live in Warsaw where he soon became known for his unusual gifts. He read people's fates, located lost articles, and furnished information about missing persons with startling accuracy. On a few occasions he supplied information in criminal cases. But Ossowiecki was no parlor soothsayer. He very generously offered himself to some of Europe's best-known parapsychologists for any tests they could design, and by 1921 he had attracted the attention of psychic researchers throughout Europe. Among his champions were the Nobel Prize winning physiologist Charles Richet, Professor Gustave Geley of France, the famous German physician Baron A. von Schrenck-Notzing, and William MacKenzie of Italy, all of whom wrote reports on his abilities. Schrenck-Notzing was particularly impressed by one of these experiments which was performed during an international convention on psychic research held in Warsaw in 1923. Eric Dingwall of the Society for Psychical Research in London prepared and sent a drawing which he had placed in one envelope and sealed within *two more*. The target depicted a flag with a bottle sketched by it. The date, August 22, 1923 was written below. The envelope was given to Ossowiecki by Schrenck-Notzing, and after holding it Ossowiecki was able to sketch both the flag and the bottle. During another notable experiment he accurately described a picture sealed in a 1¼" lead tube.

Much was written about Ossowiecki in scientific journals and books, and he became somewhat of a national celebrity. In 1937, at the age of sixty, he began his experiments with Professor Poniatowski. These tests continued for four years, even after Poland was invaded in 1939 by the Germans.

The details and results of more than thirty-three psychometric experiments carried out with Professor Poniatowski were recorded in a manuscript entitled *Parapsychological Probing of Prehistorical Cultures: Experiments with Stefan Ossowiecki, from 1937 to 1941*. This was a time of great trouble in Europe. The Nazi armies invaded Poland in 1939, so most of the experiments were conducted under strained conditions and publication of the manuscript was unthinkable. Ossowiecki's step-son now has the papers. The voluminous document is over four hundred pages long and contains two hundred drawings. Dr. Poniatowski died in 1945, and his own important contribution to the manuscript—his original analyses and commentaries— are missing and will probably never be recovered. The main portion of the document is a transcript of Ossowiecki's discourses and drawings for each of the hour-long sessions. The results speak for themselves. As he was handed stone spearheads, bone fishhooks, and ceramic figurines, the entire range of Paleolithic prehistory unfolded before his eyes in an endless panorama: from Acheulian time over 500,000 years ago when the ancestors of man first made hand axes, to Mousterian time 100,000 to 40,000 years ago when Neanderthals held sway; and from Aurignacian times 40,000 years past when modern man first appeared, to Magdalenian times when cave art reached its zenith.

Ossowiecki willingly took part in scientific experimentation; he was fully dedicated to the study of his unusual abilities. He was a sincere and spiritual man as well, who strongly believed in life after death. He was good-hearted, cordial, and possessed an inexhaustible supply of optimism and faith in other people. Ossowiecki was never a professional psychic, he earned his living as a chemical engineer. While he used his clairvoyant powers generously to help others, his psi faculty was of little personal use. He once said that "a dark wall" stood between him and his paranormal abilities when it came to anything remotely concerning himself. (There was just one exception and that related to his own death, which will be discussed later.) Andrzey Borzymowski has humorously commented in an article on the history of Polish parapsychology in the Autumn and Summer 1962 issues of the *International Journal of Parapsychology*: "When he came to Warsaw after the First World War many people did not wish to sit down with him to his favorite game of bridge, for how was it possible that a clairvoyant wouldn't know the cards his opponents held? Only when it was confirmed that [Ossowiecki] was almost always beaten was the decision taken to play with him—and then quite willingly."

Ossowiecki always seemed preoccupied and absentminded, which sometimes led to comic or even troublesome situations. Once when he had been invited by friends to lunch, he absentmindedly turned up at the wrong home. He was cordially received and his hosts' surprise went unmentioned. But just before lunch was served he realized his mistake, apologized with the utmost embarrassment, and made straight for the correct meeting place. Now, comfortably seated in the right house, with the right friends, and at the right table, he was about to have his lunch when an urgent telephone call came in—he was needed at home to welcome guests that he had invited there for lunch that very day! Zero out of three.

Despite this absentmindedness in his everyday life, Ossowiecki became completely transformed when he programmed himself for an experiment. Then he was vigilant, alert, and intense. Perhaps he compensated in his daily life for the great concentration required to harness his psychic abilities.

Most of his psychic experiments, like the one designed by Eric Dingwall, consisted of discovering the contents of sealed envelopes. Since "sealed letter reading" was the rage in psychic circles in Ossowiecki's day, the researchers always had to be wary about experimental procedures. Letters had to be carefully guarded. After all, there were people like the famous Bert Reese running about who could "read" sealed letters phenomenally—but also fraudulently! So, letters had to be sealed in thick opaque envelopes and sometimes these were placed within other envelopes. Or, as mentioned before, messages were even sealed in metal tubes. No matter how these experiments were conducted, Ossowiecki always astounded his investigators with his accuracy. He never grew very comfortable trying to receive psychic impressions from typewritten script, preferring handwritten samples. Since he could not "read" material in a language unknown to him, even if the author was present, Ossowiecki probably relied on clairvoyance rather than telepathy. In one novel experiment he sensed correctly that a message was written in invisible ink, but he could not decipher it.

Ossowiecki's clairvoyance would extend beyond the specific task set before him. He frequently was able to recreate the scenes and emotions that related to the physical setting where the messages had been prepared. For example, when Schrenck-Notzing handed him the envelope prepared by Dingwall, Ossowiecki first gave an elaborate and accurate description of Schrenk-Notzing's study in Munich where the message had been kept before the test. So it would seem that even in these "sealed envelope tests" Ossowiecki was frequently able to read the past as well as the present. In another instance he correctly described not only the room in a house in Spain where the letter being used had been written weeks earlier, but also described the physical appearances of the writer and other members of the household:

"He has a tired face," Ossowiecki observed. "He is cutting a green sheet of paper . . . I can see what and how he is drawing . . . He gets up, lights a cigarette, returns to the table, takes a pen and writes a question."

Ossowiecki noted such details as the shape of ther necklace worn by the writer's wife. He made his own replica of the drawings included in the letter, which *had* been wrapped in green sheets of paper. These were quite accuate as well.

Ossowiecki had a flare for the dramatic. During an impromptu test he was asked to locate the burial site of a Polish soldier killed in a cavalry charge. The soldier had been buried in a communal grave with 700 other men, but no one knew the actual location of his body. The dead man's brother wanted to exhume the body and transport it to the family's burial ground. Ossowiecki went into action. Clutching a photograph of the dead soldier, he immediately drew a detailed plan of the cemetery, noting just where the body lay. He even gave a detailed description of the wounds that killed the soldier and acted out a sympathetic but grim portrait of the soldier's last moment, describing the right section of the man's abdomen and groin being shot away. At the time no one could tell if Ossowiecki was right or wrong, but the brother was encouraged and asked him to help in the exhumation.

The seer walked back and forth along the borders of the mass grave site. Suddenly he stopped, pointed down and declared that the body lay before him. The spot tallied with the one he had pinpointed earlier on his drawing. The digging began and at first it seemed that Ossowiecki might have been in error as body after body was removed from the site. Then he spoke again. The next body to be disinterred would be the dead brother, he declared. It was! Although the body, like the others, was badly mangled, identification was possible because the build, army rank, clothing and a gold crown on one of the teeth all matched the description of the dead man. A doctor who was present confirmed the abdomen and groin wounds. One can note that while the people involved in this case were not archaeologists, they were in fact carrying out a simple sort of archaeological exploration.

Another less grim story comes from Dr. Wolkowski. It is a quaint tale concerning the Gordon-Bennet Balloon trophy races held in Warsaw in 1936. The weather was bad and one of the balloons was lost. Ossowiecki was called in and he positioned the crew in Russia on an island in the White Sea. In his vision Stefan saw a polar bear approaching the crew. After the balloonists were rescued unharmed, they confirmed that the most unwelcomed cordialities were paid them by a passing polar bear.

The end of Ossowiecki's life was both noble and tragic. During World War II, although he possessed a foreign visa and could leave at any time, he felt that his first loyalty was to the Polish people. He felt they would need him. He couldn't have been more correct, for scores of frightened and unhappy individuals sought his help in gaining information about the fate of loved ones. His visions were often as agonizing to him as to the people whose deaths he was depicting. There is even evidence that his psychic prowess improved during this time of superhuman need. Painting was one of his few sources of relaxation. Ossowiecki lived through the Siege of Warsaw, its fall, and occupation and was active in the Polish underground. But on the eve of the Polish uprising against the Nazis he made his first prediction about himself—he would soon be killed. He added, "I have had a wonderful life." On August 5, 1944, he was massacred with many other Poles at Gestapo headquarters in Warsaw. Most of his unpublished manuscripts were burned along with his body.

Ossowiecki's visions seem more dynamic than the Glastonbury scripts. Reading those scripts one senses that the entities were trying to recount dim memories of the past. In Ossowiecki's visions the past is a panorama. The problems of memory and confusion that plagued the Company of Avalon were absent.

If a picture is really worth a thousand words, Ossowiecki's talents are a time-travel bonanza. All he had to do was take an object from the museum's artifact cemetery, and the past was almost instantaneously resurrected. Parapsychologists call this ability "psychometry" which means "measure of the soul," a term first coined in 1842 by J. Rhodes Buchanan, an Ohio physician, who discovered that touching physical objects ignited clairvoyant visions in his subjects. Ossowiecki's discourse is not a reconstruction nor an explanation of the past. (There isn't much that can be reconstructed or explained by a single projectile-point.) There are no stone foundations or historical documents to help us answer questions about the first men who roamed the earth, or to help us verify Ossowiecki's visions directly. Artifacts from past ages tell us nothing about the personalities of the people. Stone implements constitute the vast majority of remnants that we have from this distant time, and we only know about the most elementary activities of these people—hunting, fishing, burial—but beyond that we know virtually nothing about prehistoric man. (These primitive people whom we know from their flaked stone implements and cave paintings are designated as Lower Paleolithic, Middle Paleolithic, and Upper Paleolithic.)

Dr. François Bordes, the world's foremost authority on the Old Stone Age, sums up the situation very well when he states, "Much of these men's daily life will forever remain unknown to us: their social and family organizations, their songs and dances." But this is exactly the type of information that Ossowiecki gave! In startling contrast to archaeology's almost total ignorance about man's prehistory, Ossowiecki gave potentially accurate information on the very points Dr. Bordes considers hopelessly beyond our reach. While archaeologists sit around in learned council arguing ceaselessly on such problems as whether different types of Mousterian stone tools indicate that they were developed by some cultures for different purposes, or by different cultures for a similar purpose, Ossowiecki used his psychic ability to view these mysteries directly. This is simply embarrassing to orthodox scientists because Mousterian culture, which designates the Middle Paleolithic period of Neanderthal man, is one of the most intensely studied prehistoric cultures and most of our Paleolithic artifacts come from it. Obviously, Paleolithic man had more on his mind than banging up a few stone tools or running around painting a cave or two. But this is unfortunately all orthodox archaeology has ever told us. It is not really archaeology's fault since all it has to work with are a few meager remnants.

The Paleolithic Age is an enigmatic time in man's past and one in which psychics can help immensely. It was during this period that man supposedly evolved from primitive spear thrower to the very beginnings of technological man. Yet, in the shadows of time this period remains a total conundrum. Especially baffling are the key transition periods, such as when we, *Homo sapiens*, replaced Neanderthal man as Europe's residents. How did this transition take place? What is our relationship to the Neanderthal? What became of them? Did they have language? And why didn't they develop art as did later man? Why did this transition seem to happen virtually overnight, forty thousand years ago—and simultaneously in every corner of the globe where remnants of Neanderthal man are found? Also, despite periods when man made quantum leaps in his development, were there also periods of regression? Sometimes archaeology has come up with over-simplistic explanations. As in the debate over stone tool types: there is a modification of stone tools found in the archaeological record which indicates either that similar tools were used for different purposes, or that different cultures developed the same tools independently. It is often argued that the modification of these tools over archaeological time represents a concurrent development in man's mentality, leading to the ultimate establishment of today's *Homo sapiens* and his advanced intelligence. Yet this theory falls apart when one confronts the fact that Australian aborigines are fully wise, fully sapient yet use stone age tools. The Paleolithic Age also represents a time when culture itself came into being. Unless archaeology makes some breakthrough in understanding the emergence of modern man, the public will soon be seduced by default into believing that we were seeded here, or at least taught, by ancient spacemen! This von Dänikenesque view may be fantasy, but it is a sad commentary on the failure of archaeology and anthropology to explain man's development when such theories generate public enthusiasm.

An analysis of the experiment that opened this chapter, when Ossowiecki was handed a Magdalenian projectile-point, confirms the accuracy of his psychic observations. The Magdalenian culture was one of the most highly developed of the Paleolithic Age, during the time when reindeer herds foraged Europe in large numbers. Radiocarbon dating shows that this occurred from 12,000 to 19,000 years ago which is shortly after the end of the Ice Age. With their relatively large population, the Magdalenians are one of the few Paleolithic groups that evolved into the postglacial Mesolithic culture. The Mesolithic culture immediately followed the Magdalenian stage and was characterized by delicately worked tools and the first signs of agriculture instead of simple food-gathering.

Ossowiecki said the scenes he saw occurred in the area that is now contemporary France and Belgium. This is absolutely correct—the Magdalenians did occupy that area. In fact, they were centered in France, especially in the Valley of the Dordogne, from which we have secured a rich harvest of artifacts. Ossowiecki also saw woodlands, and it is interesting to note that woods were beginning to develop and replace the barren tundra that covered Europe at that time. The cool glacial period, which had epitomized the Ice Age, was coming to its close, and Europe was becoming more temperate in climate. It is believed that this climate change cut the Magdalenian expansion short.

Contrary to the stereotype, Paleolithic Man lived in open-air sites as well as in caves; the term "caveman" is not really correct. The settlements and huts Ossowiecki described makes sense in terms of what we now know, and it is unlikely that he, who was trained as a chemical engineer, would have known these facts. Actually we have uncovered many huts similar to those the psychic described and have even found settlements of them. In some areas where Magdalenian populations proliferated, the sites cover as many as five acres. Particularly in Eastern Europe, these village huts were dug into the subsoil, covered with skins over a wood or bone framework, and contained a central hearth inside for cooking and warmth. All this is just as Ossowiecki described.

This semisubterranean type of hut still survives in the remote polar areas. There is also a parallel between Ossowiecki's comments, that the hut he saw was "very comfortable," just the way Dr. Bordes described them thirty years later, when he noted that they must have been comfortable and easy to keep warm. The dimensions given by the psychic are consistent, since huts found so far from this period have been twelve to eighteen feet in diameter and formed around a "round hole" in the top that would follow from the "central hearth." The stones that Ossowiecki described as seats are just that. At the Magdalenian site at Pincevient, near Paris, large stones were discovered clustered around the hearths as if for warmth. Ossowiecki seems to be mistaken when he described "oil lamps," since the Magdalenian period appears to be too early for Man to have come by this invention. But at one site, the cave of La Mouthe in the French Dordogne, a ground-stone dish which had once contained oil and what is presumably a wick was uncovered. From all indications it did serve as a primitive type of oil lamp. The cave of La Mouthe was not excavated until the late 1940's, a few years after Ossowiecki's vision. This type of stone lamp is exactly what modern Eskimos use today to illuminate their tents or igloos.

The Magdalenians survived primarily by hunting reindeer that they followed across the tundra. Their kills were made with spears whose heads, like the one handed to Ossowiecki, were most often made of bone. Thus Ossowiecki's vision was consistent on this score as well.

The most exciting part of the narrative, however, is Ossowiecki's description of the people. Since we do have human skeletal remains from this period, we know that the Magdalenians were by and large physically indistinguishable from modern man. The only points of dissimilarity were their facial features: they had more robust facial bones and large teeth, just as the psychic described. Also apropos is Ossowiecki's comment that the people he saw had deeper-set eyes. This would be true, since the Magdalenians' more definitive cheek and brow bones would give this illusion. These facial features were probably a result of their life-style and diet, and today we can still see the same features in Eskimo populations. The "large noses" Ossowiecki described can be substantiated by anyone who wishes to take a good look at the paintings these people etched of themselves. The representations clearly show their prominent noses. The Magdalenian Chancellade skull which was excavated at the

Chancellade site in the Dordogne Valley also has a big nose.

The skeletal evidence also backs up Ossowiecki's account of the small stature of the Magdalenians. The Chancellade man was only 5′3″, and the average height of the five female skeleton fragments we have is only 5′1″. Ossowiecki said that these women had full lips, "pointed breasts," "very nice breasts, and large hips." There is plentiful evidence that Magdalenian women did have large hips. The small statues surviving from this period called *Venuses*, depict heavy women with broad pelvic areas. This physical feature could have resulted from steatopygia the abnormal growth of fat on the buttocks associated with in-body storage. This condition can still be found among the Hottentot natives of South Africa.

Also validating Ossowiecki's vision are the fine-eyed bone needles which have been excavated from Upper Paleolithic sites indicating that they sewed leather and skins for clothing.

The "bearded" old man Ossowiecki "saw" being buried may have been one of the bearded Magdalenians who are found represented in Magdalenian cave art. And women with artificially arranged hair are depicted on small ivory carvings which have survived from this age. The hairstyling also explains the bone hairpins and offers new light on the use of some of the objects we have categorically called bone needles, awls, or pendants.

Just as with Captain Bartlett's writings on Glastonbury, Ossowiecki did not merely corroborate what was already known about a bygone culture, but he also gave an entirely new view of their world. Ossowiecki's visions don't have to be taken purely at face value; if his insights can be directly compared to what is now known about the Magdalenians, it can be seen if his visions are at least *consistent* with the knowledge gained through traditional archaeological investigation.

For example, the first new information Ossowiecki gave us was the use of the bow and arrow even at this early date in man's history. At first he seemed to have some difficulty in understanding if what he saw was a spear or an arrow. He said, "All the men have spears at their sides, I mean sort of arrows, lances." What he might have seen in this instance was neither a normal spear nor an arrow, but a smaller spear specifically made to be used with an *Atlatl*—a spear thrower. Confusion might easily have arisen due to the simple fact that

Ossowiecki, being wholly ignorant of such an implement, could not describe it properly. He finally did make it clear that the Magdalenians did have arrows and even drew a bunch of them which he clairvoyantly saw stuck in a skin hanging on a wall. This coincides with a statement of Dr. Bordes pointing out that during the latter stages of Magdalenian culture, "The spear throwers seem to have disappeared. Could this be because the bow had been invented?"

The use of the bow and arrow seems even more plausible when we consider the effects of the climatic change that was taking place at the time. Woodlands developed, reindeer herds declined, and the Magdalenians were forced to hunt the red deer and elk instead. The bow and arrow would have been a great help in hunting those more vigilant and solitary animals—animals that presented more of a challenge than had the herding reindeer. A few years ago a sensational discovery was made at Border Cave in South Africa. Some arrowheads were found that were at least *50,000 years old!* This discovery would give solid inferential support to Ossowiecki's psychic impression that the Magdalenians, who existed only 12,000 to 19,000 years ago, had bows and arrows. At the very least we know that the development of that implement was not beyond the technology of Paleolithic man.

Another one of Ossowiecki's *new* facts was that the Magdalenians had domesticated dogs. This dates the domestication of dogs back twice as far as archaeological evidence has led us to believe, for the earliest evidence we have comes from the Near East approximately 7,000 B.C. But Ossowiecki's earlier date seems quite possible since the wolf is considered, because of its dentition, behavior, and interfertility, to be the dog's ancestor. Contrasted to the Near East, Northern Europe seems to be the best place for domestication, since the wolves also followed the reindeer herds and cleaned up scraps at camps after the hunters left. Domestication might easily have developed from the close association between the Magdalenians and the animals. The skeletal record is pretty oblique, so it would be easy to confuse a large dog for a wolf. Magdalenian cave art occasionally depicts animals that have been interpreted as wolves and hyenas. But they could just as easily have been dogs.

Two of the greatest mysteries about the distant past concern the social and religious life of our ancestors. Within these mysteries lie the roots of our own social and religious attitudes. Yet Ossowiecki seemed to have had no more difficulty in recapturing these abstract events than he had in detailing such material facts as the Magdalenian huts. He penetrates where even the imagination of the boldest archaeologist has never dared to go—the reenactment of a burial ceremony. Why is the skeletal record of this era so skimpy? What did the Magdalenians do with their dead? Ossowiecki suggested cremation. But cremation at this early date is unheard of. There was simply no evidence at all for this practice until years after Ossowiecki's death, when evidence dating as far back as 25,000 years, from Mungo Lake, Australia, showed that ancient man practiced cremation.

The only information we have at all for a Paleolithic burial ceremony is based on a burial site of an even older man found in Shanidar Cave, Iraq, where pollen analysis revealed that the body was buried on a bed and covered with a blanket, both constructed of flowers. Ossowiecki detailed another possible ceremony, one in which the entire community participated, and he talked about a procession and the actions of the next of kin. He also noted that the women had red triangles painted on their cheeks. Red is a common color in the Magdalenian's elaborate cave paintings and it is associated with women. Two different figurines depicting women unearthed from this period are colored with red paint.

Ossowiecki also saw the remains from the cremation buried in a clay urn. While archaeologists know that some Upper Paleolithic men fired clay to make figurines, no pottery containers have ever been discovered. Until recently archaeologists thought that pottery developed in the Near East approximately 9,000 years ago. But new evidence from Fukui Cave in Japan proves that the Joman culture, one of the first food-collecting cultures to emerge out of the big-game hunting years of the Pleistocene, had pottery as early as 13,000 years ago. Again, further discoveries have made Ossoweicki's clairvoyant impressions more plausible, all of which adds credence to his more speculative perceptions about such things as the development of the oil lamp, the use of the bow, the domestication of the dog, and the practice of cremation.

While no clay burial urns from this period have yet been found, archaeologists have discovered something similar to the colored pebbles and the stone with the drawing of the sun which Ossowiecki described: the art uncovered from the close of the Magdalenian period seems to be limited to pebbles engraved or painted with geometric designs. What about Ossowiecki's vision of people dancing in circles with their hands behind the heads of their neighbors as the body was burned? This may be nonsense. But someday a brave young archaeologist just might open up a long-buried grotto—perhaps the one Ossowiecki described—and find a clay urn containing ashes datable right back to the Magdalenians. If so, Ossowiecki will have to be acknowledged as the prime expert on the burial practices of these ancient people. Since Ossowiecki was famous for his clairvoyant ability to locate objects, it is a shame that the experimenters never asked him to find the grotto he saw in his visions.

There is a more functional question than just what Ossowiecki knew about the Magdalenians: How was he able to gain this flow of information just by holding a projectile-point, one that to the untrained eye could have come from almost any culture? The information came in a flood of words and impressions, descriptions that almost perfectly matched a people and culture Ossowiecki probably could not even name. Whatever errors he may have made, Ossowiecki was able to "read" archaeological artifacts in thirty-three experiments with considerable success. On at least two occasions, unbeknownst to him, the same object was used again to see if the second reading would be consistent with his first. Each time the information offered was complementary. The account quoted in this chapter was from the twenty-ninth experiment, which was a rerun with the same object used in the sixteenth test. Only later was Ossowiecki told of the procedure. He informed Professor Poniatowski that he had totally forgotten what he had said during the earlier experiment and that he felt the vision of the cremation was a completely new impression.

Most of the artifacts used in these experiments are still in the possession of the department of prehistory at the University of Warsaw. Dr. William Wolkowski of the Sorbonne (University of Paris), who has recently been championing Ossowiecki and who is trying to draw renewed attention to his unbelievable career, has suggested that psychic readings on these same objects by contemporary psychics could offer a number of interesting opportunities. If these psychics repeated what was previously said, or elaborated upon it, perhaps then we would have some means of locating the burial grotto Ossowiecki described.

As in the analysis of Glastonbury, let's analyze the "psychic source" from which this information was drawn. The nature and process of contacting the source is no less complex in Ossowiecki's case than it was in Bond's. Ossowiecki described the process:

> From the first moment I stop thinking and as intensively as possible concentrate all my psychic power toward spiritual feelings, I owe the ability to attain this condition to an unshakable faith in the unity of the spirit among humanity. Then I fall into a separate spiritual state and see as well as hear everything out of space and time . . . Reading a note through a sealed envelope, finding lost articles, or creating psychometric phenomena, I always experience more or less the same feeling. Of course, at the time, I use a certain amount of internal energy. My temperature rises; my heart beats unevenly. This lasts for a moment, and then I enter real clairvoyance and images form. More often visions of the past . . . The visions are misty, and it needs an exceptionally redoubled effort to perceive the moments and scenes in all their details. Sometimes this takes only minutes. But sometimes I have to wait for many hours. It depends to a great extent on the Circle (of experimenters), since a faltering belief, skepticism or even attention too strongly concentrated on me makes it difficult for me to read documents or to reveal feelings.

The process Ossowiecki used to force his ESP impressions into consciousness stands in marked contrast to the techniques many psychics employ, which concentrate on passive mind clearing and the spontaneous production of imagery. Ossowiecki's process was more energetic, and even his physiology changed. He was frequently tired at the end of his experiments and felt that what we now call the pituitary gland played a key role in clairvoyance; "It is as if I could see that part of my brain, stripped of its coverings . . . During experiments I feel it pulsing." Ossowiecki said that it was easiest to perceive contemporary incidents, more difficult to probe into the past and most difficult of all to foresee the future. During his attempts to read sealed letters, the psychic often forbade those present from thinking about the contents. He maintained that active concentration distracted him. Ossowiecki's paranormal abilities seemed to be in best form when there was the greatest need—to help resolve a crisis or find a missing object or person—and where strong emotions were involved.

To gain access to his source, Ossowiecki needed some sort of "scent" to guide him to the requisite information. To find a missing person, an article of his clothing or a picture was needed. To recount the past of a person with whom he was speaking, he held the person by the hand to "make contact." The psychometric process—the need for some personal object to increase the signal strength of the necessary information—may explain why he did better giving psychic readings from handwriting instead of print. Ancient artifacts were the key to his personal time machine in the archaeological experiments. Once he regressed in psychic time, he could then track the whole history of the artifact and the emotions and events connected with it. When handed a projectile-point, Ossowiecki traced its original owner, the fur skins he wore, and ceremonies in which he took part. There was nothing abstract in what he saw; he described what he was actually observing.

Ossowiecki described his sources as "the Consciousness of the One Spirit." This could refer to something very similar to the Universal Memory upon which the Company drew to give historical information to Bond. In both cases, it seems the ultimate source drawn upon by the psychics is some sort of universal record that can be psychically tapped in a variety of ways. Using the source is difficult. With the Company the critical problem came from the complexity of the source itself. To Ossowiecki it lay with the investigators and their attempt to design experiments most suited to his psychic capability of making contact with the source. Controlled conditions are fine if kept within reason and are not so harsh or impersonal that they factor out the very variables which permit a psychic to function. For example, sealed-letterreading experiments "prove" ESP and little more. They lack a strong emotional appeal or human interest that may catalyze the psi faculty into operation. All sorts of miracle-mongers wanted to test Ossowiecki, but few were willing to sit down and *work with him*, find out what tests were best for him, or attempt to develop his psychic abilities and put them to good use. Professor Poniatowski carried out some thirty-three experiments with Ossowiecki over a four-year span, yet never once do the records indicate any purely exploratory experiments, practice runs, or any new procedures employed "just to see what would happen" if the experimental protocol was changed. The tests were always the same. Ossowiecki was given an object, he spoke for an hour, and when it was all over the professor left.

No one tried to discover an improved way of working with Ossowiecki or a modified technique to see if a better method even could be uncovered. This is a tragedy. He was the greatest European psychic of his day, even when tested under rigorously controlled conditions, but how much greater could he have been if he had been able to display his great gifts under the most optimal personal conditions? The professors seemed deliberately to avoid giving Ossowiecki any help, even when the aid would not have compromised the results. They wouldn't help him with vocabulary problems when confusion arose over the spear. Was there really any reason why the maid could not have been told to hold Stefan's calls? Using the same object twice, once for a "reading" and again as a control, is a neat experimental procedure, but what about giving the psychic a little feedback to help him on his way and relieve pressure? Have you ever tried to give a description of some person or of an accident without any help? Not easy, is it? There are no limits to the assistance we can give psychics that would in no way affect their impressions.

Ossowiecki would often see the actors in his clairvoyant drama talking, but he couldn't hear their words. Why not teach him to lipread? It would have been more efficient to ask Ossowiecki specific questions, instead of letting him waste valuable energy rambling on in free association. He could have been channeled away from irrelevant minutiae. Poniatowski should either have helped Ossowiecki or left the room completely to allow him total isolation so he could "read" without distraction. In four years one can vary and upgrade one's experimental technique considerably.

The biggest problem is general feedback. Who likes to answer thousands of questions to which no one knows the answers? Poniatowski could have guided Ossowiecki by asking him pertinent questions which did have archaeological answers or which would draw out the particulars the investigators wanted. Questions such as the following could be asked: how were prehistoric tools made? Where did the raw materials needed to fashion the tools come from? Was cremation a common or unusual occurrence? Other questions where the answers could have been easily checked would have been helpful. This would place the other information received in better perspective and serve to inspire the psychic. How about some information wherein excavation might offer immediate feedback? What better double-blind? Double blinds are frequently used in science. "Double blind" denotes that neither the subject nor the experimenters know much about the test—only a third party does. For instance, if researchers were testing two drugs, one to cure cancer and one neutral, during a double-blind experiment the investigator would not know which drug he was administering. This rules out the possibility that the experimenter "leaked" information to his subjects which could contaminate the results.

Digging would even provide a "triple blind" because here *no one* would know the answer until after excavation. Ossowiecki would be assured that his psychic perceptions had a direct practical application and relevance. This greater sense of discovery and adventure might have been a catalyst for his ESP. It is ironic that Ossowiecki's best quasi-archaeological feat—the location of the dead soldier in a mass grave—was carried out not by degree-heavy scientists, but by some common folks in need? Frankly, Poniatowski's 400 pages of notes, valuable as they are, reveal that the good professor was writing when he should have been digging. The location of the grotto and the burial urn would have been a natural place to begin.

The moral of Ossowiecki's work in psychic archaeology may be that, for all his remarkable powers and impressive demonstrations, he was restricted by the failings of the men who came before him. He was lucky when his skills were applied to more than parlor tricks, but he was born too soon to join in developing the mind's potency as a truly applied science.

Chapter 3

Edgar Cayce and the Akashic Records

No man has a good enough memory to be a successful liar.

—*Abraham Lincoln*

Anyone who has ever opened a book on psychic phenomena will be familiar with the name of Edgar Cayce. Cayce has been called the Sleeping Prophet because during most of his life he demonstrated his remarkable psychic gifts while in a self-induced hypnotic trance. While so entranced, he could diagnose the illnesses of people miles away, prescribe treatment for them, talk about religion and nutrition, "read" the past lives of his clients, and even discuss Atlantis and Lemuria. He is best known for his ability to diagnose clairvoyantly any medical problem his clients had, with such spectacular results that doctors would huddle by him during his trance to check out his accuracy.

Cayce also did readings on every conceivable topic under the sun. The history of man and the geology of the world were frequent topics and some of his revelations on these subjects were no less spectacular than his medical readings. Through his clairvoyance Cayce traveled back in time to ancient Egypt and sat in the courts of the pharaohs. He sailed the oceans with the first prehistoric adventurers and walked the Holy Land with Jesus. He didn't simply mention Atlantis, he gave a detailed account of this fantastic lost continent and its denizens. Cayce's readings were not mere fantasy, for many of his revelations overlap information archaeology has already collected on the history of the earth. Aware that his talks would clash with existing archaeologocal evidence about man's history, Cayce predicted that ancient records would ultimately be discovered that would resolve the discrepancies between his views and those of orthodox archaeology. He also said, somewhat cryptically, that some of these records have already been found but that we can't interpret them yet.

Cayce's view of the past radically departs from our image of it. While archaeology attempts to understand the past by piecing scattered bits of discovery into a meaningful whole, Cayce talks about entirely new pieces to the puzzle. He predicted that lost civilizations would eventually be found in the Atlantic Ocean, in the Gobi Desert, in the hills of Iran, and in the jungles of Indonesia. He clairvoyantly traveled back not only to medieval and Paleolithic times, but even further into man's prehistory. Wherever his revelations led, conventional archaeology could follow, since much of what he said could be checked scientifically. Unfortunately, though, even today archaeology has not deigned to search some of the places Cayce spoke about. This is doubly frustrating since the past thirty years of archaeological exploration has already proved that the seer had correctly prophesized *in detail* a number of key discoveries long before they were actually made.

During his trances Cayce seemed to contact a cosmic source of information that he often referred to as the Akashic Records: some mysterious hall of records where the history of man, earth, and civilization lay like the pages of an open book. Apparently Cayce had the psychic talent to read them.

Edgar Cayce either leaves a legacy as the world's first perfect liar (one who never tripped himself up, with inconsistent stories), or he was the world's first documented psychic time traveler. How was Cayce able to give 14,256 psychic readings which yielded 49,135 pages of transcript over a period of forty-three years, and at all times keep his stories mutually concordant even when jumping quickly from one topic to another?

Cayce was born on March 18, 1877 on a farm in western Kentucky where his father was a justice of the peace. The only thing which seemed to sustain his interest as a boy was the Bible, which he read through several times. He was deeply impressed by its promise that man can have divine communication with God. He prayed fervently for this mystical experience and when he was twelve years old he had a vision in which his prayers were answered. Young Cayce was far from being a budding young scholar, and he really bungled his spelling lesson the next day, for he was totally preoccupied with his vision and what it meant. Even that evening he still found it hard to concentrate on his work. At eleven o'clock that night, long past his bedtime, he heard a voice, as if in a dream. It was the same voice he had heard in his vision and it kept repeating, "Sleep and we may help you." He fell asleep for several minutes and, according to Thomas Sugrue's authoritative biography, *There Is a River*, when he awakened he knew every word by rote in the spelling book on which he had inadvertently slept. This is only one of the many strange stories that grew into the Cayce legend.

Cayce's formal education stopped at the sixth grade, and after working for awhile as a clerk he settled down to photography as his life's trade. It was during this time that he began experimenting with hypnosis. When he suddenly and inexplicably lost his voice, a hypnotist friend named Layne put him in trance and asked him to diagnose his own malady. Not only was Cayce successful in this endeavor, but he even diagnosed and prescribed medication for Layne's stomach ailment. So when only twenty-one, Cayce began giving "psychic readings" in addition to his trade, in order to help others when he could. To give these discourses Cayce entered a self-induced hypnoticlike trance. He would simply lie down, fold his arms over his chest, and by autosuggestion go to sleep. While in this state, he responded to whatever questions were asked of him. When he awoke he claimed that he remembered nothing of what he said. It is ironic that his psychic work caused this God-fearing humble man to be arrested twice; once for practicing medicine without a license and once for fortune telling. The authorities didn't take his readings as seriously as did many professional doctors, nutritionists, and others who constantly sought his help in their work.

In addition to his own religious beliefs Cayce was equally at home when discussing Christian, Jewish, Hindu, and other religious philosophies, and it is not surprising that prolific discourses on religion cropped up in his readings which offered a somewhat makeshift philosophy on the spiritual nature of man. Nonetheless, the normal Cayce was a traditional Christian. It was a shock to him when he first learned that the concept of reincarnation was appearing more and more often in his trance talks. He began by discussing the meaning of the doctrine and soon after started telling bystanders about their past lives.

While Cayce was an exemplary human being, he was by no means the saint that legend and many of his followers have tried to make him. He had all the harmless down-home vices. He liked the companionship of pretty women, and he drank occasionally, usually from his stock of homemade wine. He was a chain smoker as well, and when his startled admirers looked aghast when he lit up cigarette after cigarette, he would smile and point to the heavens, saying, "Where I am going there are no cigarettes." Cayce was a very "human" human being. He golfed, bowled, fished, put up jelly, and spent considerable time in his garden.

In the later part of Cayce's career, a hospital and a college (Atlantic University) were chartered as a way of directly utilizing the information and philosophy which had come out of his readings. But the Great Depression of the 1930's took its toll and both operations faltered only a short time after they had commenced. Cayce tried to save these institutions from financial ruin by forming the Cayce Oil Company and by also doing a series of readings on where to find buried treasure. But, like Ossowiecki, Cayce's psychic abilities didn't work well when directed toward satisfying personal goals. However, several businessmen made fortunes by following his advice, especially on the stock market. In fact, Cayce's own financial status was always on thin ice, but in times of need solutions always appeared fortuitously. During World War II, like Ossowiecki, he virtually doubled his psychic work load in order to help people in need, and on two separate occasions he was called to the White House. The seer died in his sleep in 1945 at the age of sixty-eight. It seems that he literally used himself up during the war years.

Despite the fact that it is now thirty years after his death, all the Cayce readings have been preserved by the Association for Research and Enlightenment (ARE), in Virginia Beach, which makes the Cayce archives available to all those who seek to benefit from them. Each year they sponsor a number of lectures and seminars on Cayce and related subjects, and they have recently built a multimillion-dollar library that contains one of the best book collections on parapsychology and psychic phenomena in the world. Recently the ARE has also helped Atlantic University get back on its feet and it has sponsored thousands of home study groups at which people can get together and through prayer and meditation learn to apply the Cayce concept to their daily lives. Since his death, there have been over twenty books written on Cayce, with sales numbering in the millions. There have also been countless news and magazine articles and even a Ph.D. dissertation on the Sleeping Prophet, written by a doctoral student at the University of Chicago. So Edgar Cayce has left quite a legacy. The readings, indexed on over 200,000 cards, are enough to fill over 200 volumes.

Cayce's readings of history and prehistory tread almost virgin territory. Much of the archaeological information offered about man's prehistory was not given directly, but as a virtually inadvertent by-product of his "life-readings" which included tracing his clients' past lives.

In one reading a client was told that he had accompanied Eric the Red, the Viking explorer, on his expedition to America and that he had traveled inland as far as Minnesota. Within this off-the-cuff remark lurked the theory that the Vikings discovered America before Columbus. This is a commonly accepted theory today, but the reading was made years before a number of professors discovered evidence that substantiated it.

A past-life reading would go something like this: ". . . divorced, one child in name then of Mary McClannaghan in Provincetown during the periods of questioning by those who were so orthodox as to forget God." Or ". . . during the latter part of the American Revolution . . . in the opposite sex as a man Ernest Cobb and the entity's activities in the planning of the latter portion of the campaigns through eastern and southern Pennsylvania may be found recorded in his associations with others and maybe of special interest to the entity especially associated with the family of Clarence Cobb . . ." While such bits of information may not add anything of importance to our understanding of history, these trivial tidbits of data give enough information so that any skeptic could check out the reading for himself if he wished to do so.

Sometimes the past-life readings were verified. One inquirer was told that in a former life she had been Etta Tetlow, a dance-hall girl during the boisterous Gold Rush days of San Francisco. Years later another woman, who was familiar with the reading, was browsing through some colorful old posters. The posters listed the performers at the local dance hall, and on one particular poster a familiar name stood out—Tetlow. However, there are still hundreds of other past-life readings to be checked, and investigations have failed to validate others.

In perusing these hundreds of readings, one realizes that Cayce focused on those past ages where he himself had lived former incarnations. This may explain how he was able to give such detailed portraits of the people and activities of those bygone eras. In addition to the information we can extract from these life-readings, several others were given which centered directly on the past. Six readings were specifically devoted to predynastic Egypt; sixteen to the time of Christ; one to the Mayan civilization; and thirteen to the general history of Atlantis.

According to Cayce, many thousands of years ago the Sahara area was well watered. Geological findings made since the readings bear out this claim. But more startling is the statement that "The Nile entered into the Atlantic . . ." (364-13, 1932).* This odd statement appears also in an earlier reading where Cayce claimed that, ". . . the Upper Nile regions, the waters then entering the now Atlantic from the Nile region rather than northward . . ." (5748-1, 1925). This perception of the past world seems topsy-turvy since the Nile doesn't flow westward and enter the Atlantic. Everyone knows that it flows northward, forms a delta, and enters the Mediterranean.

One of the most impressive features of the readings is just this tendency to be so at odds with established fact. One is constantly amazed at these outlandish statements and astonished when they turn out to be true. Indeed, geologists had always believed that the Nile flowed north for at least several million years, but surprising new geological studies made in the late 1960s have shown that the northward flow of the Nile from the Ethiopian highlands is only a relatively recent occurrence. It has been discovered that instead of flowing toward the north, the old Nile flowed *westward* into the Sudan and Chad and fed what was once Lake Sudd and Lake Chad. Lake Chad is over 1,500 miles closer to the Atlantic

These numbers represent the catalog number of the reading and date it was delivered. Throughout the remainder of the chapter these numbers will be given for important data which will refer the reader to the exact source of the quotes.

than the present course of the Nile, and it is in the general proximity of river systems that *do* enter into the Atlantic Ocean.

Cayce's actual story of Egypt begins with an account of a peaceful agrarian Negroid people who were invaded by Caucasian hordes from the Caucasus mountains. Here again, surprising discoveries have cast a new light on the Egyptians and also on Cayce's reading of their history. It has always been accepted that the ancient Egyptians were Caucasian. But recently a thesis based on multiple discriminate analysis of Egyptian and African Negro crania was presented at Harvard University. All possible skull measurements were taken and compared between early predynastic Egyptian, later dynastic Egyptian, and modern Negro skulls, and the results support Cayce's contention. The thesis reports that ". . . the predynastic Egyptians were more like Negroes than the dynastic Egyptians were, and that the dynastic Egyptians were more Caucasoid than their predecessors." We have already uncovered substantial evidence that the earliest Egyptians farmed, and some experts also believe that in predynastic times the Egyptian delta area was invaded by inhabitants of the Caucasus. In Volume four of his *Pyramid Texts*, Samuel Mercer states the belief that the legendary Ra and his followers, who took over Egypt, came from the northeast. Egyptologists date such an invasion at about 5,000 years ago while Cayce dates it some 12,000 years ago.

Proceeding to focus his attention on the personality of Ra, the priest of the invading Caucasians, Cayce spoke of a confrontation between Ra and the king of the delta natives which consummated in Ra's becoming priest of both peoples. According to the seer, the original passages of the *Egyptian Book of the Dead* were written at this time. He also notes that there were no real cities built at this time, but that existing settlements consisted only of tent camps and several temples.

Cayce's reading suggests that Egyptian culture sprang forward as a result of the influence of these sophisticated invaders, and in fact the existing archaeological records for Egypt also show that at some point in history Egyptian culture rapidly evolved. Likewise, Cayce discussed the early clans and how they developed animal totems, carvings of which still survive on early Egyptian pallets. These facts are really subsidiary to the main story outlined—the ups and downs of the ruler Ra. A rather Hollywoodesque plot was outlined: At first Ra is venerated by all; his words are taken as law. Then a plot involving a young girl is hatched against him. Ra takes the voluptuous bait, falls from grace, and is banished to Nubia with 200 followers. Without a strong ruler cold war develops in the delta area as different political factions vie for position. Meanwhile the Nubian area (now Abyssinia) thrives under Ra's leadership. (Cayce specifically says that the memorials left behind by Ra and his followers in the mountains they occupied may still be found.) As the cold war gets hotter, there is a split of the delta kingdom. During the chaos a counterrevolution is masterminded to force the return of Ra. Ra resumes his reign in triumph, restores peace, and reunites the kingdom, which begins to make its great leaps forward in astronomy, art, medicine, economics, and social order. During this time the great Pyramid of Giza is built and later the Sphinx which guards it.

One can only marvel at Cayce's vivid narrative. But it is more than a two-dimensional talk, for the readings take on added dimension as life and personality are breathed into these exhilarating times. Even a description of this early king of Egypt was given; his height, weight, color of his eyes, etc. These details are more useful to us today than as mere added grains of information used for dramatic effect. Just as with the geological and racial details that were offered, accurately foreshadowing revised archaeological thinking and evidence about these times, the data included in the narrative are surprisingly consistent with our view of what Egypt was like. For example, one description is given of ancient Egyptian dress:

"The robes of the priests would be blue-gray, with the hooded portion back from the head, while about the waist would be a cord of gold color, with a purple tassel—or one of the tassels—showing. The sandals would be of papyrus or woven grass. The robe of the kneeling figure would be in white (this also a robe you see), with a band about the neck or throat in blue, not too dark, and the bare feet or at least one or both showing" (585-10, 1942).

In the Old Kingdom (before the two halves of ancient Egypt were united) the priests usually wore kilts, and not robes. But Dr. Marjorie Hansen, an Egyptologist, checking on Cayce's readings in 1962 found in the Old Kingdom section of the Cairo Museum two statues depicting men in rather unusual dress. They wore just the type of robe Cayce described in his reading. This is not the only coincidence she found. Also stated was that the early Egyptians used two forms of writing. One was the ancient style of the Egyptians while the other was introduced later. On checking Dr. Hansen found the following passage in James H. Breasted's *A History of Egypt* in which he commented on two styles of Egyptian writing: "The hieroglyphics for the Northern Kingdom, for its king and for its treasury can not have arisen at one stroke with the first king of the dynastic age, but must have been in use *long before* the rise of the First Dynasty (3,400 B.C.) while the presence of a cursive linear hand at the beginning of the dynasties is conclusive that the system was not then a recent innovation."

Based on a search of historical literature, in discussion with other archaeologists, and while searching through Egyptian museums, Dr. Hansen found good evidence that the seer's perception of the ancient Egyptians was remarkably accurate. His comments on their names, religion, hieroglyphics, and tombs all panned out.

But what is the use of all this research? Can these details really help us in any way? The skeptic might throw up his hands and say, "So what?" A practical application may be made from the readings. Through them archaeologists have the opportunity to reap extraordinary guidance for the study of early Egypt and eventually give the public their first real look at the roots of modern civilization that are deeply embedded in Egypt's cradle of civilization.

Traveling east of Egypt, we are brought closer to the world which existed when Jesus walked the Holy Land. Whether one is a Christian or not, no other time in man's history has had such a profound effect upon Western culture. As with his Egyptian chronicles, Cayce presents us with many surprises that could shake theologian and scientist alike—surprises that are withstanding the rigors of scientific testing and subsequent discovery. Archaeology's greatest contribution to mankind would be to solve the emotion-laden controversies about the true historical events that rocked this critical period in our history.

Cayce's story of Jesus is long and complicated. Jeffrey Furst's book, *Edgar Cayce's Story of Jesus*, contains most of his discourses on the subject. Cayce tells us that Jesus had twenty-nine other lives and was usually incarnated as a major figure with religious movements in other parts of the world.

Cayce explains how Jesus and many of the key figures of these passionate times were associated with a secret religious sect called the Essenes, a mystic Hebraic brotherhood. Today Essene monks trace their origins back to Elijah at Mount Carmel and the school for prophets he established there.

Does Cayce know what he was talking about, or does his time machine have a loose screw? In 1936, while giving a past-life reading to a visitor, he said:

> The entity was then what would be termed in the present, in some organizations, as a Sister Superior, or an officer as it were in those of the Essenes . . . the entity ministering . . . and making for those encouraging experiences oft in the lives of the Disciples; coming in contact with the Master oft in the ways between Bethany, Galilee, Jerusalem. For . . . the entity kept the school on the way above Emmaus to the way that "goeth down towards Jericho" and towards the northernmost coast from Jerusalem . . . the entity blessed many of those who came to seek to know the teachings, the ways, the mysteries, the understandings; for the entity had been trained in the schools of those that were of the prophets and prophetesses, and the entity was indeed a prophetess in those experiences . . ." (1391-1, 1936).

This reference to a woman's having lived in an Essene community near the coast of the Dead Sea does not at first seem particularly significant, but eleven years later the Dead Sea scrolls were discovered in some isolated caves. Nearby ruins, located precisely as described in the Cayce reading, were excavated uncovering the remains of an Essene community now called Qumran. In 1936 no living person knew that these ruins were those of an Essene community and, as the reading indicated, the ground around this religious enclave contained skeletons of women as well as men. Before the actual excavation of Qumran, scholars agreed that the Essene community was composed only of cloistered celibate monks. There were allegedly no women.

Cayce's psychic insights shed new light on another controversy, for theologians and scholars have debated for years over how much Jesus knew about this community and its work on the religious scrolls. The Dead Sea scrolls now consist of over 400 different manuscripts from which scientists have pieced together nearly the entire Old Testament. They now constitute our earliest biblical manuscripts, since the Bible as we know it today was actually collected by the Fathers of the Church in the third and fourth centuries. Also, seven nonbiblical documents have been found, the earliest of which has been dated at approximately 250 B.C., while the others were apparently not written up until about 1 B.C. One of the scrolls is believed to have been written by a man of mystery named only as the Teacher of Righteousness. Another scroll makes reference to this Teacher and tells how he was once the head of the Qumran community and was killed by a "Wicked Priest." Not only did the Teacher foretell his own death and the manner in which it would come, but he also foretold his reincarnation. The scroll also suggests that this return would be preceded by a Forerunner.

The Essenes were a group dedicated to the belief in the Messiah, the savior of the Jewish people promised in the Old Testament. The community was composed mainly of very Orthodox Jews, but membership was open to anyone who would follow their disciplines and pass a lengthy initiation period.

In his reading Cayce details the communal rules and practices of the Essenes at some length. One of the discovered scrolls, which is called the "Order of the Community," sets forth the community's purpose, theology, and liturgical practice. The consistencies between Cayce's psychic perceptions and this document are incredible. It would seem that he was not only able to locate this mysterious lost group, but that he also had the ability to reconstruct their day-to-day activities and philosophy. What makes the readings even more provocative is that many of them cite the interactions between Jesus and the Essenes!

It is unfortunate that to date, twenty-five years after the discovery of the Dead Sea scrolls, fewer than half of them have been translated and published. There are many more yet to be found, even though some religious leaders would be happier if they were never translated at all. Professor John Marco Allegro of Manchester University, England, one of the key translators of the scripts, has been warning the public of what the scrolls might reveal. In a contribution to *Harper's Magazine*, he noted with apprehension:

"The very scholars who should be most capable of working on the documents and interpreting them have displayed a not altogether but nonetheless curious reluctance to go to the heart of their matter. The scholars appear to have held back from making discoveries which there is evidence to believe may upset a great many basic teachings of the Christian church. This in turn would greatly upset many Christian theologians and believers. The heart of the matter is in fact the source and originality of Christian doctrine."

Cayce's story does not focus merely on the Essenes and the scrolls. He gives descriptions and personality profiles of the disciples and also presents a physical depiction of Jesus which matches one given in a report in the Roman archives written by Lentulus nearly 2,000 years ago. Few people know about this document. In another reading, Cayce said, "For the entity was among those spoken of as the Holy Women . . . first the entity coming in contact with those activities at the death *and* the raising of Lazarus, and later with Elizabeth, Mary, Salome, Mary of Magdalene, Martha—all of those were a part of the experiences of the entity—as Salome" (1874-1, 1939). The book of Mark 15:40-41 (Revised Standard Version) refers to a woman named Salome who was present at the crucifixion of Jesus. However, John 11, which describes the raising of Lazarus from the dead, *does not* mention Salome as being present. Here an apparently insignificant statement, taken from a life-reading that has lain in the ARE archives for twenty-one years has now been shown to be startlingly accurate. In 1960 Dr. Morton Smith, a history professor at Columbia University, announced that he had found a copy of a letter while studying ancient manuscripts in Jerusalem. The letter narrated a miracle which was not incorporated in the present Gospel of St. Mark. It had been written by Clement of Alexandria, an author whose works were written between 180 and 202 A.D., and tells about Jesus raising Lazarus from the dead. A new witness to the miracle, a woman named Salome, is introduced in that letter. Even if the letter is in error, the document is certainly thought-provoking as we try to understand the mystique of Edgar Cayce.

Just as provocative is the account given about the missing years of Jesus' life. These are the much-debated years between his childhood and his return to the Holy Land at the age of thirty. We know virtually nothing of these years, and historians have come up with all kinds of speculation about them. According to Cayce's readings, Jesus spent these years studying and teaching in Egypt, India, Tibet, and Persia. Here again we have a testable theory that can act as a balm in an area fraught with emotion. And here again Cayce's readings look promising.

The Tibetan lamas possess some of the oldest manuscripts in the world. In a book entitled *Tibet*, co-authored with anthropologist Colin Turnbull, Thubten Jigme Norbu, the elder brother of the Dalai Lama, tells of an old manuscript that was hidden away in a Buddhist monastery at Hemis in Ladulch. Norbu claims that this document contains an account of the travels of a humble foreigner who had visited India in his youth and had finally come to Tibet where he resided with the monks at Hemis before returning to his homeland to preach a new religion. How apocryphal this story is we will never know, but it is Norbu's opinion that this youth was Jesus of Judea. It is reported that eventually this script came into the possession of a Russian and has since come to be called the *Chronicle of Issa* (Jesus). Jesus' possible sojourn in the Far East may well explain why he so often spoke in parables, a literary style common to that area.

Author and adventurer Thor Heyerdahl has long excited the public with his theory that our ancient forefathers were able to, and actually did, cross the oceans. As recounted in his best selling books *Kon-Tiki* and *Aku-Aku*, he sailed the seas in a craft modeled after those built by the ancients in order to prove his point. During his voyages he has traversed the Atlantic and Pacific oceans. From his firsthand adventures, Heyerdahl concludes that the parallel cultural developments that developed simultaneously in Asia and the New World, among other places, were proof that ancient peoples traveled between the hemispheres. Until a few years ago most scholars pooh-poohed this idea. It seemed to wreak havoc on the pristine schemes *they* had figured out to explain how culture developed over the globe. The very thought that Egyptians or Asians visited the natives of Peru and Mexico would send chills up the spine of any staid archaeology professor.

Long before Heyerdahl's memorable travels, the Cayce readings were also telling of such prehistoric transoceanic contact. In fact, the readings even refer to specific trips made by particular individuals. He spoke about excursions from the

Near East into the Olmec-Maya area (ranging from Mexico into Central America), and about contacts between the ancient residents of South and North America. Since most archaeologists won't even admit that there was contact between the two western continents, this was certainly bucking dogma. But time, experience, and discovery have changed all this. For example, Dr. Gordon Willy of Harvard University has been promoting the view that there was cultural contact between the ancient Chavin culture of Peru and the Olmec of Mexico. Drs. Betty Meggers and C. Evans of the Smithsonian have presented evidence that Japanese fishermen landed on the coast of Ecuador over 5,000 years ago. Dr. David Kelly, a Canadian archaeologist, has pointed out odd and inexplicable parallels between the Mayan calendar and the Near Eastern calendar. In both calendars the same sequence of animal types are used in the same order to represent each month. Even the origination date for these calendars is the same—approximately 3,000 B.C.

Recently Dr. Meggers has even gone so far as to publish an article in the *American Anthropologist* entitled "The Transpacific Origins of Mesoamerican Civilization: A Preliminary Review of the Evidence and Its Theoretical Implications." In the article, Dr. Meggers presents a hoard of evidence that members of the Shang civilization of China crossed the Pacific Ocean thousands of years ago and had a major influence on the development of the first civilization in Mexico, namely the Olmecs. The evidence is impressive since the following points of comparison can be made between the two civilizations: (1) Both cultures used the jaguar motif in art and deity depictions. (2) They had similar writing styles. (3) They placed a similar value on jade. (4) They had similar abstract concepts of physical beauty. (5) Their settlement patterns and architecture was concordant. (6) They both had the long range goal of acquisition of luxury goods. (7) The baton was a symbol of rank in both civilizations. Other parallels could be cited as well.

As Dr. Meggers emphasized, some theory of cultural exchange is needed, "for formulation of a valid theory of the evolution of civilization."

Cayce stressed this same theory half a century earlier, postulating, as had the ancient Greeks, that there once was a lost continent—Atlantis—whose civilization suddenly mothered or influenced many subsequent civilizations over the earth. If the idea of a transoceanic contact is R-rated by archaeologists, then the theory of Atlantis must be X-rated. The only reason archaeologists have ever investigated Atlantis is to prove that the belief in the lost continent is nonsense. The Cayce readings don't mince words or equivocate about the existence of Atlantis. Just as with his other readings on the past, a full Atlantean history is given, complete with specific names and events—information that might pluck Atlantis from the realm of the lost.

Literally hundreds of books have been written on the subject. Plato mentioned the lost continent in two of his dialogues, "Critias" and "Timaeus." The philosopher introduced the concept of Atlantis in a conversation between Solon (Plato's brother-in-law) and certain Egyptian priests at Sais who tell him that Atlantis was a large island in the Atlantic which sank during a volcanic catastrophe some 9,000 years before. Ever since this passage was written, Atlantis stirred fiery emotions. While some detractors have tried to show that Plato's story of Atlantis was just a myth, enthusiasts have tried to substantiate the legend. Over the years Atlanteanites have tried to locate it in every sea in the world. They have altered the date of its alleged destruction considerably, and a whole school of occult dogma and legend has grown from the original story. Rather than enter the Atlantis controversy, I will only suggest a way to resolve this emotional and controversial issue. Cayce's story of Atlantis is scattered with geographical clues to bits and pieces of information about our ancient world and its topography which we can prove or disprove and which shed light on the Atlantis story. This is all to the good, since archaeologists have troubles enough without trying to excavate the entire ocean floor!

Cayce's story of Atlantis begins 100,000 years ago on an island even larger than the one Plato depicted. Cayce tells of the great developments the first Atlanteans made. He speaks of their art, architecture, writing, and budding sciences. He describes their relatively advanced technology, founded on the use of crystals and energy conversion, which is similar to our recent discovery and use of lasers and masers. Atlantis was virtually the Eden of the physical world. He also postulates a metaphysical origin of the Atlanteans: man originated as a spiritual being, not as a physical one; these spirits or souls then projected themselves into matter and began the sequence of human evolution. According to Cayce, it was in Atlantis that our physical form took on the gradual appearance of modern men.

This lost "red race" evolved until the first of several volcanic disturbances wrecked the island. As a result, the southernmost portion of the island broke up and fell into the sea, ". . . now near what would be termed the Sargasso Sea . . ." (364-4, 1932). The Sargasso Sea is a weed-filled body of water surrounding Bermuda, and popular writers have noted with amazement how the eels of Europe swim across the ocean floor to breed there. A possible remnant of sunken Atlantean greeneries, they ask? They suggest that the eels' spawning instinct leads them back to their ancestral home, perhaps to the mouth of a great river that flowed through Atlantis.

According to Cayce, a second major upheaval occurred in 28,000 B.C. but during the interim some of the inhabitants migrated to different parts of the world. They ". . . entered rather into the Pyrenees and what is now the Portuguese, French, and Spanish land. And there *still* may be seen in the chalk cliffs there in Calais the activities, where the marks of the entity's followers were made, as the attempts were set with those to create a temple activity to the follower of the law of One" (315-4, 1932).

Archaeologists have long had trouble explaining the amazingly sudden initial appearances of *Homo sapiens* (modern man) on the earth approximately 40,000 years ago. Modern man appeared around the world virtually overnight at the same time that Neanderthal man suddenly and equally inexplicably disappeared. Could there be a connection between this postulated Atlantean migration and our archaeological records? Today the best area for tracing the sudden influx of Cro-Magnon (modern) man into Europe is in France and Spain where evidence of his unique and sophisticated art is preserved in caves. Recent research indicates that he was even making calendric and astronomical notations at this early date.

As the Atlanteans advanced technologically, they began to lose their spirituality. At approximately 10,000 B.C. the final destruction of Atlantis is said to have occurred, and all was lost into the sea's deep and mysterious waters. Again Cayce spoke about migrations of Atlanteans to other parts of the world: "Evidence of this lost civilization are to be found in the Pyrenees and Morocco on the one hand, British Honduras, Yucatán and America upon the other'' (364-3, 1932).

Ignoring cremation as a possible explanation, skeptics of the Atlantis theory have long complained that scientists lack any organic remains or evidence for such a race. If Cayce's lead that Morocco received Atlantean migrants is followed, something very startling happens when the skeletal record for this era and area is examined. Along the Algerian and Moroccan coast scientists have found the skeletal remnants of a physically and culturally unique population which physical anthropologists have called *Mouillans*. They have been found in a handful of sites which have been radiocarbon dated to approximately 10,000 B.C.! These sites provide our largest source of Stone Age skeletal remains, and populations of up to 100 individuals have been found. The remains are mostly of women and children. Anthropologists have long been baffled about where the Mouillans came from, why they appear so suddenly in the archaeological record, and how they came by their sophisticated flint and stone tools—tools which were never seen before anywhere in the world. The remains of animals *not* indigenous to the area also appear in the archaeological record concomittantly. Whoever these people were, they inhabited these sites only briefly. *But they possessed the largest cranial capacity of any population the world has ever known!* This capacity measured an average of 2,000 cubic centimeters while modern man's cranial size is only about 1,400 cubic centimeters.

Dr. Carleton Coon, the noted physical anthropologist, has pointed out that the Mouillans' physical appearance was composed of a number of features which have never before evolved in such combinations in any race at this time in man's history. These features include high, vaulted brain cases of high cranial capacity, short, broad faces with low orbits, and deep, broad jaws with everted gonial angles. Coon feels that these same features may still be seen among some Berbers, a Moslem population of North Africa, living in relatively inaccessible regions along the Mediterranean Coast. As late as the fifteenth century conquest of the Canary Islands, some of the natives, called Guanches, were depicted as being similar to the Mouillans. Yet, Dr. Coon's erudite discussions were predated by popular writers on Atlantis such as Donelly, Sykes, and Berlitz, who also drew connections between the populations of Atlantis and the Berbers and Guanches.

In Cayce's Egyptian chronicles, which are dated just after the first sinking of Atlantis, the priests of the invading Ra not only confronted the local tribes but also migrating Atlanteans. The Atlanteans first contemplated enslaving the technologically backward Egyptians but instead, due to Ra's intervention, the small group of Atlanteans helped them develop their technology. Almost overnight Egypt became the cultural center of the ancient world. While this tale has little evidential support, it is consistent with some historical facts. Plato's information on Atlantis is said to have come from records now 11,000 years old which made reference to the Atlantean threat. It is interesting to note that according to the Egyptian priest-historian Manetho, the Egyptians changed their calendric system about this very time. Of course one is left with the question, had Cayce read Plato? Friends of Cayce report that he only read the Bible and the newspaper.

The readings concentrate on the close companionship that developed between Ra and Hept-Supht, who was the keeper of the records carried from Atlantis. These records were sealed in a Hall of Records buried between the Great Pyramid and the Sphinx which were both built around that time. Cayce said that this Hall of Records is yet to be uncovered, but he gave detailed directions on how to locate it: "This in position lies, as the sun rises from the waters, the line of the shadow (or light) falls between the paws of the Sphinx, that was later set as the sentinel or guard, and which may not be entered from the connecting chambers from the Sphinx's paw (right paw) until the *time* has been fulfilled when the changes must be active in this sphere of man's experience. [It lies] between, then, the Sphinx and the river" (378-16, 1933).

No one has yet taken Cayce's directions seriously. The sealed room allegedly contains "a record of Atlantis from the beginnings of those periods when the Spirit took form or began the encasements in that land and the developments of the peoples throughout their sojourn together with the record of the first destruction and the changes that took place in the land with the record of the sojournings of the peoples and their varied activities in other lands. And a record of the meeting of all the nations or lands for the activities in the destruction of Atlantis. And the building of the Pyramid of Initiation together with who, what and where the opening of the records would come that are copies from the sunken Atlantis'' (378-16, 1933).

The discovery of these records would be a clear-cut independent check on Cayce's Atlantean epic.

During another reading, Cayce reported that the records also contain treatises on ''the ability to use unseen forces in the . . . material things of man.'' This sealed room is supposed to be a type of time capsule housing musical instruments, religious accoutrements, surgical instruments, and other material objects used by the Atlanteans. The readings go on to say that remnants of these Atlantean records existed in the great Egyptian library at Alexandria. Could it be that these records were the basis of the many discoveries made by the famous Greeks who studied there? We will never know for certain, because the contents of the library of Alexandria were destroyed when the structure was sacked by militant Christians in 415 A.D. But Cayce spoke of another link to the Atlantean Hall of Records in Egypt. He talked of a library larger than the Alexandrian, one yet to be discovered in Persia (Iran) and predicted its ultimate uncovering. Archaeologists are just now beginning to excavate in the very area he pinpointed.

Until an actual Egypto-Atlantean Hall of Records is found, the only possible mementos of the lost continent might be the Great Pyramid of Giza, one of the Seven Wonders of the World. It is unfortunate that we can't directly and clearly date stone structures, but scholars have long been aware that the pyramid was designed and executed with unusually advanced technology. The Great Pyramid is markedly different from any other. It seems to be the embodiment of a lost science. The pyramid has been analyzed extensively by Dr. Livio Stechinni, a professor of ancient history and a specialist in the history of measurements and quantitative science. Dr. Stechinni has taught at the universities of Rome, Chicago, Rutgers and M.I.T., and his precise analysis of the Great Pyramid shows that:

(1) The structure incorporates the value of pi (the constant by which the diameter of a circle may be multiplied to calculate its circumference) accurately to several decimal places.

(2) The pyramid's main chamber incorporates several trigonometric functions which were later ''discovered'' by

Pythagoras and which are revered in modern architecture.

(3) It serves as a calendar by which the length of the year can be measured to the exact minute.

(4) It can serve as a transit, enabling precise surveying measurements.

(5) It is so finely aligned with the North Pole that modern compasses can be adjusted to it.

(6) The measurements of its sides and angles accurately reflect the geographic measurements of the northern hemisphere, such as the degree of latitude and longitude, the circumference and radius of the earth—even accounting for polar flattening.

All this data was not "discovered" until the seventeenth century.

In his comments on the pyramid, Dr. Stechinni has stated; "Its architects may well have known the length of the earth's orbit around the sun, the specific density of the earth, the 26,000-year cycle of the equinoxes, the acceleration of gravity and the speed of light."

Dr. Luis Alvarez, who won the Nobel prize in physics in 1968, has carefully studied the activity of cosmic rays passing through the pyramid. In an interview in the *Arizona Daily Star*, October 26, 1975, he is summarized as saying that what was occurring was not only impossible, but that some energy was being registered that did not conform to the laws of science. Many scientists do not believe that the Egyptians were advanced enough to have come by all this detailed information normally. Did somebody much more advanced direct the construction of the pyramid? If we accept the Atlantean hypothesis, all the oddities start to fall into place.

While Ra was ruling Egypt, Cayce says, a potentate named Muzuen governed Mongolia at the Lost City of Taoi underneath the sands of the Gobi Desert. Supposedly Taoi was a great culture, more sophisticated than those in Mesopotamia (Iraq) and Egypt. If Cayce's tale is correct, its discovery will be one of the greatest events in modern history. According to the seer's description, the people invented explosives, electricity, and unique methods of transportation and communication. They coined gold, which existed in fabulous quantities and was "then as the sands to these people." Cayce described a temple built of wood that was overlaid with gold, and also said that mighty forests were located to the north where there are now only barren hills. Recently conducted pollen analysis tests have proven that the forests did exist in this area.

There are many more descriptions of lost civilizations and transcultural contact. For example, while Hept-Supht migrated to Egypt, another Atlantean named Iltar journeyed to Mexico:

> Then, with the leavings of the civilization in Atlantis (in Poseidia, more specific), Iltar—with a group of followers that had been of the household of Atlan, the followers of the worship of the *One*—with some ten individuals—left this land Poseidia, and came westward, entering what would now be a portion of Yucatan. And there began, with the activities of the peoples there, the development into a civilization that rose much in the same manner as that which had been in the Atlantean land. Others had left the land later. Others had left earlier. There had been upheavals also from the land of Mu, or Lemuria, and these had their part in the changing, or there was the injection of their tenets in the varied portions of the land—which was much greater in extent until the final upheaval of Atlantis, or the islands that were later upheaved, when much of the contour of the land in *Central America* and *Mexico* [author's italics] was changed to that similar in outline to that which may be seen in the present.
>
> The first temples that were erected by Iltar and his followers were destroyed at the period of change physically in the contours of the land. That now being found, and a portion already discovered that has laid in waste for many centuries, was then a combination of those peoples from Mu, Oz* and Atlantis . . .
>
> This again found a change when there were the injections from those peoples that came with the division of those peoples in that called the Promised Land. Hence we may find in these ruins that which partakes of the Egyptian, Lemurian and Oz civilizations, and the later activities partaking even of the Mosaic activities.
>
> Hence each would ask, what specific thing is there that we may designate as being a portion of the varied

*Oz is Cayce's term for the most ancient Peruvian culture.

civilizations that formed the earlier civilization of this particular land?

The stones that are circular, that were of the magnetized influence upon which the Spirit of the One spoke to those peoples as they gathered in their service, are the earliest Atlantean activities in religious service, as would be called today.

The altars upon which there were the cleansings of the bodies of individuals (not human sacrifice; for this came much later with the injection of the Mosaic, and those activities of that area), these were later the altars upon which individual activities—that would today be termed hate, malice, selfishness, self-indulgence—were cleansed from the body through the ceremony, through the rise of initiates from the sources of light, that came from the stones upon which the angels of light during the periods gave their expression to the peoples.

The pyramid, the altars before the doors of the varied temple activities, was an injection from the people of Oz and Mu; and will be found to be separate portions, and that referred to in the Scripture as high places of family altars, family gods, that in many portions of the world became again the injection into the activities of groups in various portions, as gradually there were the turnings of the people to the satisfying and gratifying of self's desires, or as the Baal or Baalilal activities again entered the peoples respecting their associations with those truths of light that came from the gods to the peoples, to mankind, in the earth.

With the injection of those of greater power in their activity in the land, during that period as would be called 3,000 years before the Prince of Peace came, those peoples that were of the Lost Tribes, a portion came into the land; infusing their activities upon the peoples from Mu in the southernmost portion of that called America or United States, and then moved on to the activities in Mexico, Yucatán, centralizing that now about the spots where the central of Mexico now stands, or Mexico City. Hence there arose through the age a different civilization, a *mixture* again.

• • •

> Those in Yucatán, those in the adjoining lands as begun by Iltar, gradually lost in their activities; and came to be that people termed, in other portions of America, the Mound Builders. (5750-1, 1933).

There are enough clues in this reading to keep a whole army of archaeologists busy for a long time to come! We certainly get a radically different story of how Mexican civilization advanced than is preached by the anthropological establishment. The ancient world of Mexico seems to have been a crossroads for everyone from the Atlanteans to the Lost Tribes of Israel. This may explain why the artwork of prehistoric Mexico reveals influences from many different races and cultures. It may also explain why three different blood types are manifested among the North and South American Indians. Dr. Marshal Newman, one of the country's leading physical anthropologists, has urged that we must remain open to the possibility that the American Indian had a multiple origin. He added, "There are already some indications that several biologically different groups of Indians migrated to this hemisphere."

While Dr. Meggers suggested that people from China and Japan came to the Americas in ancient times, Cayce specifically stated that the Lost Tribes of Israel surfaced in Mexico as well. Cayce says that the Lost Tribes came to Mexico in approximately 3,000 B.C., the very time which is the zero date of the Mayan calendric system. Most archaeologists believe that this date predates the development of the Maya culture and have interpreted it as a mark of some legendary or mythical event. Is this all coincidence? During excavations at the La Venta site in Mexico (Olmec) worked on around the 1950s, archaeologists discovered on a stela (an oblong stone monument) a figure which depicted what was described as a "bearded man with a conspicuously aquiline nose," a profile alien to the Mexican civilization at this time. Several leading archaeologists who have considered all the data from this site feel that this man was a visitor from another race. The Mayans also formulated the numerical concept of zero, the basis of higher mathematics which even the Romans had not conceptualized at that time.

Cayce really put himself in jeopardy when he said in this 1933 reading that, ". . . the first temples that were erected by

Iltar and his followers were destroyed . . . That [temple or temples] *now* being found . . . was then a *combination* of those people's and from Mu, Oz and Atlantis . . . This again found a change when there were the injections from those peoples that came with the division of those peoples in that called the Promised Land. Hence we may find in these ruins that which partakes of the Egyptian, Lemurian, and Oz civilizations, and the later activities partaking even of the Mosaic activities."

Cayce seems to be saying that the first temples of Iltar were destroyed but that at the time of the reading (1933) a ruined temple (or temples) was being unearthed that had eclectic architecture resulting from the influence of peoples from different civilizations. In another reading Cayce indicated that the Pennsylvania State Museum was involved in excavating this temple.

In 1933 the Pennsylvania State Museum *was* excavating in this area at the site of Piedras Negras in the steep hills of Guatemala, and the original reports on the Piedras Negras excavations are quite startling. The first site report was titled "Evolution of a Mayan Temple," since the excavated temple was the end result of three different temple building stages, each superimposed over the other. The earliest of the superimpositions overlaid ruins of an even earlier structure which was not excavated. Dr. Linton Satterthwaite, who was in charge, stated that the very first structure in the immediate vicinity of the temple had been destroyed. Could this have been Iltar's first temple?

Dr. Satterthwaite said that he was "tempted to see a mixture of Mayan and non-Mayan styles." Could this be the actual temple Cayce described in his reading? Excavation shows that there was a two-terraced pyramid that rested on a broad basal terrace. The temple building itself rested on the pyramid, and its design was a simple rectangle and severely plain. Yet it was built at the same time as the more ornate pyramid and basal terrace, and it is very much larger than any other known one-room Mayan temple. Satterthwaite feels that the temple building and pyramid were originally conceived as two independent structures and that the temple building and pyramid *originated and developed apart from each other*. Are these the influences of the Lemurians, Ozites, and Atlanteans that Cayce indicated?

During the excavations two altars, one on the pyramid

stage and another in the temple building chamber, were discovered. Satterthwaite believes that they were not used for sacrifice as might at first be thought, since their style is different in design from one pictured on a stele at the site which *does* depict a sacrifice. Cayce had stated that the altars were only used for human sacrifice in later periods. Also, the pyramid and altar before the doors of the temple building were adopted from the peoples of Oz and Mu and were separate from the other temple structures. This is just as Satterthwaite found them to be.

In general, Satterthwaite's reports coincide with Cayce's reading. If we could only read some of the hieroglyphic inscriptions carved on the four stelae at the site, we could interpret fully and validate Cayce's reconstruction.

It does seem, though, that the reading is "too good to be true." Could Cayce somehow have come by this information normally? Dr. Satterthwaite, who is now retired, recalls no news releases on the dig at the time of the Cayce reading.

Besides the Piedras Negras site, archaeologists have made other discoveries which echo this reading. Take, for example, the statement that, "The stones that are circular, that were of the magnetized influence . . . are of the earliest Atlantean activities . . ." and how these stones were used for religious purposes. Well, archaeologists *have* found small highly polished circular magnetic mirrors at one of the oldest sites in Mexico, but no one has yet been able to explain how these ancient people were able to grind them to the precision of optical lenses. Neither have they been able to discover what they were used for. Yet archaeologists also have found a figurine of a woman in a prayerful attitude, and incredibly one of these unusual stones was fastened to her breast. We are also told in this reading that the followers of Iltar ". . . gradually lost in their activities; and came to be that people termed, in other portions of America, the Mound Builders." This may coincide with a statement made by Dr. J.A. Ford, who in a study of the formative cultures of the Americas said that the Mound Builders of the Mississippi Valley appear to be a "delayed effervescence" of the first Mexican civilization.

Cayce got even wilder when he spoke about an undiscovered crystalline structure still buried in Mexico. This is the "Great Crystal of the Atlanteans," or at least a carved emblem of the device which was reportedly the major energy source for the Atlanteans. This large cylindrical crystal was supposed to have been cut with facets in such a way that the capstone would centralize the power concentrated between the end of the cylinder and the capstone itself. Cayce promised that the exact construction plans would be found with other records. These records were placed in the Great Pyramid of Egypt by Hept-Supht, in one of Iltar's legendary temples, and another set supposedly still exists in a sunken portion of Atlantis in the Bimini region. This is the area that Cayce predicts will rise again. His reading at this point may not be pure fantasy, for in the late 1960s archaeologists became interested in a stone wall and other structures that divers discovered under the clear blue waters surrounding Bimini. Now Cayce stated that ". . . time draws nigh when changes are to come about, there may be the opening of those three places where the records are one . . ." (5750-1, 1933). If this prediction comes to pass, it will not only be the ultimate vindication of Edgar Cayce, but also the ultimate scientific demonstration of psychic archaeology. Time will tell how accurate Cayce's 1933 reading was.

Edgar Cayce has been dead for over thirty years, yet looking over his readings today we get some plausible explanations for anomalies and mysteries that have troubled archaeologists for decades. During these years, we have unearthed more and more verifications of his readings, and archaeology's view of the ancient world has been constantly modified.

If archaeologists would rely more diligently upon psychic guidance, we might finally get a less foggy window into the past.

What was the source behind Edgar Cayce? And how did he contact it? More than with any other psychic, Cayce seems to have been able to make contact with some memory bank of the past which he called the Akashic Records.

According to his own readings, Cayce's subconscious mind contacted the Universal Mind. (This is a term used by the great Catholic theologian Pierre Teilhard de Chardin.) This Mind would appear to be analogous to what Ossowiecki called The Consciousness of the One Spirit, and what the Company of Avalon termed the Universal Memory. It also suggests what C.G. Jung called the Collective Unconscious. The term "Akasha" in the Cayce discourses is a Hindu appellation. It was also called the *Book of Life* or *God's Book of Remembrance*. Cayce's concept of this pool of information is similar to the Yogic one—a "Scheme of Time and Space" upon which all entities impress their thoughts and actions. One may contact the record by attuning oneself to it. However, this source can itself contact the subconscious of each individual. Cayce indicated that the source exists physically somewhere in the Cosmos, and he once remembered upon coming out of trance that he had traveled in a bubble of water to a Hall of Records where he was given books he had requested by a "Keeper of Records." Commenting on the reading, Cayce emphatically claimed that this information was stored in actual books, but he did not know if these volumes were physical or symbolic.

Cayce felt that some aspect of himself actually left the body during the readings. At the end of one trance talk he said, ". . . may ye in watching close see the entrance again of the entity, as the body lies here, and in the seeking has it been drawn far from the vault. Watch as it hovers near and enters, as the light of the body" (2126-1, 1932). In another reading the doctrine of out-of-the-body travel was expounded upon, "each and every soul leaves the body as it rests in sleep." The out-of-the-body state did not keep him from an occasional cough or movement during his trances.

The Akashic Records and the subconscious records of an individual were not the only sources Cayce drew upon. During a talk given in Washington, D.C. on February 3, 1935, Cayce commented on the role the questioner played and how he could affect the source:

"I believe that if the source is not wavered by the desires of the individual seeking the reading, it will be from the Universal. Of course an individual's desire is very intense to have a communication from grandpa, uncle, or some great soul, to contact as directed that way, and that becomes the source. Do not think that I am discrediting those who seek in that way. If you are willing to receive what Uncle Joe has to say, that's what you get. If you are willing to depend on a more Universal source, that's what you get."

There seems to have been no question that Cayce could not answer while in trance. He even dictated several plays while in that state. When asked a technical question, he frequently answered in technical terms. If appropriate, Cayce would speak in a foreign language even though he only consciously knew English. Once he even spoke in Homeric Greek for an inquiring scholar. He could also pick up the thread of a reading on one subject just where he left off, even if the readings were separated by several years.

Cayce's mental, physical, and emotional states prior to giving a reading were also important. A great deal of strain was caused if he gave more than two readings a day. Someone trusted, such as his wife or his secretary, acted as his ground control by directing the reading and asking the questions. Sometimes he specially prepared for certain readings. When readying himself for the Atlantis revelations, he went on a three-day juice diet which he felt would improve the clarity of his channel.

Reincarnation and the power of thought are frequent topics in the Cayce records. His powers were credited as being the ultimate result of his previous incarnations, despite the fact that as a youth Cayce received a hard blow to the head, as have other psychics.

Another common theme in the talks is that of Fate—that there is a proper and planned time for things to happen. Cayce stated, for example, that the Great Pyramid could not be opened until a specific date. He told one treasure hunter that the bounty he sought could not be located until the proper time, the proper attitude, and the proper conditions were reached, and that the hunter was now going through a test.

If more than one individual were involved in seeking information, for either financial or spiritual growth, "unity of thought" was necessary. The motivations of the questioner and the practical application of the information were also important factors in the quality of the readings produced. The attitudes, skepticism, and interpretive ability of the questioner, the stenographer, and anyone else present could drastically affect the quality of the results they would get from sitting to sitting. If those present were incapable of understanding what was being said, the session was cut short and the blame fell on the sitters. Further, Cayce felt that his own attitudes and desires as the psychic channel were also a key factor in the quality of the information received. An unselfish desire to aid one's fellow man was important.

Finally there is one more factor that could effect the session, involving Cayce's deep devotion to Christian thought. This is the concept of grace. In Christian theology, grace is the term used to designate the gratuitous help of God in the affairs of man. We find a peculiar variant of this idea in the Cayce readings, which state that sometimes a person could ask the "wrong" question and yet receive the "right" answer. Cayce's psychic responses were not just answers to questions but answers to needs, and the seer believed that this "grace" factor was sometimes a product of the humanism or spirituality of the inquirer.

If anything, the readings of Edgar Cayce make it clear that the researchers are just as responsible for the quality of the results as the psychic himself. We must keep this in mind when evaluating the errors Cayce apparently made. Just how capable were the questioners of following and interpreting what he was telling them? Advice was once given to an inquirer on where to drill for oil. Many of the subsurface geological details that were described checked out. There even was a good show of oil, but not good enough for a commercial well to be sunk there. One source of error may have been Cayce's reliance on physical measurements. Even a minor error of this sort could permanently ground a project. The fact that years later geologists drilled a location adjoining Cayce's former property (where drilling had been attempted) and struck oil would suggest that the problem was not in finding the oil, but in pinpointing its exact location.

Unfortunately, no expert on archaeology ever questioned Cayce, nor has any real expedition been mounted to verify his visits to the past. There has been so much sensational verbiage written about him that professional archaeologists have shied away from taking him seriously. Cayce himself always stressed that research should come before enlightenment. Maybe the Association for Research and Enlightenment, which carries on the Sleeping Prophet's work and legacy, will someday sponsor professional level research on the clues he gave about the past. Remember, we were not only given clues to the past but also an actual primer about prehistoric times.

There is more than just archaeology to glean from the Cayce readings, for they also contain a spiritual message. When he tells us how man was first created as spirit, depicts the rise and destruction of Atlantis, or surveys the life of Jesus, he is telling us about the grace and dignity that personify the nature of man. The accounts offer a spiritual guide to our life's journey.

Once, while very much awake, the Virginia Beach seer

said, ''If we were as anxious about where we came from as we are about where we are going, we would be in quite a different position as to what we are doing with ourselves, now, wouldn't we?''

Wouldn't we?

PART II

My Story—The Flagstaff Dig

The story of my own adventures in psychic archaeology. How I discovered the Flagstaff site and the experiments I have done that provide basic "how to do it" guidelines for psychic archaeological time travel and research.

Chapter 4

Flagstaff—The Discovery of the Earliest Evidence of Man in North America

(Round 1)

> Is it really any wonder, the price of significant scientific advance is a commitment that runs the risk of being wrong?
>
> ——*T.S. Kuhn, The Structure of Scientific Revolutions*

The terrain was very rocky. The whole area was spotted with huge boulders, and some cliffs made the spot look even more desolate. The cool green pine trees scattered about stood in sharp contrast to sandstone cliffs which ranged from yellow to almost red in color, and I was just below the cliffs working my way down the steep hillside. My dog was my only companion as I explored for man's earliest ancestors. Somehow I "knew" the people I was looking for were hunters, and that they either practiced head deformation for beautification or that they had unusually small heads for their size. I can't remember for sure.

As I stood atop one particularly large boulder I compulsively pointed to a dry creek bed below me. Although no one was around to hear me I shouted, "That's it. That's the place. It's a bonanza!" I was jumping up and down, my enthusiasm verging on delirium. As I rushed down to the creek I knew this was the place I had been looking for. I just knew that there were not only many, many artifacts to be found here, but even entire skeletons. Complete, blackened skeletons. I also knew that these remains had diamonds or some other jewels with them. Suddenly I noticed that other people, archaeologists and scientists were present, and I excitedly told them that if we undercut the creek we could secure a rich bounty. I was so excited I thought I had better show them, so I cut under the creek at an angle and then lifted one bank up from the creek like a trap door. To our amazement, bones and skeletons lay there in some strange black soil. It was carbon or something. . . .

Then I woke up.

It was April 30, 1971. Most of my dreams are run of the mill, but this one was strikingly different. What sticks in my mind even years later was how excited I was in the dream and the surges of energy I felt. I didn't know where the location designated in the dream was, nor did I know what it all meant. I just knew that it was different—different from any dream I had ever had.

I thought to myself, maybe this dream has something to do with what I had dreamt several weeks earlier. In this earlier dream I was calm and I worked at a dig site partitioned off from the rest of the area. I was able to pick my own site and chose a small central area that was clear of trees. I was a little worried about getting the area dug up in time, and I told the man in charge that I planned to have my cousin Jay come in and help me. I also saw a geological map of the area in the dream, and strangely, the faults and volcanoes on the map matched up with those shown for the Four Corners area of the Southwestern United States where New Mexico, Colorado, Utah and Arizona meet. The only thing that seemed wrong was that while I had a cousin named Jay, the last thing in the world he was interested in was digging.

Reflecting on these two dreams, I felt intuitively that I was being given a message. But if that were true, what message? My mind raced over various interpretations. Perhaps they were some sort of rationalization or confirmation of the decision I had made that spring to return to graduate school to study archaeology at the University of Arizona. I had spent the last five years in oil exploration, and this was a big change for me. Just as Pharaoh had consulted Joseph, I talked to friends about these dreams, but nothing became any clearer. Wherever the dreams came from and no matter what they meant, I simply tucked them away as innocent curiosities.

A couple of weeks later, on May 25, 1971, I was waiting by my mailbox, like a child who has dutifully sent in his boxtops and is anxiously expecting his Captain Marvel decoding ring to arrive any day. The mailman didn't let me down. My package from Oregon had finally come. Inside was a cassette tape recording, and in a matter of minutes I had whisked it into my machine, started the tape rolling, and off I was catapulted into an archaeological odyssey that would preoccupy my life for the next several months.

I was expecting the prehistoric riddles of the first men to set foot in America to be decoded for me. This might sound like a rather tall order but, you see, the tape had been made several days earlier by a psychic while in a state of meditation. Several of my friends who studied parapsychology had promised me that he could help me in my research. I doubted that a psychic could be of much help but it was too good an opportunity to pass by. But since people I respected said he was a real psychic, as good as Edgar Cayce, I sat down and wrote him a letter enclosing a series of questions. My answer came astonishingly soon, and the psychic, named Aron Abrahamsen, seemed astonishingly kind. He said his taped replies to my questions were in the mail. Excited, but not truly convinced, despite the man's sincerity, I told myself it would be for the good of science if I invested in a small tape player so I could hear the man's predictions.

As the psychic's mellifluous voice with its Scandinavian accent rolled on, my initial vague excitement grew more deeply emotional. This guy—this psychic, mystic, or whatever you want to call him—knew what he was talking about. He was using the right terms in the right ways, and what he was saying about the earliest inhabitants of America made sense. But then he came to the question that had led me to contact him—directions on where to discover a new excavation site to find the remains of early man in the Southwest. His directions to search in the mountains near Flagstaff, Arizona; Pueblo, Colorado; or Kino, Mexico seemed reasonable enough. But as he started to give details about the civilizations I might uncover, he dashed my hopes just when he was gaining my confidence.

How and when the first Indians got to America is one of our most intriguing and debated puzzles about man's prehistory. But this psychic, Aron Abrahamson, had thrown tradition to the winds by dating ancient man's landing in America ten times earlier than any current evidence indicates. He said America's first inhabitants were a people archaeologists don't believe ever existed, and they were not from Asia, as we believe. Instead of saying that the ancestors of the American Indian migrated across the Bering Bridge from Siberia into Alaska and hiked down the ice-free corridor 10,000 to 30,000 years ago, he was relating an entirely new sequence—one beginning as far back as 500,000 years ago.

I was trying to be a scientist, and Aron was talking about a migration from the lost continent of Atlantis!

This startling but uncorroborated new information given through Aron's ESP was doubly frustrating because the rest of what he said was so reasonable and logical. I thought to myself, "No way his prehistoric picture could be right." No one could sit in his study in Oregon and pretend to give details about events that took place in these areas in the distant past. I was in double jeopardy: on one side, I had to contend with the uncertainties of what really took place during America's ancient past; and on the other, I had to contend with the notorious capriciousness of a psychic's presumed abilities. Yet the voice on the tape was so engaging, and what was being said sounded so intriguing. After all, my friends had told me that this psychic was no dummy. He was an aerospace engineer and was one of the project leaders for one of the country's major contractors involved with the first moon landing. He was an ordained minister, as well. Aron wasn't simply telling a story to be believed at face value. Perhaps we could test his information archaeologically, for Aron was even describing possible dig sites.

This led me to consider some of the major anomalies we find when trying to pinpoint the origins of the first Americans. Maybe discovering one of Aron's sites could help us explain (1) Why the American Indians have entirely different blood genetics than the Asians. (In fact their blood is different from any other ethnic group in the world.) (2) Why the American Indians have such unique dental and skull parameters. (3) Why the American Indians have over 200 languages, none of which bear any resemblance to those of their supposed Asian ancestors. (4) Why corn pollen over 80,000 years of age has been found in Mexico City, when domestication is not supposed to have started until 9,000 years ago in the Near East. (5) Why there are so many Indian myths which narrate how their ancestors came from across the seas and not overland. (6) Where *Homo sapiens*—modern man—came from when he suddenly appeared in the Old World (Europe and Asia) 40,000 years ago without any evolutionary precedent. (7) Why archaeologists are finding sites in America bearing dates older than when the Bering Bridge, an ice-free corridor, was opened. Maybe in the mind of Aron and in the mountain areas he mentioned we would find the answers.

It is true that there are already more than enough people running around claiming that they have discovered the earliest American archaeological site, and every one of them is trying to win anthropological laurels. It also seems that every day the tabloids are screaming about some superduper psychic discovery. These claims, both psychic and archaeological, never pan out when investigated closely. I had to be cautious about all this since I was supposed to be embarking on a new professional career as an archaeologist, not joining a bunch of nuts who patronize tearoom fortune tellers.

The mountain areas that Aron described covered quite a bit of terrain, so I wrote back to him and asked for more specific help. In particular I asked about a suspicion I had. I asked if the dream I experienced in April was related to one of the areas he mentioned—the Flagstaff area. Aron's answer was yes and he encouraged me to have confidence in the information I had gotten through *both* my dreams. I had not even *mentioned* the earlier one! In some mysterious way things were piecing themselves together, but I still felt like Moses setting out in the wilderness. But I was too impatient to spend forty years finding my way at satisfying my soul. Already the possible accuracy of my dream and Aron's information was being hotly disputed by my scientific associates.

Following up on my application, acceptance and decision to attend the University of Arizona, which I made in the spring, late that summer, I drove to Tucson where I would begin my graduate work in archaeology in the fall. After getting unpacked, I immediately made the five hour drive north to Flagstaff, Arizona. Upon arrival I visited the head archaeologist at the local museum. I told him what I was up to, how I wanted to test this psychic material and possibly find some remnants of early man in the process. He was blunt. No way, he said. He told me that there were no early man sites in the Flagstaff area, and politely pretended that he didn't hear the part about the psychic at all. He asked why I didn't want to be a nice conventional type of chap and dig a site in search of one of the prehistoric cultures *known* to have lived in the area. Weren't these early enough for me? Our conversation deteriorated rapidly. He was branding me as a kook, so I graciously bowed out of his office.

The next day I set out into the field to try to locate the area Aron had spoken about. Instead of being equipped with a staff and entourage, my only companion was a tape recorder with Aron's tapes. All about me were very large jagged peaks covered by dense stands of stately ponderosa pine trees. After six hours of walking and exploring, I started to have some doubts about my mission. Here I was, looking for a new archaeological site just five miles from the Museum of Northern Arizona. Acre for acre, the southwest United States is the most explored and excavated area of the world. Because of the museum's location, the Flagstaff area is the best and most widely studied area in the Southwest. Could the museum have missed something so important laying right under their noses? Well, by the end of the day, I hadn't found anything that resembled what I had seen in my dream. All I could find were volcanic deposits. Great Expectations be damned!

The next day it was back down to Tucson and to the University of Arizona for fall registration. I also had a conference with the head of the anthropology department about my course plans. In my naïvete I confessed to him about my Flagstaff venture. Since I didn't want to upset him too much, I left out the bit about my dreams. It sounded so much more scientific to talk about how I was merely testing Aron's information empirically. Could you imagine some top nuclear physicist telling his staff that he had dreamed the other night about a crucial experiment they were working on, and the dream had influenced him to make some major revisions? I doubt that this would go down well. But the work with Aron had scientific promise since he could contact his "source" whenever he desired. Perhaps we could refine the information we were getting, so I simply told my department head that I was trying to check Aron out in as open minded a way as possible. In return I got one of those "Lord, what did we get ourselves into with this guy!" looks. I listened to a few stern and carefully chosen words. If I envisioned myself as Moses, out to set archaeology free from the tyranny of orthodoxy, then I had just found my pharaoh, shining bald head and all.

I quietly retired to the college library to go over the geological maps and reports available about the Flagstaff area. The key was to find sedimentary deposits somewhere in the volcanic mountains of Flagstaff. Without sedimentary deposits there could be no sandstone cliffs. Without the cliffs, there could be no site. After hours of searching, I found what I was looking for—one map showed that deep within the mountain range there were three places where sedimentary deposits were faulted up. And one spot had a dry creek by it, just as in the dream. I breathed a well-deserved sigh of relief, feeling like someone who blindly jumped into a swimming pool and was relieved to find water in it. The fault, the dry creek, the volcanic area, and the sedimentary rock cliffs—all the components from my dreams were there. I couldn't wait to drive back and field-check the area.

Early the next day I set out to find the actual place where all these key components came together. On the drive up my mind was fixed upon the images from my dream. I didn't play the radio, I didn't chew gum, and I didn't talk to anyone. I slipped into Flagstaff like a ghost. My four wheel drive vehicle got me close enough so that it took only one hour of hiking to reach the general target area. Soon after I began looking about, I suddenly started to tremble. I saw a big boulder above the creek. This was the boulder I had seen before in my dream!

I must have set a new land speed record as I scrambled up the hills and darted through the trees to see if the rock cliffs were also going to look just as I dreamed them. They did! I raced back down the hill into the creek and started to dig—digging like crazy with a little folding shovel I had with me. I was unearthing black stuff. My thoughts instantaneously turned to the bones that had to be there. My digging became more furious and frenzied. Only after I skinned my hand raw did I calm down enough to realize that there would be no bones, for this black stuff was just ashes from a recent campfire. Aron had said that what I sought was buried very deep, and I wasn't about to lift the bank up from the creek with a folding shovel in an afternoon or two as I had done in my dream. And I was not sure just where on the creek I *had* cut.

Sobriety finally prevailed and diminished my intoxicated enthusiasm, so I was content to draw a map of the spot and return to Tucson. I mailed the map to Aron for a check reading. He said that I had found the right spot, gave me some more encouragement, and then proceeded to deliver a detailed geologic history of the area for the last one million years along with instructions for excavation. His geologic history included descriptions of earthquakes, faulting, ice flows, volcanic eruptions, flooding, and fire. Upon returning to the library at college I quickly verified that Aron's rather complex history was accurate. He really had picked the area. The only difference from what geologists knew about the area was the date of the last major volcanic activity. Aron said it occurred only 250,000 years ago while the literature cited a radioactive dating of not less than 500,000 years ago. A year later I was to learn that another dating was made, and the date of the last major volcanic activity was corrected to 250,000 years ago. The accuracy of this geologic history made it clear to me that Aron wasn't simply reading my mind. He was either really tuning in on the area or engaging in some backbreaking historical research of his own.

The tape of his psychic reading spoke about the fault, the creek, and the sandstone of my dream, but he added something new. A new fact that was confirmed by another quick peek into the literature. He said the site was "near the granite, near the mountainside." Apparently he sensed, accurately, that the mountain just opposite the creek was not of volcanic origin as were all the others in the range. Instead, this particular mountain had a composition and origin much like granite. This mountain was the result of an intrusion and slow cooling, something quite different from the extrusive and quick cooling volcanics.

Aron said the first people in this area came in small numbers 500,000 years ago. They had high ideals and were a priestly and peaceful people who lived in communes. In time other people arrived, having heard about the good new land. He said the different groups of people came from the lost continents of Lemuria and Atlantis. Some worked their way first through South America. He said they had a symbolic writing similar to Egyptian hieroglyphics, and that one of their key symbols was the ankh. He said the later groups also had cultivated seeds, domesticated animals, and cured leather. Instead of some prehistoric Buck Rogers culture, he described a quiet, sleepy community which was technologically advanced in more subtle ways. He described how the culture rose and fell several times in this one area; that buried deepest was the highest civilization. The big fall came as the population grew larger, an unequal distribution of land and property took place, and a ruler was set up by some self-appointed power grabbers. Here was this rabble-rousing talk again, but after seeing how accurate Aron was on the geology I was coming to respect his words more and more.

During my course work at the University of Arizona, I learned that an archaeology professor at the University of Michigan, a Dr. E. Greenman, had written an article in *Current Anthropology* suggesting that man had come to the New World much earlier than we have generally believed. He cited evidence which indicated that people from the Upper Paleolithic of Europe crossed the Atlantic Ocean in kayaks and canoes and populated the Americas. Kayaks and canoes? Perhaps Aron was not so wild after all. This professor even said, ". . . certain artifacts from the southwestern United States indicate that region as another focus of Upper Paleolithic influence." Maybe Lemurians and Atlanteans were Aron's terms for Neanderthal and *Homo sapiens*. An ultimate answer wasn't necessary, as any artifacts found in Flagstaff would in a way speak for themselves.

Even more provocative than Dr. Greenman's article was the mythology of the Hopi Indians of Northern Arizona. This tribe's tradition teaches that three worlds existed prior to the one in which we now live. Legend says that a very long time ago, in the first world, their ancestors came onto this continent from islands across the sea. The first world was destroyed by fire, the second world by ice, the third by water. To the Hopi these worlds existed in the San Francisco mountains, the mountains outside of Flagstaff. These peaks are just seventy miles from the Hopis' present home in Oraibi, the oldest continuously occupied village in America. This all makes good geologic sense. The destruction of the first world by fire could represent the volcanic activity that took place in the Flagstaff mountains over 250,000 years ago. The destruction of the second world by ice could represent the glacierlike activity that took place in the peaks approximately 100,000 years ago. And the destruction of the third world by water could represent the wet period and corresponding inner-mountain basin damming and flooding that occurred approximately 25,000 years ago. I had to be careful here, though, in trying to use a myth to back up a psychic's story. I might be criticized with the old saying about the blind leading the blind.

More upsetting to me than the revolutionary prehistoric picture that Aron painted were his directions calling for a very deep, large-scale excavation. How was I going to get such an immense psychic treasure hunt founded? One thing was for sure: I now needed some direct check on the archaeology of the site. There was water in the pool I jumped into, but now I had to know whether it was deep enough to dive safely. There was no indication on the ground surface that Atlanteans and Lemureans had once frolicked along these slopes. In fact, independent searches over this area carried out by myself and later by friends didn't turn up any evidence that this area had once been inhabited by anyone. Later I learned that survey crews from the museum had searched the area unsuccessfully as well. Indeed, there were no sites uncovered *anywhere* in the Flagstaff mountains at this 8,000-foot altitude. A simple test pit was in order, so I asked Aron to pick the spot. Another tape came in answer. Aron directed me to move northeast from the spot where a trail crossed the riverbed. As precisely as possible, I pinpointed the location he was urging me to. I knew I could be criticized unless my verification of Aron's readings were scrupulously validated, so I proceeded with the utmost caution to document everything that Aron said before actual excavation was to begin.

First I distributed complete transcripts of all of Aron's readings and my dreams to a number of members of the academic community. Then I invited my department head, the head of the state museum, and whoever else would listen to witness the unveiling of a new archaeological site. Aron's reading on this 10′ x 10′ test pit only predicted the discovery of some crude stone tools buried from four to six feet down. While the mind-boggling cultures he called for were to be found at much deeper levels, here was a chance to test his ability to peek back into archaeological time quickly. I might as well have asked the archaeological hierarchy to come watch a sneak preview of the Loch Ness monster gargling at 2:00 A.M. in a stock tank right here in their very own Arizona mountains!

I set out to Flagstaff with an Air Force colonel, a high school science teacher, and a few fellow students. We were all equipped: shovels, spades, screens, enough food for a migrating civilization, and even a transit with which I planned to follow Aron's directions to the nearest inch, or so I thought. But when we arrived at the site in early November, we were greeted by the first snowstorm of the season. I could only reap disappointment from my seeds of expectation. The local residents said that once the mountains got snowed in, there was no getting in or out of them until late spring. All painstaking ceremonial digging was out of the question. It was a matter of finding the artifacts and getting out of there as fast as possible. We were only able to get a small part of the test pit dug. We did find some crude objects, but I didn't know how to distinguish a crude lump from a genuine artifact since I was just then taking the "we make you an expert in just three semester hours" lithic technology course as part of my archaeological training. Contrary to what you might think, it is very hard to determine whether a time-battered object is really a man-molded implement or only a hunk of rock. It takes a real expert to pronounce a find an artifact, and the expert needs a laboratory. Some crude stone objects such as spearpoints and arrowheads are not hard to identify, but the identification and interpretation of man's earliest stone tools is another matter altogether. In these cases appearances may be deceiving, especially with such crude tools as choppers and hide scrapers. Through quite normal geological processes nature can produce stones that look like man-made objects. Analyzing these objects is a touchy business, so I decided to consult with an expert on my finds. I took my "possibilities" to my professor, Dr. Arthur Jelinek, one of the world's leading authorities on such matters, to get his opinion. His opinion on each object I handed him was the same. Negative!

My growing depression was soon lightened by new rays of hope. The weather took a turn for the better, and my crew and I could go back and finish the pit. This was a much-needed reprieve not only from the weather, but from a storm looming in my mind. When we got to Flagstaff, a storm was raging again, and we knew this would certainly be our last chance to discover anything. When we reached the site, I decided that we should concentrate our efforts on just *one* part of the pit. The problem was *where?* When in trouble, ask Aron. I needed a reading pronto, but I didn't have time for tapes or the mail, so I decided to phone him. I left my crew and returned to town, where I found an outdoor phone. Chills were soon running up and down my spine, not from the cold, but from what was coming over the telephone as my tape recorder rolled. It was the source—I was talking directly to the source which Aron had contacted to get information about the past. The source through Aron told me to draw an arc with a radius of six feet, 20 degrees to the north of due east, thus making a wedge. Since we were running out of time, we would excavate just the pie-slice area of our dig.

I scurried back up to the test pit and played the new tape for the crew. About halfway through the tape, I thought I was about to lose the younger members. It looked as though they were getting set to run off the mountain. You see, the source encouraged us not to worry, and that there were "many" standing by "watching" and trying to help. Eerily, the tape stated that those "watching" knew what the crew was up to while I was in town at the phone booth. The crew got pretty spooked and more than a little self-conscious. The eyes of Big Brother were upon them. The source had said that a red marker had been moved while I was away. This was correct. Luckily, everybody settled down enough for us to collect some better-looking possible artifacts which we uncovered about five to six feet deep within the wedge-shaped area.

When I arrived back in Tucson, rumors were flying that I had flipped out and was looking for Australopithicenes, humanoids that had lived in Africa several million years ago. When I took my latest artifact contenders from the test area to my professor, I got a very cool reception. But all was forgiven when he held out one object and pointed out that it had *retouch* (patterned edge modification). This meant that it definitely was of cultural origin.

In other words, it was an artifact!

The creamy colored object involved was a small scraper tool used because of its sharp edge. When the edge became dull, the user resharpened its edge by removing a series of slivers from its edge which produced a new sharp scalloped edge. Nature never produces such a patterned edge. I now knew for sure that we were onto something. Aron had done it. Either he had pinpointed artifacts below the surface from his room several thousand miles away, or it was a million-to-one lucky strike. Visions of sugarplums, Atlanteans, and excavation permits danced in my head.

Yes, permits. One of archaeology's ten commandments goes: "Thou shalt not excavate on federal property without a permit." For the next few months I seemingly went to work for the government—I filled out form after form and tried to follow the status of my permit application. At the same time I worked on getting some funding help. I was going to teach an introductory seminar for a small eastern college on southwest archaeology, using the Flagstaff site as a field school. But it soon became clear that I was being given an official runaround by the Department of Agriculture to whom permit applications are made. First I was told that it could take up to eighteen months to process a permit. Then, after a long delay, I was asked for more information about my work. Then I was asked why I wanted an excavation permit since there really wasn't any site involved. Just when I thought I had answered all their questions a new set was put forth. Each exchange took an even longer period of time, until the summer was at hand and I still had no idea if I was going to receive an excavation permit at all. Further, all the red tape scared away the patrons willing to help finance the project. Needless to say, no permit, and no money meant no dig. Instead I went fishing and visited Aron in Oregon. A year later I learned just how big a runaround I had received. My department head could have cleared my fieldwork with a simple phone call. My permit application never reached the Smithsonian Institution, which acts as an adviser to the Department of Agriculture on such matters. "Certain people" didn't want me poking around with "witches and mystics looking for cavemen" in Flagstaff. I even was to learn that a certain nabob was on a certain federal advisory committee also involved in the permit-issuing business! Most important, though, I learned an old but unwritten commandment which tyrannizes any bold adventurer, "Thou shalt seek a permit if thou hast a new idea."

The next year, the fall of 1972, I completed my course work for a M.A. degree in anthropology. When I took my oral exams, the subject quickly turned to my ideas about psychic archaeology and using psychics to aid archaeological research. (I had just done a course paper on this subject which had received an A+.) One of the members of my Master's committee wasn't quite as enthusiastic about psychic archaeology as I was. He wanted to know: Why dig at Flagstaff? Why use psychics? I explained that Aron had helped in some research on the three-story abandoned Indian ruins at Chaco Canyon, New Mexico. I told how I had used Aron to review the skeletal record from which we have based our theories about human evolution, and I had used the psychic's ability to review Mexican prehistory. In all cases he showed a sophisticated knowledge of the archaeology involved and gave hypotheses which had the potential of resolving some major controversies in these areas. I explained that Aron did not just ramble on about Atlanteans and Lemurians, but that his going back into time also encompassed those prehistoric records that archaeologists are presently familiar with.

Instead of an evaluation or critique of my monologue, I got a harangue in reply. Flagstaff was too far away, they argued. Why didn't I find a new site in the Tucson area upon which to try a psychic instead? If a Tucson site was what this professor needed to convince him of psychic archaeology's vast potentials, that was okay with me. So we set up some test procedures and several weeks later I consulted with Aron about a new Tucson site. Every time I tried to get this professor into the field to check our information, he just couldn't seem to make it. He was like the proverbial man who was blind because he didn't wish to see.

Even with all these headaches I was awarded my master's degree, and I was accepted into the Ph.D. program despite my idiosyncracies. The university had little choice: I had gotten an A in every archaeology course I had taken. And there really was no legitimate way they could turn me down, or *any* way for that matter, without putting themselves in a bad light. But a sort of cold war was developing between the few professors who could see the potential of what I was doing, and the others who just wished I would go away. While one professor asked me to become his research assistant, good old Pharaoh asked me why I wasn't transferring over to the psychology department—to get my head examined. The most open hostility came from the department's senior cultural anthropology professor. He was very offended by my statements about how anthropologists were arbitrarily excluding psychic ability when they studied the nature of man. I really irked him when I wrote a paper on this topic for his course. In red ink he wrote three pages of comments in which he said I was engaged in mystical speculation. He said the paper was unacceptable and he made an impassioned statement that he would defend his opinion of it to the death. This seemed blindly extreme since the key idea of this paper had received very favorable comments from several other professors. I just couldn't bear to tell him that one of his own colleagues had had these "unacceptable" ideas Xeroxed and placed on file in the Arizona State Museum Library! I was to hear from this professor again, though.

For my doctoral project I planned to concentrate on developing the empirical practicality of psychic archaeology and set up a series of special study courses. Some of these courses were organized along with Dr. Cecil Rogers, a professor in the psychology department, so I became almost one step removed from the anthropology department and their love-hate attitude toward my work. Dr. Rogers was an expert on research design and learning theory, and these were the very areas in which I wanted to experiment with psychics and archaeology. I wanted to carry out tight research and also see if I could develop psychics as practical research tools. Under my professor's guidance, I began to put Aron through a series of work sessions and experiments. The experiments were designed to test the range and accuracy of his ability under controlled conditions. At the same time, they were designed to help Aron learn how to better give the archaeological information I needed. The design was rather simple. For the most part, I merely buried artifacts or other objects in my yard in Tucson or in nearby fields and would ask Aron in Oregon to locate and give details about them.

For a typical experiment I would bury a set of objects and then mail Aron's wife, Doris, my questions about them. Aron never handled the letters I sent pertaining to these experiments. At his convenience he would meditate and seek to make contact with his source. After he signaled that contact was made, his wife would ask him my questions—asking for the descriptions and locations of the buried objects—and tape-record his replies which were then forwarded to me. We also communicated by telephone. If I had any doubts about Aron's ability before, these tests made me a true believer. With few difficulties he located, described, and identified these objects. One of them was just a piece of pottery less than one-half-inch square in size with a white stripe down the middle. Aron accurately gave the location of this small fragment, gave its size, and noted not only the white stripe but also its other unpainted side. He would also give extra information. For example, after identifying that I had buried a seed, he even told me its correct species—a summer squash. And after correctly identifying that I had buried bones, he accurately told the age and sex of the person from whom the skeletal material had come.

Sometimes I supplied Doris with a few answers to my questions so she could give Aron immediate feedback on his replies. The only direct feedback we gave him was innocuous. A firm, "You are right," or, "You are wrong—would you care to try again?" was all we offered, and this helped him gain confidence in his ability and improve his accuracy.

Apparently a great deal of psychic information is available to Aron's sixth sense when he is in meditation, and during these tests he felt he was becoming better able to select the most pertinent information we needed. His accuracy would improve during a single test, and over a series of tests, and during some experiments, his accuracy ran as high as 90 percent. In a fifty-square-foot "test" plot in my yard, Aron was able to locate objects buried in it to within a foot horizontally and vertically. Curiously, he *consistently* measured short vertically and long horizontally—scant criticism for predictions coming to us from a man in Oregon.

Dr. Rogers emphasized the role of imagery in these tests. He urged that we try to do everything we could to enhance Aron's ability to induce imagery, and avoid doing anything to impair this ability. The professor seemed very sensitive to Aron's psychic sense, and one day he made a little confession to me which explained his obvious insight into this tricky business. He told me that he once saw psychic images himself, images so profuse that they were interfering with his work, and he had to make a concentrated effort to stop the flow.

The test sessions quickly revealed that Aron was affected by a number of psychological, physical, and subjective factors. For example, boredom was the greatest curse. When he was tired or anxious, his accuracy fell off. This is amazingly consistent with laboratory ESP tests where it has been determined that ESP often falters after a tiring session or when boredom overrides the subject's motivation. Aron handled part of his boredom problem in a rather novel, but no less remarkable, way. After he answered all the questions we had heaped upon him for a single test, he would add a clairvoyant weather report for the Tucson area, or—much to my embarrassment—describe the jumbled contents of the metal sheds in my yard. He described how my camping equipment was jammed behind the garden tools and bicycles!

Aron seemed to receive his psychic information from a number of different sources. Sometimes he said he could envision objects he was asked about even though they might be thousands of miles distant from his Oregon home. This is the faculty he relied upon when describing artifacts or locations. At other times he said he got his information from some universal record. When he needed to draw upon information from the past, this is the source he contacted. But certain types of technical information were hard to find in these records, so in the last experiments he tried something new—contacting spirits of the dead.

Aron claimed that there were always a number of "spirits" ready to give us any information we needed. Calling upon discarnates was like opening floodgates. If we asked a question about prehistory a whole entourage of spirits might come forth to aid us: spirits interested in prehistory, spirits interested in the culture we were exploring, or intelligences who had lived in the area we were interested in, spirits trying to help Aron or myself, and others who came just to *kibitz*. Aron had to learn not to pick those spirits who just spoke first or the loudest. Rather, he had to learn how to tell the difference between benevolent and deceitful or ignorant intelligences.

As these tests proceeded, another channel of communication began to open—our ability to understand one another. We worked up a mutually convenient vocabulary but even so, parts of Aron's readings were hopelessly obscure. For example, there was the time that we put a yardstick in one hole to help him sharpen his measuring. In this test, Aron's wife, who relayed to him the questions I had composed for each session, asked him if he was taking time to measure the coordinates he was envisioning to find an object. He said yes. She then asked if he were using the yardstick we had placed there. He said no. Instead, he said he was "in" the hole and was using his hand. But what hand? Whatever part of Aron that might have traveled from Oregon to the hole in Tucson couldn't possibly have had a "hand."

In these sessions, I began to use human skeletal material to bear out something I had in mind. I felt that if Aron could pinpoint objects in my yard, he could also pinpoint objects on a small-scale excavation I had envisioned to prove out Aron's psychic abilities and views on prehistory. Maybe he could pinpoint the bones in Flagstaff and we could get to them with just a test shaft, which is an excavation a little more elaborate than a test pit. This was quite a tall order, but the tests using my backyard had worked beautifully, and a small excavation in Flagstaff was something I didn't need major funding for.

Aron's abilities would now be put to the severest of tests. The target zone was a lot bigger than my backyard, with many more objects underneath the surface which might confuse Aron's ESP as he tried to locate an artifact, not to mention the tremendous psychological pressure that would be on him while giving the information. But Aron was willing, and I had witnessed too much with him to walk away from the Flagstaff project.

Before proceeding with the next obvious step in my research, we had to contend with the permit problem again. The same rules that apply to archaeological excavations apply to archaeological test shafts. But I had an ace up my sleeve. I wasn't going to apply for an archaeological permit—I was going to apply for a *geological* permit. I could avoid the red tape, and since I was a geologist by earlier training, no one was going to refuse me. With a geological test permit it didn't make any difference if I were looking for oil or tapioca—I could even "tight hole" them and not let them know what was coming up out of the hole! I got a permit for a 35-foot-deep test shaft, but I found I really wasn't fooling the Department of Agriculture since any geological permit application initially went through the same personnel channels as my earlier archaeological permit application. Instead of the standard permit form, the Department of Agriculture wrote one up just for me and they put the knife right to my throat. On the last page of the permit was a clause that said that if during excavation work I discovered items of substantial archaeological value I would cease excavation until given further approval. This was okay with me because they didn't exactly define "substantial." I smirked as I remembered how during the earlier runaround I had been told that it might take "eighteen months" to process my application for a permit—well, maybe it would take me eighteen months to process my information after I finished the test shaft!

Early that spring, Aron attempted the impossible. From his home in Oregon he selected *just one ten-foot square* in the dig area and made a series of predictions concerning the geological and archaeological materials that we would uncover. He made specific predictions for each level of digging and even predicted the age of each level. He told of major changes in the geology at eight feet and at fifteen feet. He also predicted that throughout the test shaft we would find hammerstones, cutting tools, choppers, and scrapers. He also thought that we would find one piece of fabric and some potsherds in one section. At twenty to twenty-three feet, Aron said that we would find the bones of three different individuals. They would be the bones of a mother and two children who had perished while huddling together against an avalanche of ice and water coming from the snowfield above them. He said that they were overcome so quickly that even their horse fell beside them. This is all trivial enough—except for the fact that according to orthodox archaeology, there were no Indians on the American continent until 85,000 years after the date Aron gave for this depth, and there were supposedly no domesticated horses until 7,000 years ago. For each level he told the story of the culture from which the artifacts we would find had come.

The main target, though, was human skeletal material. Skeletal material alone would tell us how physically evolved these people were, whose ancestors they were and, once we radiocarbon-dated them, how long ago they had died. In all honesty, though, I knew I would be happy to find *any* kind of deeply buried evidence that man inhabited the Flagstaff area long ago. If you buried a small community—or even New York City—there would be plenty of places you could sink a ten foot shaft and fail to unearth any evidence that the area had once been occupied. The accuracy of the geological predictions would serve as a good control—or at least a poor second—in case Aron was off and we didn't hit any artifacts.

I had the predictions notarized and distributed copies of them to friends and enemies alike. Following the advice of my psychology professor, I sought an independent control on the predictions. He warned that If I were successful some people might come forth and say that archaeologists could also have fairly well made cogent predictions. He also wisely pointed out that even if I didn't find all that I hoped for, I still might be able to show how much better my psychic technique was than more "rational" techniques employed in orthodox archaeology. So, I had a friend of mine who teaches college in Phoenix take Aron's predictions to the Department of Anthropology and Archaeology at Arizona State University for an evaluation. He was able to consult with two top archaeologists there, both of whom were familiar with the Flagstaff area. They were a bit taken aback and declared that they weren't about to select a specific ten-foot square and make specific predictions about it. They thought this was impossible if not downright crazy. But they did make their own predictions and offered a professional evaluation of Aron's. They felt that the geological and archaeological predictions Aron had made for the first seven feet were doubtful but possible. After seven feet, one professor said we would hit solid rock, and all the other archaeological predictions were impossible to no matter what depth we explored.

The other professor concurred but did not think we would hit bedrock. He was quick to note that the twenty-foot level probably didn't go back that far in time anyway. They both emphasized that man was nowhere in America at the early dates Aron designated. In short, they felt that his predictions were farfetched and that there wasn't the remotest chance for any success. This demonstrates that Aron's predictions were not rationalizations, nor based on a little geological homework. They were unique—unique enough to incite the utter contempt of professional archaeologists.

About this time I also did a series of lectures on psychic archaeology at the junior colleges around the Phoenix area. There was always a hush when I announced Aron's predictions for the upcoming geological test shaft.

In May, Aron came to Tucson for a visit. He couldn't wait to see my backyard in person—with his *physical* eyes, that is. Most of the objects I had used in the tests were still buried in the ground, and Aron felt that being there in the flesh made his clairvoyance even clearer. After meeting with Dr. Rogers, whose guidance was a key factor in our success, we visited the State Museum and looked at the archaeological displays. This helped us to sharpen up some of our working vocabulary. Then we were off to Flagstaff, where Aron's psychic process could work right on the spot. I wanted him to do a reading on the target spot, to check up on the square I had staked out. I wanted to make sure that the shaft would be dug in the exact spot Aron saw in his earlier reading on which his predictions were made.

After rolling through the Arizona countryside, we finally arrived at the site and I decided to use a formal test procedure to make sure Aron was in top form. We began with a control test to make sure he could contact his source. I secretly buried an object on the site and then asked him to locate and identify it. To help speed things up, we agreed that Aron should also try and use the discarnate experts we had found to be so reliable in some of our earlier work in addition to following his normal procedure of inducing psi-mediated mental images. Among these spirit guides was one who had expertise in surveying, one experienced in biology, and one familiar with archaeology.

As we began, Aron grew still. I was a little on edge.

Usually he only took a few moments to locate and identify something, but as the minutes rolled on there was still no response. Thoughts of an impending fiasco darted through my head. I started to get nervous—very, very nervous. Here was the acid test, the focus of all our work and pilot research. If Aron blew it, I could kiss the whole project (and perhaps even my Ph.D) good-bye. Aron was at the site area; his predictions were already recorded and distributed. There was no way out. I wanted to run only a simple check, but nothing was coming through. Maybe there was a change; perhaps Aron realized some mistake. Maybe there was nothing in this psychic stuff after all—I didn't know what to think. I began to sweat, the beads of perspiration rivaling the steady melting of the ice still on the ground. Finally he spoke and quickly and correctly told me where I had buried the object. He said it was the left hipbone of a dog. I was relieved and marveled at the extra detail. We then moved on to the check reading itself. After a cursory examination, Aron said I had staked the correct spot, and he confirmed his earlier predictions. After the reading, we kidded Aron about the delay. He explained that it was due to the fact that his spirit experts couldn't make up their minds about the object, so he had left them to their argument and used his usual clairvoyant procedure to answer the control question. It seems that even after death experts can't agree on anything.

Almost jokingly, I asked which two experts couldn't make up their minds, expecting to hear that it was the biologist and the archaeologist. But, it wasn't—it was the biologist and the surveyor. "The surveyor?" I said. "What did he know about bones?" Aron said that the surveyor was just standing around. Well, I figured, so much for our new superduper spirit technique.

A month later my crew—which consisted of myself, two female undergraduate students, my wife and our two daughters—were all set for the groundbreaking. A number of friends were also present to lend encouragement, as well as the pessimistic president of the State Amateur Archaeological Society. We started to follow Aron's directions. From the intersection of the road and the creek he said that I was now to go to the northeast. At twenty feet I drove a stake, as Aron instructed. That was to be the southwest corner of the hole.

No one knew what to expect as we plunged our spades into the ground. I didn't have any surface geological information for the area. As we removed the first shovelsful of soil it seemed that our chances of digging down a full twenty-five feet to unearth a skull were incredibly slim. I, at least, took solace in the fact that our stated purpose was to check a wide range of Aron's psychic predictions. Consistent with this goal of our excavation and the limited budget and time available to us, I planned to dig in a very simple way, with any finds cataloged only in relation to the levels Aron gave in his predictions. We used shovels and picks to bring the soil to our screen tables through which the soil could be sifted. Trowels were put to the side, should they be needed. I also arranged to have the work I did on the dig be the basis for a special problems course in archaeology I was taking at the university.

We didn't exhume anything interesting in the first four feet. Aron predicted that nothing would be found, so it was hard to be scientifically faithful and screen all the dirt and material we were digging up for any man-made remnants. We were torn between our fervent desire that Aron be correct in his first prediction and our anxiety knowing that at any moment we could hit pay dirt. As soon as we dropped below the 4 foot level we expected to uncover the crude stone tools that Aron had predicted for the four-to-seven-foot zone. Eureka! We encountered several stone flakes that were clearly manmade. When man chips flakes from a rock, the rocks have a set of distinctive characteristics which Mother Nature, despite her limitless variety, rarely if ever duplicates. Some of the flakes we found were waste material from the manufacture of other tools. Some were used as tools themselves; their sharp edges made them very handy. Some flake tools were typically used for cutting and scraping fat from animal hides. A few of them even had been retouched or resharpened. Right now, though, it didn't matter to us what they were used for. We were delirious with joy. These flakes were the product of man's hand, proving that he had been in this area at the time period represented by this level. We had knocked at a deserted house and found somebody at home!

Approaching the seven-foot level meant either digging with shovels with seven-foot handles, or developing some other bit of technology. We attached a boom arrangement to a nearby tree, and this boom lowered a bucket into the hole. After the bucket was filled, it was winched up and swung over the screen tables. We also placed shoring in the hole to keep the sides from caving in. The hole finally took on the shape of a bona-fide shaft, and our engineering arrangements gave the onlooker the impression that a big-time big-budget operation was going on.

At this time there was also a changing of the guard. Digging isn't much fun even when discoveries are being made. The drudgery and tension of this tedious digging easily matched the initial excitement the crew had shared. My two undergrads departed and a philosopher-carpenter named Dennis joined me. With all the construction that had to be done, Dennis was a godsend. As we began to work he remarked that his nickname was Jay. I was dumbfounded. The dream! "Jay" was the cousin I wanted to help me in my dream so long ago! I didn't understand what was going on, but I prayed that the dream script, with its more than gracious ending, would continue to be followed. On the weekends our help came from interested housewives and businessmen. After giving them a quickie artifact identification course, they were turned loose on the screen tables, and we prayed for the best.

At eight feet I was getting anxious again because this would be the first chance to check one of Aron's major geological predictions. His ability to predict the geology was a necessity because he said that bones would be found in a unique geological zone. Aron predicted that at eight feet the haphazardly deposited soil and rocks would be abruptly interrupted by a one-foot thick finely bedded zone of silt and sand. Tension mounted as we inched downward, and then there it was. I stared at it in disbelief. Out of a nearly infinite number of possible geological configurations, Aron had pinpointed the exact depth and composition of a major change in deposition. This fine-grained claylike deposit was the last thing one would expect to find amid the unsorted jumble of boulders that had been working its way down the mountainside over the ages. When Dr. Henshaw from the University of Arizona, who had been following my work from the start, visited us, he, too, stared at the zone in disbelief. Also at this time, several geologists from the United States Geologic Survey, who specialized in the geology of the Flagstaff area, made the first of their many visits to our site. They could only shake their heads in wonder. They were particularly interested in following the progress of the dig from a geologic standpoint, since it would provide the first subsurface information on this area. At least here was one body of academicians who weren't scared off by the psychic aspects of the project. Even if Aron turned out to be all wrong in every other case yet to be checked, the amazing accuracy of his predictions about the artifacts which we began to find at four feet and the sudden geologic change at eight feet alone made the dig a success. Round one for psychic archaeology.

At nine feet we had unwelcome company: an enormous boulder that filled a third of the hole. We dug and dug and at thirteen feet we were still stuck with the monster. It seemed as if the rock were endless. I called a halt to the digging. Either we or the rock had to go; there was no doubt about it. This was easier said than done, for neither would budge. Trying to pry it loose was fruitless. This was no time to be bashful, so with trembling hands I read the instructions on a brand-new case of dynamite. While training as an engineer I had studied blasting, but I had never ignited explosives before. These were not firecrackers. The ups and downs of this project had taught me how to pray, but I never prayed as hard as when I placed the fuse in the first charge of dynamite. The first blast removed only part of the rock. We blasted twice more but the behemoth stayed firm. And we were up against a new problem. Since we were directly under the shoring, we couldn't blast any longer. So in came the air hammer and compressor, a sledgehammer, and finally a chisel.

After effecting a compromise with the boulder, we were back in stride. Our perseverence was immediately rewarded when we hit the second major geological break Aron had predicted: a second fine-grain bedded zone at fifteen feet. And in this fine grained zone we got an extra prize—carbon specks. By gathering and analyzing these bits of carbon, we could date the age of the geological level. How far back in geologic time were we—5,000 years back? or 10,000? Or a minimum of 20,000, as Aron predicted? No one knew; so with tweezers and dental picks we began the tedious task of collecting all the specks we could find. After a full week of picking, the sample was sent off to Teledyne Isotopes for dating.

We had recovered one piece of hand-molded wood, and what looked like crude stone tools from four feet, six feet, eight feet, ten feet, twelve feet, fourteen feet, and fifteen feet. We had no idea at what depth we would stop finding these tool remnants, but I figured it was as good a time as any for a little show-and-tell. So I phoned Dr. Charles Hoffman, the senior archaeology professor at Northern Arizona University in Flagstaff. His specialties were early man and stone tools, and I thought he could give me a good readout on our finds. Art Gilliam, the Air Force colonel who had been digging with Dennis and me for the past few days, accompanied us to our rendezvous point, a pizza parlor. It was a smorgasbord day. While Dennis handed Dr. Hoffman pizza slice after pizza slice, I handed him lithic artifact prospect after lithic artifact prospect. Dr. Hoffman spoke in superlatives. He thought everything was very good. I wasn't sure whether his praise was for the pizza or for the lithic materials. Needless to say, good artifacts are a lot harder to find. Dr. Hoffman was really impressed with the materials we showed him. I made a habit of cataloging anything that even remotely resembled an artifact and he agreed with me that a good number of my samples from each of our levels were artifacts. Later the materials were shown to another archaeology professor at Northern Arizona University, and he, too, agreed that many of the crude bits of stone we collected were hand-fashioned.

I drove back to Tucson on a cloud of air. I joyfully showed the materials to three different archaeologists there, and only one showed any reluctance about giving the materials his full stamp of approval. The odd man out felt certain only about a few objects and said he wanted to see more. Even though I still didn't have a radiocarbon date for my specimens, I felt he was scared off by the implications my finds would have on our concepts about early man. When I told him from what depths these materials came, he gulped and cooled off toward me in a hurry.

Back in Tucson, it was now time to take my doctoral exams in anthropology. As it turned out, I passed my exams in archaeology, physical anthropology, and linguistics, but not in cultural anthropology. The chairman of the examination committee happened to be a personal friend and he told me on the sly that there actually was a split decision on that one exam. He said that ordinarily three passes and a split decision will get a student through, but unfortunately this was not true in my case. He said that the cultural anthropology group wasn't ready for my brand of anthropology, even though my major was archaeology and my minor was physical anthropology, the exams for which I had passed with little trouble. I learned that the senior cultural anthropologist with whom I had had the run-in months before over the gist of one of my papers finally had his say. From another faculty member I learned that this professor even made a bet with someone that I wouldn't pass. Friends wanted me to take the case up with the American Civil Liberties Union or some similar group, but I still had the dig to finish and didn't want to take on people whose heads were even harder than the boulders I was encountering.

Resisting the temptation to bemoan my martyrdom, I turned my attention back to the dig. We excavated a quarter of the hole from fifteen feet down to twenty feet in depth. The president of the State Amateur Archaeological Society visited again and after seeing what we were unearthing, dropped his skepticism and offered his encouragement and whatever help we could use. We gave him a shovel! Dr. Hoffman also brought one of his archaeological classes up to the site on a field trip. He marveled at the unusually long and continuous sequence of artifacts we were getting. He felt we had some more winners from our excavations at the new and deeper level. He invited me to organize and present a research colloquium on the dig and on psychic archaeology for the anthropology department at Northern Arizona University. At this colloquium students and faculty alike showed a sincere interest and excitement over the many implications my work was offering.

There was a big question as to what the Flagstaff data meant in terms of early man. If Aron continued to be right, the controversy would be even touchier. A faculty member informed me that a few weeks earlier Dr. Roald Fryxell, an archaeologist at Washington State University had presented a paper to the Geological Society of America (November 1973) in which he said that he and two other scientists had data indicating man existed in North America as long ago as 250,000 years ago. This is a date ten times earlier than believed possible. Fryxell told the society that his team used several independent methods to date a number of stone tools (scrapers, knives, and spearpoints) found in an ancient Mexican stream bed. The outcome always was the same. The objects were 250,000 years old. He said, "We have no reason to suppose that over decades, actually hundreds of years, of research in archaeology in the Old World and in the New World, that our understanding of human prehistory is so inaccurate that we suddenly discover that our past understanding is all wrong. On the other hand, the more geological information we've accumulated, the more difficult it is to explain how multiple methods of dating which are independent of each other might be in error by the same order of magnitude."

Fryxell was also troubled by the fact that the tools were considerably more sophisticated than contemporaneous tools used in Europe and Asia 250,000 years ago. Whether we were going to hit the right spot or not in Flagstaff, to me Fryxell's remarks were a sort of independent confirmation of Aron's ideas about early man in America.

Fryxell's ideas also reinforced Dr. Louis Leakey's ideas about early man in America. Leakey gained fame by digging at Olduvai Gorge in Africa. For twenty years he ignored the establishment views and eventually discovered conclusive evidence supporting his ideas that the first ancestors of man walked the earth over a million years earlier than had been thought. But few know that Leakey also came to the United States to prove that man walked the Americas much earlier than we believed possible. In the late 1960s he excavated a site at Calico Hills, California, and said he found evidence for man being in America over 250,000 years ago. He found very crude pieces of stone that he believed were handcrafted, but a fierce debate arose among archaeologists as to whether these were the products of man or nature. Debate over the interpretation of lithic material was nothing new to Leakey; at Olduvai he also had found very crude stone tools that invoked a similar argument. But Leakey stuck with it, and after many years finally discovered human skeletal evidence there and won his point.

Dr. Greenman, Dr. Fryxell, Dr. Leakey—Aron was certainly in good company when his psychic source informed him of the early dates man walked the American continent. At such early dates, the Bering Bridge and the ice-free corridor were not yet available and could not account for *any* Asiatic migration. There is simply no explanation of how man could have reached America from Europe or Asia at such an early stage in man's evolution. Or was primitive man infinitely more advanced than we have given him credit for, as Fryxell and Aron indicated? Were they Neanderthals, as Leakey believed? Were they from some lost race or civilization, as many Indian myths and Aron indicate? Did they have a skull type we have never seen before? The only way to answer these questions was to find human skeletal material, and with this in mind I became even more anxious to finish the Flagstaff dig.

My increasing desire to dig deeper and finish the shaft was cooled by the icy winter weather that was moving into the area. Money and sunshine grew rarer. Any bones deep within the ground would have to wait a few more months to be discovered. We would have to postpone our meeting until the next dig season.

I was closing up the site when the radiocarbon date on the fifteen-foot level came in. The results wouldn't make the wait seem shorter. Aron was right again, for the fifteen-foot level was older than 20,000 years. Teledyne Isotopes determined a date of approximately 25,470 years in age. This was a minimum date because the sample I sent wasn't large enough to remove all the contaminants which could complicate and unduly contemporize the date. The United States Geological Survey geologists were also happy with this date, since it agreed with the date they had arrived at for the fifteen-foot level by independent means. I wondered if Aron could also be right on his predictions for the twenty-foot level. Did we already have evidence for man's existence in North America 100,000 years ago?

All in all, I was quite satisfied with the results of round number one at Flagstaff. Dr. Rogers, who helped me earlier and is now the head of the psychology department at a large eastern university, was the dig's official statistician. He calculated that at this halfway point Aron had done incredibly well. Out of thirty-four geological predictions that could be scored at this stage of the game he had gotten thirty-two correct (94 percent). Out of twenty-three archaeological predictions, Aron had gotten eighteen correct (78 percent). Overall, he was batting 87 percent on his predictions. The two distinguished professors who served as controls were batting a meager 10 percent at best.

Aron's most notable misses concerned the pottery fragments and fabric that he predicted but which we did not find. Were these errors of measurement or objects outside the shaft? Or were they lying in unexcavated soil, or destroyed over time by disintegration? Could these errors even have been identification errors. For example, once Aron confused a straight piece of root for what he saw as a wooden handle.

But the most intriguing question was were the bones going to be there when we excavated the twenty-to-twenty-three-foot level in our next dig season? I decided to reconfirm this information and asked Aron to do a check-reading for me. To do this reading Aron went to an Oregon beach for a few days so he could clear his mind. He confirmed that the bones were still there in a layer of black stuff which he said was carbon resulting from the rapid burial (before oxidation could occur) of the organic materials when the avalanche precipitated. He described a unique type of rock that would be encrusted with carbon and said this would be our number-one tipoff when we were getting close to the bones.

The discovery of the bones would put an icing on our archaeological cake. I had to resist the temptation to make an impulsive haphazard dig right then and there to go after them. But as Aron reminded me, the bones had been there for a long time—they could wait a little longer.

Frederick Bligh Bond From *The Quest at Glastonbury*

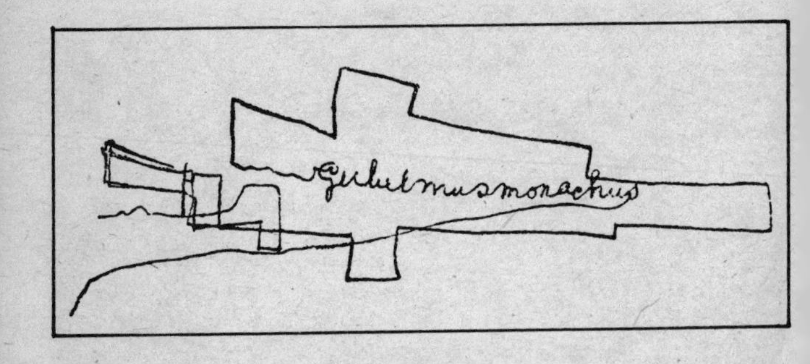

Automatic drawing received by Bond of the Abbey Church with the Edgar Chapel on the left

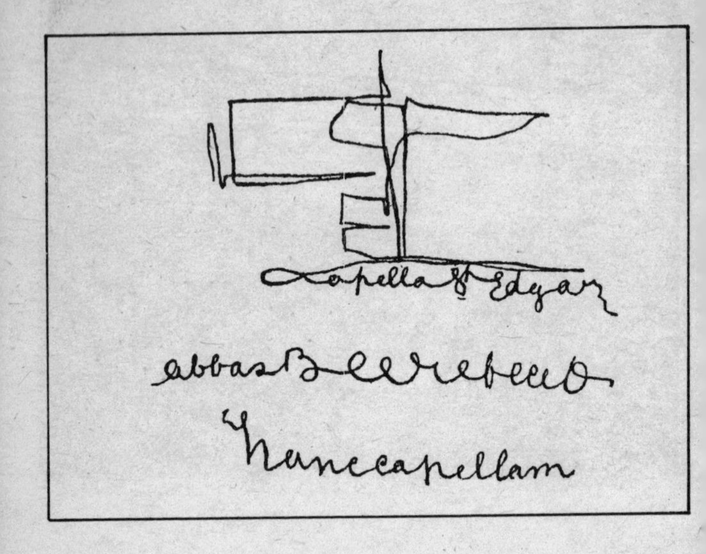

Automatic drawing of the Edgar Chapel From *The Gate of Remembrance*

The Edgar Chapel, discovered and reconstructed by Bond
From *The Quest at Glastonbury*

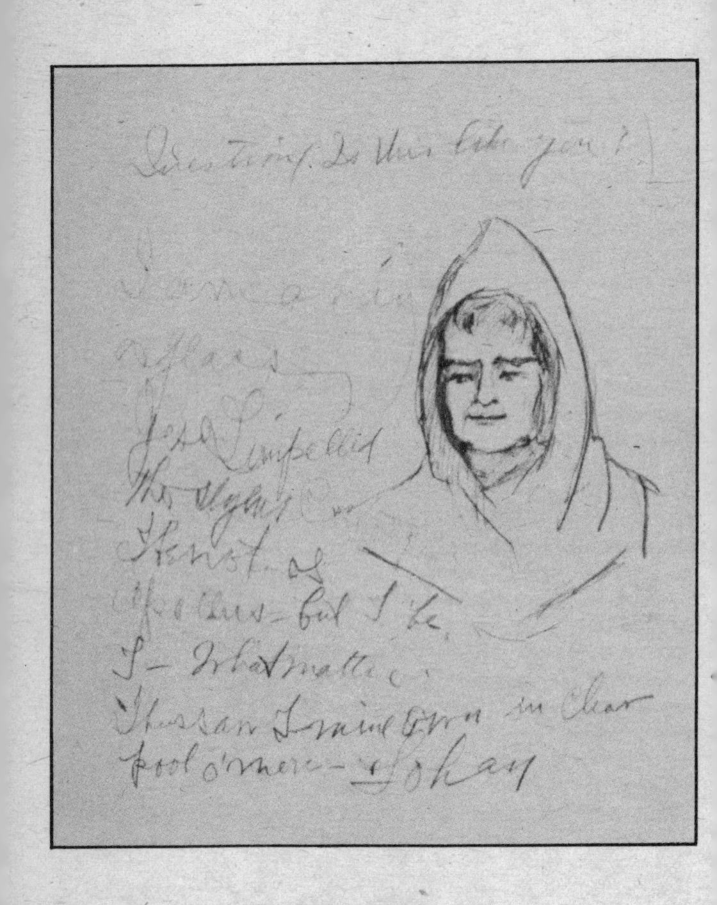

Automatically drawn, self-portrait of the monk Johannes
From *The Quest at Glastonbury*

A Magdalenian sculpture. Ossowiecki spoke of large-hipped women in his psychic visions. *Moravske Museum V Brne*

Ossowiecki sketch of a Magdalenian woman from a vision
Courtesy Marian J. Swida

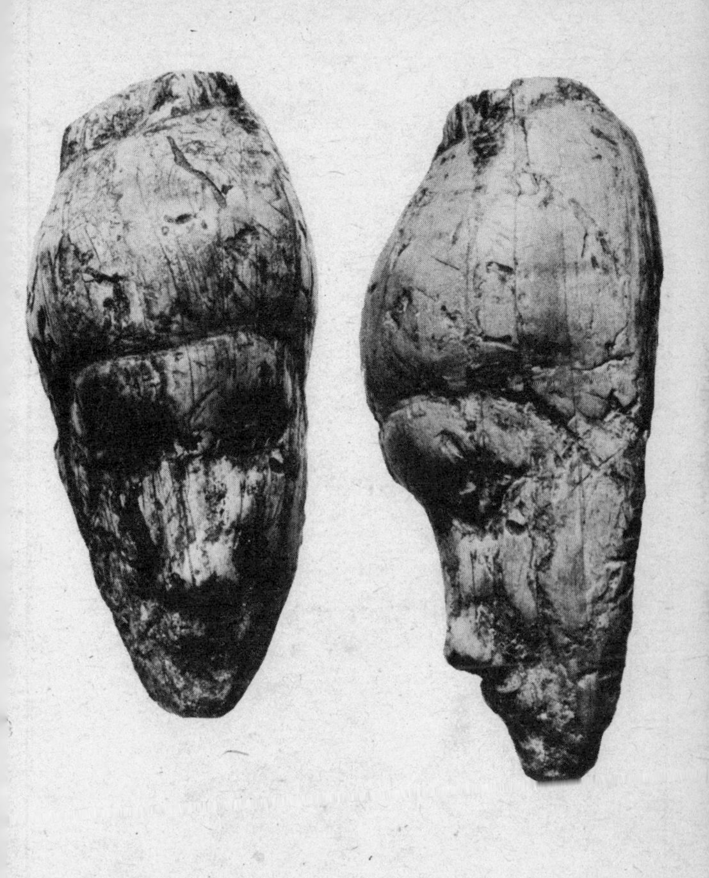

Bust from the Magdalenian period. The artifact and the drawing both emphasize the elaborate hair arrangement. *Moravske Museum V Brne*

Edgar Cayce

Targets used to test Ingo Swann's out-of-the-body vision, with his drawn responses alongside. *Courtesy Janet Mitchell*

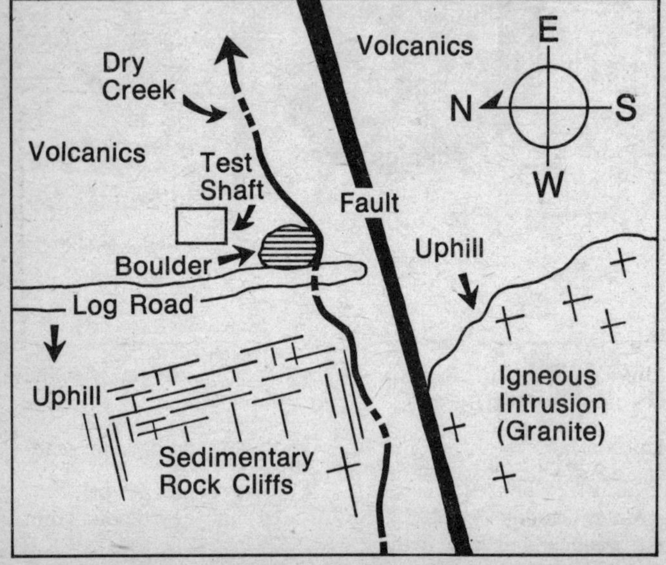

Dry
Creek
Volcanics
E
N
S
W
Volcanics
Test
Shaft
Fault
Boulder
Uphill
Log Road
Uphill
Igneous
Intrusion
(Granite)
Sedimentary
Rock Cliffs

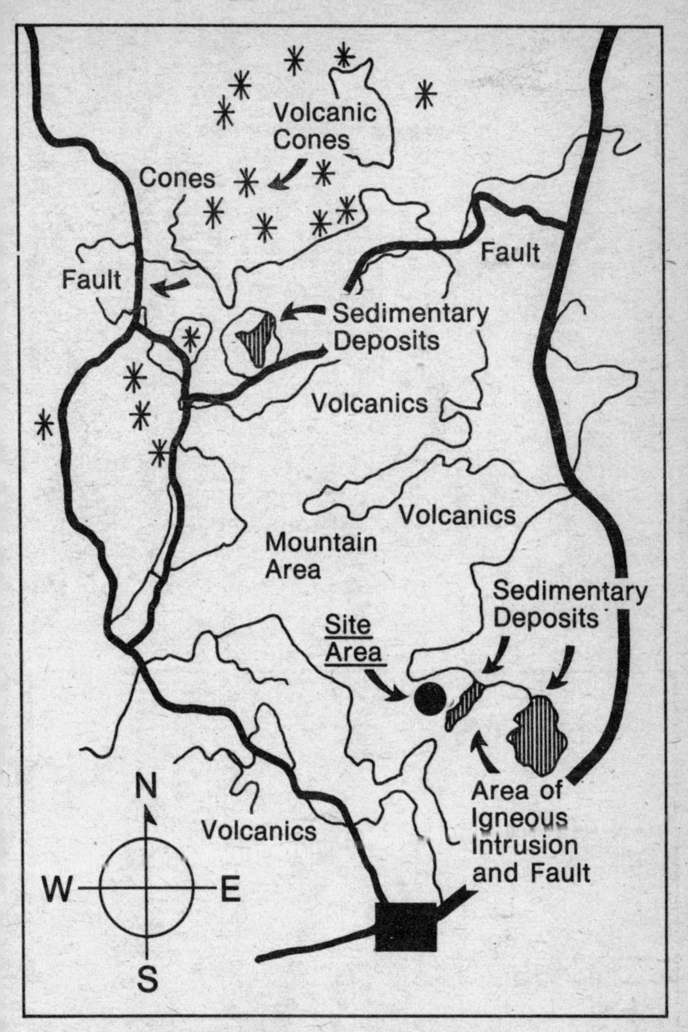

(top left) The actual site from Jeff Goodman's dream, with the dry creek bed and boulder *Jeffrey Goodman*

(bottom left) Geological details from dream and psychic reading, all of which were later found in the field

(above) Geologic map of Flagstaff area with key details from the dream and psychic reading.

General Psychic Predictions Made By Aron*

Geology	Time (Minimum years B.P.)	Archeology	Added Behavior
sandy loam w/bldrs (alluvium)	2,000-3,000	Absence	absense of occupation at site
4'	4'	4'	4'
—as above w/more bldrs (platty basalt, dacite and basalt, lms & ss bldrs) —rotten igneous mtl. (granite comp.) —some mtl. with sharp edges.	5,000-7,000	**tools:** 10-15 chipped stone —size range ½-6" —color almost dark —some w/glassy sfs sheen —some of obsidian —incl. sharp edged cutting tools, hammerstone —wood: some pieces—handle remnants	seasonal occupation summer low cultural level (declining culture)
	7'	7'	7'
8'			
—silt, sand & loamy soil (from presence of water)	9,000-10,000	**tools:** 2-3 more than in 4-7' zone and similar **potsherds:** some pieces **fabric:** cotton—1 piece	—permanent occupation —trade centers on trade route —ceremonial activity —low cultural level (declining culture)
9'			
as 4-8' above w/fewer boulders			
	12'	12'	12'
	20,000	**tools:** 4 ground 2-3 chipped, some obsidian **potsherds:** more pieces **fabric:** cotton **dom. seeds:** corn, rye, wheat at least 10-12 seeds of each type **dom. pollen:** as above and mustard	perm. occupation (incl. school of religious thought) medium cultural level (declining culture)
15'	15'		15'
Disconformity	Disconformity		Disconformity
15'	15'		15'
compacted soil (paleosol)	72,000	**wood:** some pieces —some stones w/high glassy sfs: obsidian (15-20') **Note:** most of above artifacts are deeper than 15'	—permanent occupation (of long standing) —medium cultural level (declining culture)
20'	20'	20'	20'
—as 15-20' above —glacial activity —disturbance —area much flatter w/brooks	100,000	**human skeletal material:** 3 different individuals —Homo sapiens sapiens **animal skeletal material:** —horse—(pony) (domestic) —**wood:** some pieces	—permanent occupation (of long standing) —trading center & resid. —had language & writing —lived in peace w/o fear —highly intuitive —knew where man came from —religious —orig. from Lemeuria & Atlantis —cult. source for Peru Yucatan, Hopi
23'	23'	23'	23'

1. Water flotation for seed recoverv will only be done on a selective basis.

* This was the set of predictions which was notarized and distributed **before** excavation began.

General Predictions Made by Aron

General Predictions Made By Two Professors Serving as a Control*

Geology	Time (Minimum years B.P.)	Archeology	Added Behavior
sandy loam w/bldrs (alluvium)	2,000-3,000	Absence	absense of occupation at site
— 4' —	— 4' —		
—as above w/more bldrs (platty basalt, dacite and basalt, [illegible] & ss bldrs) —[illegible] igneous mtl. ([illegible] comp.) —some mtl. with sharp edges. *Possible*	5,000-7,000 *No*	**tools:** 10-15 chipped stone —size range ½-6" —color almost black —some w/glassy [illegible] sheen —some of obsidian —incl. sharp edged cutting tools, hammerstone —wood: some pieces—handle remnants *Possible but doubtful*	seasonal occupation (summer) low cultural level (declining culture) *Possible but doubtful*
	— 7' —	— 7' —	— 7' —
— 8' — —silt, sand & loamy soil (from presence of water) *No* — 9' — as 4-8' above w/fewer boulders	9,000-10,000 *No*	**tools:** 2-3 more than in 4-7' zone and similar **potsherds:** some pieces **fabric:** cotton [illegible] piece *impossible*	—permanent occupation —trade centers on trade route —ceremonial activity —low cultural level (declining culture) *impossible*
	— 12' —	— 12' —	— 12' —
No	20,000 *No*	**tools:** 4 ground 2-3 chipped, some obsidian **potsherds:** more pieces **fabric:** cotton **dom. seeds:** corn, [illegible] wheat at least 10-12 seeds of each type **dom. pollen:** as above and mustard *all impossible*	perm. occupation (incl. school of religious thought) medium cultural level (declining culture) *all impossible*
— 15' —	— 15' —		— 15' —
Disconformity *No*	Disconformity *No*		Disconformity
— 15' —	— 15' —		— 15' —
compacted soil (paleosol) *No*	72,000 *No*	**wood:** some pieces —some stones w/high glassy sfs: obsidian (15-20') **Note:** most of above artifacts are deeper than 15'	—permanent occupation (of long standing) —medium cultural level (declining culture) *doubly impossible*
— 20' —	— 20' —	— 20' —	— 20' —
—as 15-20' above —glacial activity —disturbance —area much flatter w/brooks *No*	100,000 *No*	**human skeletal material:** [illegible] different individuals [illegible] Homo sapiens sapiens **animal skeletal material:** —horse (pony) (domestic) —**wood:** some pieces *all impossible—never*	—permanent occupation (of long standing) —trading center & residence —had language & writing —lived in peace [illegible] —highly intuitive —knew where man came from —religious —[illegible] from Lemeuria & Atlantis —cult. source for Peru Yucatan, Hopi *doubly impossible*
— 23' —	— 23' —	— 23' —	— 23' —

1. Water flotation for seed recovery will only be done on a selective basis.

* Written over Aron's predictions.

General Predictions Made by Two Professors Serving as a Control

Artifacts discovered at the site. (top) Chopper with serrated edge (bottom) Blade *Jeffrey Goodman*

(top) Flake

(bottom) Core *Jeffrey Goodman*

(top) Setup at the Flagstaff site
(bottom) View of the shaft *Jeffrey Goodman*

Chapter 5

The Return to Flagstaff

(Round 2)

> If it were on any other issue, one-tenth of the evidence reported would have been enough to convince me. As it is, ten times that would not do it.
>
> —*An unnamed scientific acquaintance of Dr. Louis Rhine, on psychic applications to science*

The dig site was snowed in shortly after I had closed it up at the end of the first season's excavation. Frankly, this worried me. I didn't know if the shaft would stand up to the added pressure and moisture, so the possibility of a cave-in was a real and frightening threat. Since we were now closing in on the key target zones designated in Aron's readings, any accident would be disastrous. The radiocarbon date we had for our dig (25,000 years old) had already pushed back the accepted date for man's first appearance in North America by 10,000 years. Of course, my worries did not focus only on Mother Nature and her unpredictable antics. There were money problems as well. Just where was I going to get the money with which to finance the next dig season?

My spirits were soon lifted by an unexpected visitor, Dr. William Kautz, a research scientist at Stanford Research Institute. Dr. Kautz had been encouraged to make an informal inspection of my work by John White, director of education at The Institute of Noetic Sciences. IONS was founded by Apollo 14 astronaut Edgar D. Mitchell to study the nature of consciousness and human potential. When I learned of its existence, I applied for a grant to support further work. White told me later that my application was given high priority by

IONS, but as things turned out IONS itself found its funding sources drying up as the national economy went into a tail-spin, so I never got the money I applied for.

Dr. Kautz spent a weekend with me, going over everything I'd collected and talking with other archaeologists and anthropologists in the state who'd visited the site. At the end of his inspection, he told me that he was impressed. He said that he was pleased to find my project wasn't all just a "tall story" like most of the psychic phenomena he checked on turned out to be. I was also pleased to learn from him that the professors from Northern Arizona University and from the University of Arizona who had followed my work and visited the dig really stood up for "Flagstaff" when he had checked with them.

As the summer dig season drew closer I was still without funding. Every time a funding possibility arose, I jumped for the bait, but it always seemed to be pulled away as I was about to bite. Finally in March 1974, friends with whom I was visiting in Virginia insisted that I approach the Smithsonian and see what they could do. What they would do, I explained to my friends, was throw me out unceremoniously on my ear. The Smithsonian Institution is the country's official and foremost museum, not to mention a particularly conservative one. Luckily, though, one of my friends had an "in" there and marched me right to the office of the seminar director. The next thing I knew, appointments were being jockeyed around for me to meet with some of their head archaeologists and anthropologists. I was getting VIP treatment for a change.

I showed the artifacts from my dig to Dr. Dennis Stanford, head paleoanthropologist (expert on early man), and I just couldn't believe what I heard. He liked what I had brought. Not only did he have nothing against revising the date for man's appearance in the Americas, but he didn't even have anything against psychics. He was constructive as well. He felt that the key problem ahead of me in my next dig season would be to thoroughly work out the geology, thereby canceling out any arguments to the effect that our artifacts might have somehow gotten mixed in with the wrong deposits and been faultily dated. Undercutting an ancient stream bank could do this. Dr. Stanford wondered why I had confined myself to the limitations of a shaft rather than taking a bulldozer to the area. I had to explain to him about my permit hassle. Nuts, Stanford responded. The antiquity laws were not designed to keep serious people from digging, he explained. If I had any further troubles, I should go directly to him. He regretted that the Smithsonian had no funding money to hand out beyond its own projects. I left encouraged, but encouragement doesn't pay the bills. Even with all my background in the psychic field, I didn't know any psychokinetic way to conjure soil up from the bottom of a deep shaft without the aid of a properly equipped crew. Mind over matter has never gone that far. One cannot buy new winches and wood bracings with good wishes alone, and archaeologists—especially psychic ones—are not generally known for their credit ratings. Whatever was down there would have to wait yet another year.

It was also at about this time that Aron and I started to drift apart. The demands of my tests and constant queries for refined information were taking their toll. Since his part in the Flagstaff project was completed for all practical purposes, the diversely gifted Aron showed little interest in pursuing psychic archaeology. Aron's personal readings for clients and a new series of tests he was carrying out with Stanford Research Institute were keeping him busy enough. So I had no money, lost opportunities, and little to encourage me. I was beginning to feel like the heroine in the *Perils of Pauline*.

At least the delay had one merit, it gave the financial scars from the first dig season a chance to heal. So the following year, in the summer of 1975, I relied on the most generous, understanding and reliable funding source I knew of—myself.

When I returned to Flagstaff, the first thing I did was set up a briefing session for my new crew of four archaeology students from Northern Arizona University and Dennis (Jay). Joining us was Pete Pilis, the newly appointed chief archaeologist for the forest service. After going over the artifacts we had unearthed during the first dig and the new dig plans, sparks began to fly from an unexpected source. Pete Pilis told me that I was in violation of my permit and that he could stop me from digging if he wanted. There was no doubt in his mind, he told me, that I was dealing with ancient artifacts; and since Flagstaff was already a full-blown archaeological site, I now needed a proper archaeological excavation permit. No longer could I rely on my compromise geological permit. Sharp words ensued. Finally Pilis said that since I was so willing to keep him posted on my work, he would let the permit issue go for the time being.

When we finally reopened the shaft I was pleased to see that all the shoring had held and that the bottom was dry. In fact, after a lapse of almost two years, the shaft was in the same shape as we had left it.

One day as we were setting up at the site, some Hopi Indians came by. One of their religious leaders told us that they had come to gather spruce boughs for the upcoming ceremonial dance *Niman Kachina* from the very slopes on which we were digging. At this dance the Hopi bid farewell to the *Kachinas*, spiritual beings who since the beginning of the world of the Hopis come to help them for part of each year. When not assisting the Hopi, the *kachinas* reside in the mountains outside of Flagstaff. We were digging on the very slopes the priests believed the *kachinas* favored. So if the parallel between Aron's readings and Hopi mythology was correct, we could rest assured that we had good ethnographic control on the location we were digging.

It soon became evident that our goal for the second dig season had to be compromised. While I had been able to pull together some money for this new effort, I still did not have enough to procure a full-size crew, nor to buy all the proper equipment we needed to finish checking out all of Aron's specific predictions for the test shaft completely. We had to plan for a six-week excavation season during which we would dig just one-quarter of the shaft down another five feet through the key zone which Aron predicted contained the human bones. We would dig from the quarter of the hole at twenty feet down to the twenty-five foot level, giving Aron a two-foot margin of error on the twenty to-twenty-three foot depth where he had psychically seen the bones. This, of course, assumed that some of the bones were to be found in this particular quadrant. Thus the long shot of finding the predicted bones in the shaft would be four times greater.

The rest of the shaft was still fifteen feet in depth, so to gain working room we had to first dig out another quarter of the shaft down to twenty feet. During our first field season, we had already found artifacts in the fifteen to twenty foot zone. These discoveries pushed back the date for the entry of ancient man into America to over 25,000 years ago. Since we had already made our breakthrough in artifact hunting, digging in this zone again didn't hold much excitement for us, especially since all our minds were set on finding the bones in the deeper zone. Nevertheless, dig in the zone we did.

Just as we got under way I came down with pneumonia, not a very pleasant way of avoiding digging. Since two members of the crew were experienced in excavation work and also had expertise in stone tool analysis, I entrusted direction of the digging to them. As it turned out, I didn't miss a thing because nothing was found. All this didn't do anything to spur on the crew. As the doldrums set in, the two less experienced members of the crew turned in their shovels. Apparently they thought my whole spiel about psychic archaeology and what we had found at Flagstaff during the first excavation was baloney. I couldn't really blame them: here we were digging in the middle of nowhere at a depth where nothing was supposed to be found.

Just as things were ready to crumble, my reduced crew and I were inspired to keep the faith by a report I had just received from a group of psychics in St. Louis, led by Beverly Jaegers. In order to satisfy my own curiosity, I sent the group a set of soil samples from the shaft. This exercise would enable me to get some more experience in dealing with psychics and psychic information. Knowing how to separate the good guys from the bad guys before beginning normal testing is a usefull skill for psychic archaeologists to have. Self-proclaimed psychics were always coming up to me and telling me all sorts of wild things about what I would find at Flagstaff, predicting that I would find everything short of the Taj Mahal. So developing a better screening process of potential psychics would be of immediate value.

It quickly became clear that Beverly Jaegers and her group were different from the attention-seeking ego-inflated prophets who frequent the psychic scene. They had already demonstrated some potential in the service of a midwest archaeology professor, and they seemed truly interested in using their abilities to further a good cause. They showed a sincere desire to develop whatever abilities they had in the area of archaeology, and indeed the report they sent back provided me with some interesting information. Beverly had told the group nothing at all about the site, yet two of their psychic impressions confirmed my hopes. They reported that "primitive stone tools" and "skeletal material" were to be found in the shaft. Several of the members had the impression that the skeletal material included the deteriorated skull of a child.

The report from Bev Jaeger's group made me recall a reading I received from a Florida based psychic named Fran Farley several months earlier. I gave Fran an artifact recovered in the first dig season at Flagstaff to psychometrize.

Fran said that the stone scraper I had handed her was over 60,000 years old. She went on to report that the stratigraphy of the site (the order and relative position of the strata on the earth's crust) would break sequence at a level representing 70,000 years. Some animals came to her mind; she couldn' be sure if they were small horses or goats. Then her attention spotlighted on bones—human bones. She said that bones of several individuals were buried in a small area. I was stunned when I realized that Fran was reporting in no uncertain terms the same "predictions" given by Aron. Her dates were similar to his; she, too, saw the "horse" which Aron said had perished in the avalanche, and she also described the bones of several people. The coincidence was so perfect that I immediately thought Fran was reading my mind—no mean feat in itself! But then her reading veered from what Aron had told me. She said the bones were buried thirty-nine feet beneath the ground while Aron had isolated them at the twenty to twenty-three foot level. My hands ached in memory of the blisters which had rewarded my first dig, so I silently prayed that Aron's predicted depth would be the correct one and tucked Fran's reading in the back of my mind.

Also about this time I received a series of readings from a psychic recommended to me by the Michigan Metaphysical Society. Several months earlier I had met Sol Lewis, the president of the Society, who had told me about a new and promising woman psychic who was a member of his Society. Sol told me that Dr. Norman Emerson of the University of Toronto had given her a series of artifacts to psychometrize, as sort of an informal test and that Emerson reported that she did well. Emerson apparently was impressed enough with her abilities to take her out to a site he was digging in the Great Lakes area. Again he found her to be effective. I didn't think it would hurt if, through Lewis, I gave the subject a map of the Flagstaff site to psychometrize. The readings I received were fascinating. She spoke of a small colony of artistic people who originally left their primary settlement and came to the Flagstaff site area to live by the creek which at the time flowed more like a river. She added that upheavals in the ground had caused the creek to diminish in size. She spoke about several other groups who once lived in this area, including a "black race of people" who had traveled through Flagstaff en route to South America. I immediately recalled a point of corroboration: The colossal Olmec carvings in Mexico that depicted people with Negroid features.

The psychic also said that I could find some remnants of this black group "for some were lost trying to cross the river." Was this the proper interpretation for the "blackened skeletons" I pictured in my dream? Her readings also described artifacts we would find in specific locations, and she had even marked them on the site map. I was tempted to probe for a few of them, but since I already had my hands full with the primary dig I couldn't spare the time or energy. I also wondered if some sort of mass telepathic leakage from me was contaminating the psychic impressions I had obtained from Aron, Fran Farley, Beverly Jaegers's group and now Sol Lewis's psychic friend. In our different ways we were all predicting the unearthing of bones of very great age. A young nurse who visited the site with some friends added to the puzzle while meditating in a special tent we had put up specifically for this purpose. Although she had just arrived at the site, she envisioned a mother kneeling down in the creek bed with her arms around her two children, shielding them from an avalanche rumbling down the slope above. I would like to add that the nurse knew virtually nothing about the site at the time.

When we finally got down to digging out the chosen quadrant, the work proved to be slow and arduous. We had little maneuverability in only a five-foot square, but this discomfort took a back seat to our concern about a very real danger. This was the only portion of the shaft being dug out, so the dirt bucket had to come up and out right over our heads. The original cable we were using to lower it soon became too short, so several times we had to substitute a longer and thinner one. Each change lowered our safety margin, and the possibility of the cable snapping became more and more threatening. If the cable broke, there would be no place to run. It would crash on our heads. The weight of the bucket became too much for the motor (a 7/8 horsepower drill) on our winch, so we could only fill it up halfway. This arrangement eliminated the need for a more elaborate and expensive power setup, but we had to repair the drill constantly since it just wasn't designed to lift a several-hundred-pound bucket all day long. While working in constant fear of having our skulls smashed, the cold also started to get to us. While it was 70-80° during the day up above, it was near freezing at the bottom of the shaft. It was like digging in a cold storage locker.

Just as Aron had predicted, we no longer had many boulders to contend with, but one day at the twenty-one foot level an exception showed its knobby head ominously above the ground on the creek side-wall of the shaft. How do you get a four-foot boulder out of a five-foot hole in a three-foot bucket? It was time to call in the demolition squad, which consisted of Dennis and myself. Our previous blasting practice paid off, and we made short order of the boulder blocking our way.

When the last of it was pried out of the wall, we were greeted with a major surprise: a paleosol. A paleosol is a fossil soil, the ground surface is buried and preserved just as it was ages ago. If man or beast once inhabited the area, it was upon this thin veneer that they would actually have trod. Finding a paleosol is very rare and exciting to an archaeologist. What made this particular find even more impressive was that Aron had predicted it.

A paleosol represents a period of stability. This is fascinating to the archaeologist because it is the best place to look for remnants of primitive man and beast. It is a welcome contrast from most geologic deposits where the thin surface layer of soil and everything that has been lying upon it has usually been stripped away by erosion. If ancient man was present in Flagstaff at this time, we now had a zone where his tools and implements could be found just as he dropped or left them. This zone came in striking contrast to the long series of deposits we had already cut through, which for the most part represented material jumbled together and moved down the mountain side by gravity, mud, ice, and/or water. Dr. Thor Karlstrom and several of his associates at the United States Geological Survey who visited the site got quite excited when they saw this paleosol, and the excitement grew when they saw how the total geological section was developing. It became clear that the fine grain zones (at fourteen-to-fifteen feet and now at twenty-one feet) represented relatively warm periods of the past, which would be equivalent to the interglacial periods of the Great Lakes region. Based on the dates for the Great Lakes glacial sequence and correlating from the 25,000 year old date we had for our fourteen-foot level, the date for our twenty-one-foot zone was at least 40,000 years old. (Later we found still another fine-grained zone which contained artifacts from over 100,000 years ago!)

We were right in the midst of the most ideal target zones in which to continue our search. We weren't disappointed. We quickly began to find crude stone tools and their flake debris (waste material from the manufacture of stone tools) just as we had during our first excavation season. But now the stone artifacts were more plentiful and of better quality. We were tremendously excited. One specimen was long, thin, and bladelike in shape. Mother Nature could *never* produce a blade by normal geologic processes. It *had* to be handmade. In contrast to producing a stone flake, a very definite and well-placed carefully struck blow by a human hand is required to produce a stone blade. Making stone tools on blades, rather than on flakes, marked the replacement of Neanderthal man by *Homo sapiens* in Europe.

As we dug down and through the twenty to twenty-three foot level where Aron had designated the human bones would be found, the excitement mounted. We already knew that somebody had lived at the site during this ancient period; we were finding the remains of his tool-manufacturing activities. It was not unreasonable to expect to discover human bones at any moment in this paleosol. But, alas, we found no bones.

I didn't know whether to be happy or sad. On one hand, it was sad that our hitherto-reliable psychic information seemed to have failed on this very key point. But on the other hand, we had found evidence of human activity at the depth and age Aron had predicted, in a paleosol he had also predicted, which just happened to be the ideal place for human skeletal material to be preserved. This was something to be very happy about, even if Aron's accuracy was not perfect. I now knew that bones *could* be found somewhere in the vicinity. It seemed unlikely that there wouldn't be any bone material at the site. It was merely a matter of looking hard enough for it. We still had three-quarters of the shaft to dig out. Possibly the bones lay in one of these quarters. Maybe the bones lay just beyond the periphery of the shaft. The bones could be five feet away or two hundred feet away. Or perhaps Fran Farley was right and the bones were buried thirty-nine feet down. I just couldn't say, but at least I knew that man walked the lands of the Americas over 100,000 years ago (that is, taking into account the next fine-grained zone we discovered later) at dates far, far earlier than archaeological texts have dared to speculate about. Somewhere embedded in this Flagstaff paleosol lay the ultimate evidence. It mattered little where these people originated. The skeletal remains of one of the ancient inhabitants was calling out to be found. If only our psychic ears were just a little more sensitive. . . .

"What should we do now?" I asked myself. We still had some time and a little money left. I could either begin digging another quarter of the shaft down to this depth, or I could keep digging the same quarter even farther. I chose to keep going down, if only for just a peek at what I might find.

We emerged from the paleosol at about twenty-four feet, but three feet later we struck another finely bedded zone which seemed to be the start of another paleosol. This was a zone correlating to a date not less than 100,000 years old. Not only was the zone older, but it also contained strong carbon deposits which the first paleosol didn't. In this deposit we also found pieces of *scoria* (volcanic cinderlike material) encrusted with carbon.

My mind wandered back to the special check reading Aron had done on the bones at the close of the last dig season. In this reading, not only did he confirm that the bones would be at least 100,000 years old, but *that they would be found in a strong carbon deposit*. Just as I had pictured in my dream. Aron added that some "black lava fused hard . . . much carbon" would be our tipoff when we were getting hot. Was this carbon encrusted *scoria* the "black lava fused hard" tipoff Aron had promised we would find several feet above? This was what my crew anxiously wanted to know when they brought up samples of this material along with an exceptionally nice stone tool. This artifact showed prolonged wear and was found on the edge of the carbon deposit. It was sent back to me in town where I was spending the day nursing my ailing lungs. Whether or not we were ready to make the great breakthrough, I couldn't say.

When I saw the deposit myself, it seemed to be developing more strongly in the direction of the dry creek adjacent to the shaft. Some undercutting into the creek wall side of the shaft quickly confirmed this. Could the bones lie under the creek-bed itself, some ten feet from the shaft wall? Aron's first set of psychic instructions told us to dig a wide trench right down the center of the creek for several hundred feet. "You will proceed in the direction downstream," he envisioned, "you will then dig quite a wide trench . . . you will start going downward." This was the very large-scale excavation that I was originally forced to put aside for lack of sufficient funding and lack of a full-scale excavation permit. Excavating down the middle of the creek for several hundred feet required a very elaborate system for controlling spring runoff to prevent flooding. The test shaft only constituted a meager substitute for a full-blown excavation (especially an excavation in the creekbed.) I wondered if Aron had actually shown some real engineering insight when he instructed us to drop a shaft next to the creek in order to discover the carbon zone and follow it to the bones by undercutting the shaft wall. This avoided the water-control problems we would have if we excavated down the creekbed itself. Time and time again I vainly tried bringing back my dream images to see exactly where and how I undercut the creek to find the bones. It was frustrating!

I could feel that we were nearing the icing on the cake—bones. But the situation was still a complex one. Let me pursue this by citing an analogy. For my professional degree in geological engineering, I had written a thesis on the geology of the Hall Mine near Georgetown, Colorado. Here the Colorado Central vein provided millions of dollars in silver ore, but just as the vein substantially grew in size, it was interrupted by a fault. Huge sums of money had been spent unsuccessfully in trying to ascertain where the vein and its rich deposits continued. The only reliable prospect was to dig up the entire mountain concealing it. I felt we were up against a similar problem trying to follow the carbon deposit we had found at Flagstaff. While the bones could still lie in the unexcavated confines of the shaft, the only reliable way to find them would be to excavate the entire creek section and its margins. It was like Monopoly. "Go to Jail . . . Do not collect $200.00." In our game, "Go to Jail" meant all the way back to the original excavation instructions Aron had given before he gave his instructions for the compromise test shaft. From the test shaft we had artifacts which proved the potential accuracy of these earlier psychic perceptions made by Aron. We even recovered one oddity, at sixteen feet—an "Apache tear," which also supported the accuracy of Aron's perceptions. Apache tears are drops of obsidian that were collected as ornaments by early man in the Southwest. Since there were no Apache tear deposits in the dig area we could assume that it had been carried in and left at the site by an ancient collector who either lived at the site or visited it over 25,000 years ago.

I had another decision to make. Either I could finish the test shaft and also undercut the creek wall as much as possible in a sustained effort to discover the skeletal material under my compromise permit, or I could renew the fight for full excavation and dig down from the creekbed itself. My decision would be influenced by how accurate I suspected or wanted Aron or my other psychic contacts to be. Two more complicating factors were the ever-depleting state of my bank account and the attitude of the Department of Agriculture which issued excavation permits. Time and money helped me make my final decision. I ran out of both! I couldn't resume my excavation at all. No decision had to be made.

This interlude in our work allowed me to do some mental stocktaking of our entire effort. It was uncanny how well Aron's story was piecing together. My archaeological concepts about early man's entry into the Americas had been shaken by Aron's pinpointed discoveries, but I now placed more confidence in some of the more remarkable features of his readings. Aron had said that the early Flagstaff inhabitants had domesticated plants. While as yet we have found no corn pollen at Flagstaff, the initial pollen studies conducted for us by Dr. Richard Heavely of Northern Arizona University, one of the nation's most respected palynologists (an expert on pollen and spores), implied that the Flagstaff inhabitants may indeed have practiced plant cultivation. Dr. Heavely found that the samples from fourteen to fifteen feet, fifteen to sixteen feet, twenty-two to twenty-four feet and twenty-five to twenty-seven feet were dominated by pollen from herbacious weedy types of plants. Therefore it is safe to conclude that at one time the immediate area had weed growths even though it was in the middle of an enormous forest. As Heavely pointed out, so far as is presently known, we only get this type of pollen record in ". . . areas which have been burned and in which secondary succession has proceeded as far as the weed stage." This would mean areas which have been highly disturbed. Now; who did the burning? Man or nature?

Man is known to burn in order to clear areas to plant his crops. Nature can cause fire with lightning storms. Could lightning have hit the specific Flagstaff site area successively at 25,000, 30,000, 45,000 and 100,000 years ago (the estimated ages of the different zones from which the pollen samples were taken)? Or did the people who made the stone tools we found at these intervals cultivate as well as hunt? It is interesting to note that some varieties of fungi were also presented in the samples which are usually associated with litter and decomposition.

According to Aron's psychic story, the bones of a domesticated horse would be found during our dig, and we know that horses were present in North America at this early time. But just as with plant cultivation, the domestication of animals is not supposed to have taken place until about 9,000 years ago and once again in the Near East. More specifically, the earliest date we have for the domestication of the horse comes from the Ukraine in southwestern Russia 6,000 years ago. This carving on horn dates back to the Upper Paleolithic age in Europe circa 15,000-30,000 B.C. This in itself is not unusual since the horse is a constant figure in French cave art. But what makes the Arudy horse different is that the markings carved about the head seem to depict a muzzlelike rope halter. This is an obvious clue to the possibility that the horse was domesticated even at that time. There is no argument about the authenticity of the Arudy head; instead most scholars simply ignore the remarkable detail of the halter. Scientific traditions must be honored at all costs. Those who do take the muzzle into account try to explain it away by a bit of circular reasoning: the markings couldn't depict a fiber rope halter since the art of twisting a fiber rope was unknown before 8,000 B.C. In other words, if you can't find a good explanation for an exception to a conventional pattern, merely quote another convention! If our "Flagstaff man" had domesticated the horse, this would be consistent with several Northern Arizona Indian legends which speak of the horse.

Another remarkable aspect of Aron's readings where prior literature offers some credence is his impression that the Flagstaff people knew how to weave fabric. This art is supposed to have been developed in the Near East some 7,000 years ago, yet at the Kostienki site in the Soviet Union objects suspiciously identical to spindle whorls and items with fabric pattern designs on them have been dated back more than 80,000 years.

Putting aside these specific anomalies, our biggest question concerns the whole culture of Flagstaff man. If Aron's story is correct, how could these inhabitants have possessed such a remarkable set of advanced concepts long before scholars have dated these developments in other parts of the world? Aron's readings on the hypothetical full-scale excavation said that we would find evidence of other sophisticated practices as well—carvings, paintings, wooden ankhs, cured leather, and parchment scrolls with hieroglyphiclike writing. He even cited a mysterious underground tunnel system. This had also been predicted by a number of the other psychics who gave me information about the site. (Underground tunnels play a key role in Hopi mythology.)

Could this assemblage of sophisticated concepts be the product of some "Mother civilization," as Aron believes? Could our general archaeological concepts about the origins of world culture and civilization be just as much in error as Aron had proved about the date man first showed up in the Americas? Aron's impressions predict that at Flagstaff we will eventually discover remnants of a colony from a full-fledged civilization—a remnant of the very first civilization of the world. How I longed to run a bulldozer down the middle of the creek! If only the Department of Agriculture, the permit god, would turn its back for one week!

As our second dig season came to a close it was once again "show-and-tell" time. Psychic archaeology was winning another round at Flagstaff, so I wasn't about to be defensive about our work when visiting academic celebrities began to look in on our site. This time I wanted to get the most unbiased opinions possible from these experts. I kept mum about my training in both archaeology and geology. To the geologists I presented myself as an uninformed archaeologist, and as far as the archaeologists were concerned, I was merely an uninformed geologist. The visiting geologists were open and honest. They thought that the shaft covered what could be the best geological section in the western United States. There was no doubt in their minds that we had dug back over 100,000 years. They were anxious for me to keep digging and hoped to return to try some paleomagnetic dating techniques in the shaft. They also felt that the obsidian Apache tear which we found deep in the shaft was foreign to the area and probably came from a location at least 75 miles away.

But some of the visiting archaeologists were tainted by bias. Our early dates coupled with the wilder facets of Aron's story clearly colored the opinions of some of them as they evaluated our stone materials from the deeper levels of the pit. Acknowledging the existence of these tools was equivalent to admitting that the archaeological traditions they had grown to respect were nonsense. While none of these frantic experts actually denied our findings, some of their tortuous interpretations bordered on the absurd. One archaeologist even suggested that the Apache tear found its way to our site in the gizzard of a nomadic turkey!

Dr. Dennis Stanford of the Smithsonian visited the site with several of his associates from the museum. Dr. Arthur Jelinek and Dr. Vance Haynes of the University of Arizona did not visit the site, but they studied the materials. Along with Stanford, they felt that nature could possibly have struck the required blows to produce the stone flakes from the deeper zones during violent stream or downhill tumbling, abrasion, and frost action. But this ran counter to the fact that some of the deposits were found in parts of the shaft representing periods of great geologic stability and gentle deposition. It is just a matter of expertise. Some archaeologists just do not understand all the geological mechanics involved in producing the Flagstaff deposits. Since they could not appreciate the different types of deposits that occurred at Flagstaff, they just weren't sure if some of the materials we were finding were made by man or by nature. Some of our visiting experts were not acquainted with the research several archaeologists have carried out concerning the exact nature of alterations to rock materials which result from stream or downhill movement. At Flagstaff there was a distinct absence of materials altered by these processes.

In order to prove this point, I always invited visiting archaeologists to make a surface collection from the best concentrations of lithic material exposed in the area surrounding the site. I challenged them to come up with some candidates nature had produced to vie with what we were finding in the shaft. The results were always the same: no one could do it. Nor could anyone explain why the tools we found were concentrated in certain zones, why one quadrant had tools while an adjoining one did not. Why one depth interval had tools while another depth interval didn't. Why the paleosol had been so much more productive than the other zones. And more.

I was lucky to have the opportunity of showing the Flagstaff materials to Dr. François Bordes, the famous French archaeologist and the world's foremost stone tool expert. Even though he didn't visit the site, he understood some of the geologic mechanisms involved, or which were *not* involved. As he held the bladelike tool we had found at twenty-seven feet, he eschewed the "downhill Mother Nature theory" by pointing out that the delicate blade couldn't have been moved very far from where it was struck or else it would either have been broken or its edges would show signs of abrasion. To sum up, you just can't understand the archaeology unless you first understand the requisite geology.

The situation also offered the usual and expected irony. Our few doubters readily admitted that if the stone materials found at Flagstaff had been found *at a previously known site*, there would be no doubt in their minds that true artifactual finds had been made. Few doubted the authenticity of the artifacts we had found at—say—fifteen feet. It was the deeper material that emotionally offended them, that caused all the trouble. In other words, the finds that were 25,000 years old were okay. But the finds that were 100,000 years old had to be denied or explained away, even though they were the same material! Maybe it was only an act of conscience, but some of our critics went so far as to admit that our materials were better contenders and remnants for evidence of early man then what Dr. Louis Leakey had uncovered at the Calico Hills site in California.

Dr. Stanford, who at first was rather enthusiastic about our finds, was quite reticent when he visited us at the site. This perplexed me, but Dr. Hoffman, who was with us at the time, interpreted this as a good omen. He felt that Stanford's uneasiness indicated that he could not find anything he could legitimately attack. On the other hand, Hoffman was perplexed at the conservative reaction of Dr. Vance Haynes, one of our doubters. Haynes couldn't commit himself about our finds one way or another. Hoffman wondered how any archaeologist could deny the telltale man-made characteristic features on some of the tools, and Dr. Richard Ambler, another expert from Northern Arizona University, had no doubts at all. Neither did Pete Pilis, the Forest Service archaeologist, or Paul Fish, the stone tool expert from the Museum of Northern Arizona. (Fish, by the way, was a former student of both Dr. Jelinek and Dr. Bordes.) The gamesmanship of academic maneuvering was obviously now coming into play even more. Dr. Hoffman had warned me of this problem long ago, as had Dr. Richard MacNeish, director of the R.S. Peabody Foundation for Archaeology. Dr. MacNeish is not only one of the United States' most outstanding archaeologists, but also a long-time champion of the theory that man walked the Americas long before archaeologists conventionally believe. He warned me that "certain archaeologists" at "certain institutions" wouldn't accept these earlier dates even if they saw the ancient technicians making the tools with their own eyes.

Over the next few weeks we showed the materials to a number of others, and there was no doubt among them that man was the rightful sculptor. It seems that as long as the viewers had no vested interests at stake, they didn't doubt the authenticity of our interpretation of the finds. Bonnie Fine, a graduate student at the University of Arizona, took the Flagstaff materials to Lubbock, Texas, where a group of archaeologists who specialize in early man, and who call themselves the Friends of the Pleistocene, were meeting. Returning, Miss Fine reported that Dr. George Carter of Texas A. & M. University, who was in charge of this meeting, was tremendously excited by our materials. I phoned Dr. Carter directly and he reported that he felt that about half of our material was definitely "flake debris," that is, the results left from the manufacture of tools by prehistoric man. Dr. Carter was not at all upset by the 100,000-year-old date involved. In fact, he opined that when all the evidence is in and accounted for the date for early man in the Americas would go back over 250,000 years.

Ironically, some of the archaeologists who visited or spoke to me about Flagstaff were more keenly interested in the psychic aspects of the project. Not only had this interest grown among the professors at Northern Arizona University, but Dr. Richard Ambler told me how one day he had even gone out digging with a dowsing rod himself! Maria Wormington, a former curator of archaeology at the Denver Museum and one of America's most respected early-man experts, asked for information on the psychic aspects of the dig several times. Dr. Bruce Bradley of the Smithsonian, who had visited me with Dr. Stanford, admitted that he was a member of the Cambridge Society for Psychical Research in England and said he would be very interested in participating in my next psychic archaeological extravaganza. Beatrice Von Rotz, a professional archaeological artist who sketched some of the artifacts from Flagstaff, told me that she once worked on a medieval dig in Switzerland and the director of the excavation, one of the leading authorities in that area, had relied on his own psychic abilities for guidance.

Dr. Paul Martin from the University of Arizona, one of the nation's leading authorities on the Pleistocene age (the geological time period which encompasses the supposed entry of man into the Americas), provided a surprising turn of events when he visited the site. He has long been known as a devil's advocate against new early-man sites and early dates for man's archaeological emergence in the Americas. His arrival on the scene could have been destructive, but his main interest did not lie in analyzing our finds. Instead, he surprised us by concentrating his attention on the psychic aspects of the project. He got more and more excited by the potentials of psychic archaeology and felt that the doubt cast on some of the tools by a few of the archaeologists was unimportant. If such tools could convince better than nine out of ten professional archaeologists, this was a good enough majority vote for him to give Aron full credit as a master psychic. He admitted that our "total" case was pretty hard to argue with, and was also pleased that we had left standing some of the unexcavated columns in the shaft. This meant that there was plenty of site area still left for independent investigators to reproduce our results to date. I had to add a rueful note, though. I confided to Martin about my troubles and ultimate demise as a doctoral student at the University of Arizona. Dr. Martin was sympathetic and surprised me once again when he invited me to complete my doctoral work on psychic archaeology under him in the department of geochronology. I was flattered, but I had really endured enough of official university hospitality and politics. Dr. Martin persisted and we finally agreed that I would at least make a presentation on the Flagstaff project to all the graduate students in his department, many of whom were working in the area of archaeology.

These students didn't blanch at my premises and had no doubts at all about the artifacts. One student's support was extremely noteworthy. He had completed all his course work for a doctorate in archaeology, having specialized in study of the altering effects of nature on stone. He was quick to tell me that he could see no evidence for such a process in the material from the site. This presentation was sort of a tryout. The next thing I knew, Dr. Martin had me give a research colloquium on psychic archaeology and geology to the entire College of Earth Sciences at the university—psychic archaeology was opening up at the University of Arizona.

The Flagstaff dig offers great implications for two key issues within archeology: (1) The power of psychic archaeology itself; and (2) the existence of hitherto-unknown ancient peoples in the Americas. My work at Flagstaff is not complete, and I am quite anxious to get back to it. I would like to make things even clearer and more conclusive on both of these key issues. In fact, the most interesting aspects of the project are yet to come. I still must explore further for the bones. Even now my main worry is whether I can get the necessary permits to carry on a larger-scale and more complete excavation.

I feel Aron's psychic perceptions are consistent from one point to the next, thus I expect his present level of accuracy to hold when large-scale excavation is carried out. I feel we will find human bones in one of the black carbon deposits lying between twenty-three and forty feet in depth: not just the remains of several individuals, but the remains of a large number of individuals who died on the spot as they were overcome by a watery avalanche when the lake which likely existed at the head of the stream valley the site lies within broke its icy dam. Geologically speaking, we could expect such a lake to have formed below the type of massive snowfield which existed in the mountains at this time, and we could expect this lake to break its damming in an exceptionally warm summer. This is just what the Bear Glacier in the Soviet Union precipitated on a hot summer day in 1963, when it caused dammed lakes in side valleys to wash out and send a huge mass of melt-water and debris to sweep thru the Vanch Valley, which had a population of 10,000. I suspect that some of the black deposits at the site were formed when the organic material buried by the avalanche never had a chance to see the air again and oxidize. This deposit could be anywhere from 100,000 to 500,000 years old.

Analysis of this skeletal material should show that they are the first antecedents of the genetically unique American Indians. This realization should go a long way in clearing up the anomalies regarding the population dynamics of early man in the Americas.

I believe we will find that these people had an advanced civilization with technological developments that party-line archaeologists don't believe were discovered until just 10,000 years ago. They will likely have domesticated animals such as the small horse and dog, and domesticated plants such as corn and rye. They will probably have pottery, leatherwork, artwork, and some sort of symbolic writing system. I believe these will be the people the Hopi refer to as their ancestors who came from islands across the sea—Atlantis and Lemuria, if you like. Wherever they came from, the fact that they had an early advanced civilization should help resolve the mysteries associated with the origins of civilization on a worldwide basis.

Interpolating from what natural resources the Flagstaff site area offers, Aron's readings, Cayce's readings, and even portions of my dreams that I haven't yet confessed, I think we will find that these people were engaged in mining crystals from the zone where the fault, the granitic intrusion, and the sedimentary limestone deposits intersect. This is a classic environment for crystals, since the great amounts of heat and pressure required for crystal formation are associated with these geologic features. I suspect these people used these crystals for healing and for energy purposes in ways which we today are just beginning to imagine are possible.

My beliefs may appear to outstrip the physical discoveries at Flagstaff so far. And some may complain that scientists must advance on fact alone. But I know it is perfectly natural to have a vision extending beyond what is in front of your face. I have told you what I found, and I have told you what I think I'll find next. Without theories to question and pursue, I might just as well be poking blindly in a mud puddle. For I have not been seeking merely to justify personal predictions—I am seeking discovery itself.

The Flagstaff project directly challenges the intellectual honesty of all archaeologists. But for now, this issue is secondary to proving the vast potentials of psychic archaeology. There is no need to belabor Flagstaff now; as psychic archaeology begins to live up to its potential, many more discoveries will no doubt be made. A new and deeper understanding of the past stands ready to be grasped, whatever that past will be.

Chapter 6

On Using Psychics in Archaeological Research

Using psychics to help us make archaeological discoveries is not simple. Only by understanding the pitfalls can we overcome them and further the growth of psychic archaeology. Problems of accuracy, communication, and consistency all hamper the use of the psychic sense as a viable research tool. But even these are not the only variables that confront us. There are also physical, physiological, psychological, and ESP-based complications, the development of proper work and test procedures, the affects of practice and feedback to help learning, the pitfalls into which one can fall, and other problems. I only began to understand a few of these problems and their possible solutions, after having worked so long with Aron. Consultation with Dr. Cecil Rogers of the University of Arizona psychology department also helped make things clearer.

Communication

Probably the biggest problem we face is that of communication between the psychic and the investigator. Compare the psychic to someone who has just witnessed a traffic accident. The archaeologist or researcher is the note taker trying to reconstruct the accident on the basis of the witness's verbal reports and subsequent interviews. In a way we never measure the accuracy of just the psychics alone but rather the accuracy of a "team" composed of the psychic and the interpretive researcher.

During my work with Aron, most of our communications were carried out over the telephone or through the mails. I can only wonder how many of the problems we faced could have been eliminated if Aron had been present at the site while we were digging? I would have settled for a telephone at the bottom of the shaft.

Information Retrieval

The psychic has his own problems to contend with as he tries to retrieve the desired information. First and foremost, he must be able to get to the scene of the accident (that is, get into a psychic state where he can make proper observations and relate them). Different types of psychic information may be obtained in different ways. Aron, for example, feels he uses discarnate entities to gain some types of information and the Akashic Record for yet other types. Furthermore, it seems he induced out-of-the-body travel when he psychically visited my back yard. The psychic may gain the *same* information through different processes as well. From his point of view, relying on different processes may keep him from getting bored, or becoming overly dependent on one particular technique. This might just be a blessing in disguise. From the investigator's standpoint, it allows a perfect opportunity to cross-check the psychic's information internally.

My Flagstaff work has already revealed how Aron had to learn to discriminate between the different spirit entities ready to help him, and not to react to the one who seemed to communicate the most obtrusively. Aron learned to take his time. He ultimately learned how to obtain some of this information himself directly, information which he usually sought from discarnates. However, discarnate help can be used efficiently. In one reading we were told that in dealing with specific entities (such as calling them in on a project) it is best to "make an appointment," since they could already be occupied. While working at Glastonbury, Bond was once told that Abbot Beer would not be available to him for some time as he was busy on something else. The great psychic researchers of the past such as Dr. Richard Hodgson and C. Drayton Thomas, who worked with such great mediums as Mrs. Leonore Piper and Mrs. Gladys Leonard, also advised making specific appointments with the communicators before engaging in subsequent sittings.

As I said, a psychic will use very unique techniques to

retrieve information. Once I asked Aron to date some bits of charcoal we had recovered from the shaft. Aron said that he pictured a very large and beautifully furnished room. As he began to concentrate on the age of the charcoal, the room suddenly filled up with spirits. It seemed as if everyone and his brother-in-law was ready to offer advice. Aron then said that one of his contacts, who usually guides him, asked if anyone in the room knew anything about dating. The room emptied as quickly as it had filled! After a short interval, Aron said he noticed a blackboard in one corner of the room upon which was written the dates being sought.

The symbol of the blackboard is not as unusual as it might seem. Aron often obtained his information in novel ways. If I questioned him about the presence of pottery at a site, he might not only describe the pottery as it lay now, but might also describe a scene from the past when the pottery was broken and originally came to lay in its present position. When giving readings on the physical health of an individual, Aron reports that he goes to what he calls his laboratory and examines the person's body on a special screen. (This technique is similar to one from a Silva Mind Control procedure.) It must be emphasized that the use of such specific techniques are not ends in themselves, but rather various procedures which aid in tapping the psi-source.

Another problem of information retrieval is that a different psychic *modus operandi* seems to be involved when Aron makes psychic observations than when he makes psychic measurements. During our controlled back-yard experiments Aron appeared to be under more of a strain when he had to make measurements ascertaining the exact location of an object than when he just had to describe the object. Similarly, it takes greater effort to land on the moon than merely to orbit around it.

While object identification grew easy for Aron, measurement taking always remained difficult. He once compared making measurements to flying a high-speed jet over an area where even the slightest pressure or disturbance would throw the jet off course. Here the mental pressures on Aron seemed to take their greatest toll. To help minimize this problem, I learned to make Aron give measurements in several different ways. Ideally, the measurements for finding a hidden object were given from three different points of origin (triangulation) so that a triangle of error was produced. If this triangle of error was large, we immediately knew that there were inaccuracies given in the measurements. We then had the opportunity of having Aron attempt to improve on his psychic perceptions.

Aron feels the basis of any problem in his readings lies not with his source, which he believes to be always accurate, but with the filtering mechanism of his own personal psychic channel. New York psychic Ingo Swann agrees, referring to the principle as "analytical overlay." A psychic may accurately see a target such as a paring knife, but instead of saying that he saw a knife, the psychic may say that he saw a peeled apple. In this case the knife triggered an *association* in the psychic's mind. Thus the mind may have a significant modifying or symbolizing effect on the actual psychic impression.

Research Design

The research design employed during any project can have a significant effect on the accuracy of the information retrieved by the psychic. Unfortunately, too many parapsychologists do nothing but direct callous questions to their psychics and hope for the best. The exercises in my yard and the test case at Flagstaff illustrate how, in the long run, a more humanistic research design can produce better results.

Before using a psychic, the researcher should try to help develop his ability. Again, pioneer investigators such as James Hyslop always had a great hand in developing the psychics they worked with. An associate of Hyslop's, Dr. Titus Bull, personally developed three of the four psychics he eventually used in his research.

No one likes to be tested. It produces a lot of anxiety which can block a psychic from demonstrating his best abilities. It is here that the role of the experimenter is critical. First, the psychic should be put at ease. You should explain to him what you are trying to do, familiarize him with the testing procedures and, above all, design the experiment to accommodate the way the psychic feels he can best work. The psychic must have a word in the design of the experiment, not merely be subjugated to the experimenter's whims. A research design may call for five months of exploratory development and just one week of testing. When archaeological testing begins, the researcher should be careful not to rule out the very factors that produce or enhance the abilities he is seeking to test. A cold, impersonal atmosphere or noisy equipment are just two factors that may doom an experiment before it has even begun. No one knows what roles these and other seemingly peripheral factors can play.

Once testing has begun, the researcher should make sure that he doesn't overquestion. When I began our controlled sessions with Aron, Dr. Rogers, of the University of Arizona, emphasized that mental imagery is the key link between the psychic and his source, and that questioning should never jeopardize the imagery. One could literally question the image away yet the image is the psychic's reference point. For example, in one experiment during which Aron correctly identified a buried test object as a tooth, I inquired about the sex and age of the person from whom it had come. I could then have asked a series of questions about the culture and background of the person. But if I were to do so, it would be best if I periodically asked Aron for more details about the tooth itself, since it was *that* impression which was the springboard to the other information. I might have even asked him to visualize a grid over the tooth to aid in giving us more details.

During another experiment, I observed a phenomenon about which Dr. Rogers had also warned me. He pointed out a factor which can be demonstrated with subliminal perception tests in which images are flashed before the subject's eyes at too rapid a speed to be observed in detail, but which can be vaguely recalled. (For example, elements may appear in subsequent dreaming over the next week.) When the subjects were asked to retrieve the image from their brief memory of it, they tended either to *enhance* the image or *flatten* it. If a picture of a square with a bump on one side was quickly shown to a person, he might report a nice even square (thus leveling off the bump), or he might report that he saw a figure in which the bump was exaggerated over the entire square. Aron often did the same sort of thing. Once when we asked for a description of a piece of pottery we were using as a target, immediately after Aron acknowledged the image, he distorted it. This served as an excellent warning that if we rushed him our information would be inaccurate in some details.

The researcher should also be cautious about overtesting.

Ingo Swann told me that after all his work with the Stanford Research Institute, he wasn't even sure of his own name. A researcher can actually test a psychic's ability away. When J.B. Rhine started his ESP tests at Duke University, virtually all his star subjects eventually lost their abilities. During the sessions I periodically had with Aron, his wife Doris would ask him if he felt anxious, tired, or bored. If he felt hampered by any of these feelings, we interpreted it as a danger signal and backed off. His responses also serve as clues to the accuracy of his information, as well.

The greatest help a researcher can give in developing his psychic is immediate feedback to the responses to test questions. With such feedback the psychic can learn to improve his performance. This of course assumes that the psychic has the desire to learn and improve. In some of our experiments I gave Doris the answers to the test questions I was relaying to Aron. That way she could answer simply yes or no when the information was given. When Aron was wrong, she merely asked him if he would like to try again.

In the measurement tests, Doris would occasionally give Aron more specific feedback by telling him if his measurements were too long or too short. Caution had to be employed, since this type of feedback could become a crutch and even cue him to the answers. In the long run, this *could* impair his ability to measure under uncontrolled conditions. Dr. Charles Tart, of the University of California at Davis, has now carried out research showing that if a subject has a good deal of ESP ability to begin with, learning as a result of feedback can be fairly steady. However, the ESP talent must be present to reinforce the application of feedback. If the subject has only intermediate levels of ESP talent, Tart reports that we can expect either increased variability or stabilization of performance for some time, but little actual learning. He also found that if a subject has only minor ability, feedback will often serve no purpose at all, and might even constitute a kind of noise that could sap the subject's motivation or confuse him, impairing learning and even extinguishing his abilities altogether.

Aron is a gifted psychic. Consistent with Tart's laboratory research, we found that with immediate feedback his ESP became even more accurate. Aron knows how to use his talent.

During testing, the researcher must keep the work as

informal, novel and intriguing as possible. It must be fun. A variety of different tests would be helpful in reducing boredom and fear of failure. Once again, Rhine uncovered a similar principle during his Duke University testing. The introduction of a novel test often ignited his subject's enthusiasm and helped him to score better. The psychic should be given time to redo some of the tests on his own and at his leisure so he can get the "feel of things." For example, I always left many of the test artifacts I had buried in my yard still in place so that Aron could psychically revisit them whenever he felt like it. A researcher might even set up some tests which the psychic can conduct on his own, and supply the answers so that he could check his accuracy.

Another often overlooked point is that the researcher should make an effort to give the psychic a good working knowledge about the subject matter at hand. He should be taught about artifacts and the different raw materials used to make them. A general understanding of the prehistoric cultures involved would also save a lot of sweat and tears. Usually experimenters are paranoid about telling their subjects anything. They fail to realize that a psychic's ability to be articulate what he is saying can make all the difference in the world.

Psychics must always be treated as human beings, not just as machines. After someone has shown that he can lift a ten-pound weight, why must he do it ten thousand times? Researchers must fulfill moral responsibilities they have to their subjects. Patience and a willingness to help are always in order. All too often psychics are treated like guinea pigs. Ingo Swann, described in his book, *To Kiss Earth Goodbye*, the way most parapsychologists feel about working with gifted psychics: "The tactic heretofore has been to capture a subject exhibiting some paranormal potential and grind the subject through the research mill governed by fashionable . . . ideas of human possibility. The paranormal potential of the subject . . . usually was extinguished promptly and the subject himself fed out the back door in some sort of pulp form."

Another interesting phenomenon the researcher must recognize is that the psychic and his source may have some information they want to deliver regardless of the specific questions being asked. I learned this during some of my initial work with Aron. As he answered each of my questions, he kept referring to the first government of Atlantis. Finally I caught on and asked him what he had to say about the Atlantean government. He then gave an eloquent discourse on the subject and got it all out of his system so to speak. The channels were now clear, and I could go on with the particular questions I had in mind. The researcher must respect the psychic's world and the things he values. Ideally, the researcher shares the spiritual concerns that are a psychic's motivating force.

Since psychics gain impressions during altered states of consciousness, a researcher should familiarize himself with such states. He should practice meditation, imagery generation, and dream recall to get a good idea what his psychic is up against. The researcher may even set up a dialogue between two or more psychics at the same time, each in his own particular psi-conductive state. The investigator himself may attempt to join in. Once I participated in just such an experiment with a psychic who was a Ph.D. in psychology and who had great expertise in the use of hypnosis. The psychologist first hypnotized me, and then he and Aron entered into their own psi-conductive states. All three of us tried to move to the same point in the past. I described what I saw, then the psychologist had his turn, and then Aron, with his more masterful ability, was able to fill in the details. The staid experimentalist may question the scientific validity of this experiment, but the experience gave me an increased sensitivity to Aron's work.

Model of Key Variables

When working with psychics, there are several variables which will affect the overall success of the project. I've learned to divide them into four areas: (1) physical and physiological variables; (2) psychological variables; (3) spiritual variables; (4) engineering variables. These categories are not mutually exclusive and are only a preliminary guide to all the problems confronted in psychic archaeology. Let's look at each of them in turn.

(1) Physical and physiological variables.

The entire physical and physiological setting in which the psychic is placed can have a great effect on the information obtained. Such factors include the size of the room, the temperature, and even the lighting. Certain colors, and even the odor of incense, for some, could foster greater ability. Ossowiecki felt he could do his best work when skeptics were not present.

The main concern should be to set up an environment in which the psychic can shut off his conscious mind, or at least make it passive so that the ESP retrieving layers of his mind can operate more efficiently. Automatic writing served this purpose for Bond and John Alleyne. To help obtain this deeper state, Aron uses prayer at the beginning of each reading and then follows it with meditation. Sometimes he will use a "deepening tape." This tape, adapted from a Silva Mind Control technique, contains a series of clicks duplicating the rate of the human pulse with the heartbeat superimposed. Sometimes Doris, his wife, will speak softly to him in order to guide him into a deeper state and might tell Aron to see himself descending a long flight of stairs or going deep within himself.

Edgar Cayce, on the other hand, used a self-induced hypnotic trance. Aron has also done readings while under hypnosis, but he prefers to use his meditation procedure. This has certain benefits. After a reading Cayce did not remember what had transpired. Because meditation does not require trance, Aron isn't faced with this problem. I don't know whether this is good or bad.

I might add that for some reason Aron did better when he held a piece of azurite during his readings. This may only be a psychological crutch he picked up from Cayce who once said that azurite helps one tune into the psychic. In one reading Cayce noted that azurite, *lapis lazuli*, and other minerals containing copper had this property. So just to test this curious statement we tried a combination of the deepening tape and azurite on another psychic. Using these two aids seemed to help the psychic speak louder and more clearly during his reading, and when we asked about their use, his source felt that they were helpful. Of course, whether or not these procedures were only confidence-building aids is another question that we never resolved.

Every psychic has his peculiarities. Sometimes Aron would run out of "energy" during a reading. When he became tired, it was best not to proceed any further. To help, we learned from Aron's source that brewer's yeast would be beneficial. So just before a reading Aron would mix some brewer's yeast in a glass of orange juice. Dr. Rogers, who is a physiological psychologist, felt that the vitamin B-12 complex found in the yeast was supplying added energy to Aron's nervous system. (Cayce also recommended "mummy food," a gruel made of figs and dates; we were willing to try anything, but unfortunately Aron could never develop a taste for that!)

Besides daily prayer and meditation, Aron has also found other activities that help. He paints in oils to help him get in touch with his inner self. Aron's source has noted that any creative activity such as playing an instrument or singing can be of great help.

Even with all this, though, there will be times that a psychic will simply not be able to function at all. The psychic channel is a human channel, not simply a radio that can be continually switched on and off. There was a period in Edgar Cayce's life when he couldn't do readings at all, and many other psychics, such as D.D. Home, went through dry spells. Once a business problem upset Aron so deeply that doing any critical readings didn't feel right. To help overcome such personal stresses and pressures, Aron found going to the beach for a few days was a great help.

Obviously, all sorts of physical and physiological matters affect psychic ability. The best overall rule to follow is, that if a psychic says he works best under a certain set of conditions, go along with him! You won't be sorry.

(2) Psychological variables.

The greatest block for any psychic comes from his culture. This is but one aspect of another of our primary variables—the psychological considerations. A culture imposes certain norms of behavior, and in our modern Western society, being a psychic is abnormal. This weighs heavily on the personality and psychology of every psychic. In our culture there is a natural tendency to suppress rather than discuss and develop extrasensory ability, while in some cultures psychic abilities are encouraged. Among the peaceful farming Senoi of Malaysia, for example, dream interpretation is a regular aspect of child education and is held in great esteem. According to research psychologist Dr. Kilton Stewart, breakfast in a Senoi house is like a dream clinic. Certain members of this culture spend a great deal of time in a trance state and are considered specialists in the use of ESP. A great many actions taken by the Senoi are based on information which they feel is extrasensorily received—certainly a far cry from our own culture!

A psychic's personality plays an important role in his willingness to communicate the information he receives to others, especially to generally impersonal researchers. As pointed out before, being tested is always anxiety-producing and this will negatively affect the quality of any information received. Not only can feedback and development help overcome this problem, but testing also should be kept to real-life situations where the information has a direct application and need. Ossowiecki seemed to work best in these circumstances, but unfortunately this, too, can be a double-edged sword. Too much emotion can contaminate the psychic's ESP, causing him to latch onto the experimenter's own wish fulfillments and parrot them instead of making a genuine contact with the psi-source.

Allowing and encouraging a psychic to try his hand at teaching others during the research or using a team of psychics are other means of reducing pressure on any individual subject. The psychic may even have his confidence strengthened when other subjects in the group have similar psychic perceptions. This, however, is good only as long as what the psychic learns does not bias his subsequent impressions.

In conclusion, every psychic uses a personal procedure for retrieving psi-based information which is probably based on his personality and unique concept about what he must do to obtain his information. So psychological considerations must be involved in virtually every action taken by the psychic and the researcher.

(3) Spiritual Variables.

Spiritual variables are a little more abstract than psychological ones. While it is hard to give an operational definition of "spiritual," this term will at least serve to classify a wide-ranging group of variables whose importance we are just beginning to recognize. Several of these factors were noted in the chapter on Edgar Cayce, so I will mention them here only briefly.

We encounter spiritual factors when a psychic talks about the "vibrations" involved as he gains his impressions, and how they can effect the quality of information he seeks. Cayce felt that everyone cooperating in a session should be "in tune." Cayce may have been telling us something very important. Maybe there is a spiritual factor which is a sort of correlative to emotion and thought. The ultimate goals and ideals held by all those seeking psychic information, as well as their intentions, is yet another spiritual variable. We have also noted Cayce's concept of "grace," a higher directive which may come into play and determine the results that are achieved.

Akin to spiritual variables are psychic variables. A psychic often has a "feel" for a certain subject area because of a dramatic experience in his own life. For example, the Dutch psychic Gerard Croiset is especially good at clairvoyantly tracking down lost children, since as a child he himself was once lost and almost drowned in one of Holland's many canals. If one accepts reincarnation, these factors can be stretched to include events which occurred in past lives. Edgar Cayce claimed that he developed his psychic ability over a series of different past lives. This could explain why a psychic may have a specific ability to retrieve archaeological information from a specific time in the past instead of a more global ability. Dr. Emerson's key psychic informant, George, seems to be best at giving information about the Iroquois Indians.

Another psi variable may be the discarnate helpers so many psychics feel guide them. By constant prayer and meditation Aron tries to keep his channels to them open and clear; he feels these procedures will attract the appropriate entities. He claims that he has already made contact with three different sets of helpers, each group taking him through a different aspect of psychic development.

Aron believes that "spirit" is the most important force contributing to either the development or ruin of a culture. This spiritual factor is reflected in the honesty and integrity of a people, the loss of which led to the fall of the Atlantean, Egyptian, and Roman civilizations. As Aron says, these cultures evolved technologically and materially, but not spiritually. A similar concept pervades Cayce's readings on prehistory.

(4) Engineering variables.

Engineering variables encompass the effects of practice,

training, and procedures used to retrieve psychic information. With experience, a psychic and a researcher working together should be able to improve their joint ability to harness the psi-channel efficiently. The only difference between a master and a novice is practice. For a psychic who can occasionally make contact with a psi-source, practice will make all the difference. I have worked with several psychics who weren't as good as Aron. Still, they were picking up useful pieces of information, and I think with practice some of them could learn to retrieve a whole body of psychic data, not just bits and pieces.

In one of our first experiments Aron reported that three buried test objects were all six inches in size. While this was true for the first two, it was much too large for the third object, which was a one-inch pottery shard. It was easy enough to see that Aron, in his altered state, seemed to be looking through a six-inch lens and that everything was naturally measuring out to six inches. He had forgotten to find an independent point of reference before he gave the measurements.

Vocabulary and semantics are two other possible sources of error that can be reduced with practice. From our backyard experiments we learned that a control question served as an excellent indication of the quality of information Aron would give in a subsequent reading. This control simply consisted of asking Aron a question to which we already knew the answer. If the reading was going to be on a measurement, we might ask him to make a psychic measurement between two stakes set up at some distant location. Once before, in a reading on ancient astronomy, I asked him to give me the relationship between the earth, sun, and Mars on April 18, 1906. Reference to the 1906 *Ephemeris* quickly confirmed the accuracy of Aron's answer. We then knew he could be accurate on the subject of ancient astronomy.

Edgar Cayce had his own control when he did a reading. He never proceeded until he saw a blue light go on—his personal signal that he had made contact with his source. So two controls can actually be employed—one by the psychic to make sure he is properly tuned in, and one by the researcher to make certain the psychic channel is functioning clearly.

When the psychic is actually giving a reading, some sort of "ground control" is helpful in order to conserve his psychic ability. For example, if only a brief answer to a question is required, the ground controller (the questioner, in this case) can cut him off if he starts to ramble about unnecessary details.

Constantly cross-checking the psychic's information is also extremely important. If the researcher is sharp, he can save himself many hours of digging, if right then and there he can cross-reference the psychic impressions to a site upon which he already has data. The following example will serve as a good illustration of a type of cross-checking:

During one reading, Aron was describing Atlantean technology, especially use of crystals. I remembered that in an earlier unrelated reading he had given instructions for growing some special crystals. Were these the same as the Atlantean ones, I wondered? If they were, we could grow them to see if they had the attributes of the legendary Atlantean ones. As a cross-check, I took the information Aron had given for crystal growth to a specialist in crystallography. He, in turn, was immediately impressed by the readings' extremely sophisticated information, some of which had only just recently been uncovered, and it became a research guide for a group of interested physicists.

However, there is one danger to all this. One must be wary of unnecessarily oversharpening the psychic to the point that he becomes "muscle-bound" and loses his more general ability. While it is fine to let the psychic specialize, as Cayce did with his medical readings, several areas (such as archaeology, medicine, and astronomy) should be included to insure that the psychic remains rather versatile. Further, there should be some pragmatic aspect to every research project. The project should not consist merely of tedious irrelevant experimental tasks. Allowing the psychic to visit an actual archaeological site to watch the digging is much better than sitting with him in some dingy museum and handing him one artifact after another.

I also find it helpful to ask Aron for self-critiques. I would ask Aron about the errors and contradictory statements he had made in the course of different readings over the preceding months. I was constantly amazed at the insight shown in these critiques, but I also cringed when I saw how hard they were on Aron as the strap always fell on his personal disciplines and practices. Even with his ability, there was no way for Aron to improve other than hard work. While such self-criticisms can be very helpful, one must be cautioned from overusing them. Like feedback, they, too, can become a crutch.

One aid we were not able to employ during our controlled tests was what parapsychologists call "confidence ratings": seeing if Aron could determine the accuracy of his own psychic readings and impressions. Some research carried out in parapsychology laboratories has shown that gifted subjects can determine to a statistically significant degree when they are reacting to a psychic impression and when they are only guessing. If Aron could have given this added information, then we would have had some way to factor out and control the effects of inaccuracy and separate good readings from bad ones. But this would have required more elaborate experiments than we were able to engage in.

Development

Keeping all these considerations in mind, I still do not believe that we have any truly research-oriented psychics available to us. What is needed is sort of a school where what I call "second-generation" psychics can be developed. Contemporary sensitives—even Aron—developed on their own, work on their own, and have learned very individualistic ways of using their abilities. It really is presumptuous for a researcher to step in and start making demands on a psychic who has been getting along quite well without him! Should we expect the psychic to harness himself to the rigors of scientific investigation when he can already bask in the accolades of his own hugging and kissing clientele? But if a sensitive were taught early in his life to have great interest in science, a sense of commitment and dedication will surely override any trepidation about the hard work required by scientific research. This is the second-generation psychic: an individual developed for the express purpose of research and application in whatever area he has chosen.

The roots of such development can be seen in Ossowiecki's apprenticeship under his teacher Vorbej, in Aron's teaching of others, or in Dr. Ross's and General Elliott's ability to teach archaeological dowsing to others. The biggest question is, what price are people with some initial psychic ability willing to pay to develop this talent? The conscious

Edgar Cayce, in a talk given in Norfolk at an open meeting on Feb. 6, 1933, said:

"Apparently I am one of the few who can lay aside their own personality sufficiently to allow their souls to make this attunement to this universal source of knowledge but I say this without any desire to brag about it. In fact, I do not claim to possess anything that other individuals do not inherently possess. Really and truly, I do not believe there is a single individual who doesn't possess this same ability I have. I am certain that all human beings have much greater powers than they are ever conscious of if they would only be willing to pay the *price* of detachment from self interest that it takes to develop these abilities. Would you be willing even once a year to put aside, pass out entirely from your own personality?"

Indeed, Cayce trained several students to interpret their dreams more proficiently than he believed he could do himself. One student, a successful businessman, merely had to close his eyes a moment to retrieve information psychically, but unfortunately he and others like him became too infatuated by this miraculous ability and went from the zenith of success to total ruin. This convinced Cayce that the development of psychic ability had to go hand in hand with the concomitant development of a strong personal ethic, and the Sleeping Prophet never again helped train anyone psychically without first helping him develop spiritually. Being able to tune into the sensations and substance of the past, or the emotions and thoughts of those around us, may not be such a blessing if the sensitive hasn't first learned to appreciate this information. This is not to say that people who lack character can't be good psychics; rather that the development of character and psychic ability should go hand in hand.

Conclusions

Cayce taught that "through the application comes the awareness." I present psychic archaeology as one of the best examples of the practical use of psychic ability and as the best possible demonstration of the value that psychics offer science and society in general. Parapsychologists, by working together with archaeologists, may achieve just the psychic breakthrough they have been waiting for. The entire history of science shows us that new discoveries and proofs never really become accepted until there is a genuine need for them. There is a great difference between proving your point to others and selling it to them—and I mean *selling*, not simply communicating. If more archaeologists take advantage of psychic aids and employ them successfully, a need for and recognition of psychic science will soon follow. The reality of psychic phenomena will finally be acknowledged. In its present state, archaeology needs the use of good psychics, and parapsychology needs a bold new frontier. Working hand in hand, they can sell the reality of psychic phenomena. As Dr. Emerson, I, and others find more sites with the help of psychics, other archaeologists struggling with traditional techniques will follow.

PART III

Contemporary and Future Research

Psychic archaeology is presently being employed across the breadth of the United States and in Russia, Ecuador, Mexico, Canada, Britain and France. On a worldwide basis, archaeology is undergoing a revolution, where ESP is replacing the spade as archaeology's primary tool. But even more exciting is what the future may bring. New brain research and the continued development of lasers and holography may yet create a time machine to the past which is available to all men—one as handy as the family TV set.

Chapter 7

Psychic Archaeology from Canada to Mexico

> A universal proposition can be made untrue by a particular instance. If you wish to upset the law that all crows are black, you must not seek to show that no crows are: it is enough if you prove one single crow to be white.
>
> —*William James, Founder of American Psychology*

"At a meeting of the department's archaeologists we agreed that we wished to welcome you here. . . . Please rest assured that I am personally enthusiastic, excited and interested in your work and genuinely impressed and will lend you every help I can."

These were the words that struck my eyes in the spring of 1974 when I opened a letter from the University of Toronto. The note was signed by Dr. J. Norman Emerson, the well-known president of the Canadian Archaeological Association and head of the archaeology section at the University of Toronto. Many people consider this division to be the best center for archaeological studies in the world. It was certainly a flattering invitation. I had not made formal application to the university, so the letter came as a double surprise. I had applied to Simon Frazer University in British Columbia, and the school sent my transcripts to its neighbor college. I applied to Simon Frazer University hoping to find a more suitable milieu in which to complete my doctoral work. They were at least frank with me. They labeled my plan as "unusual research interests" and warned that I would not receive a very sympathetic ear within *their* department. However, they were trying to be helpful—a pleasant relief from the earlier

Arizona machinations—and informed me that the only archaeologist in Canada working to coordinate the dual disciplines of archaeology and parapsychology was Dr. Emerson. They had taken the initiative of sending my files on to him.

Whatever the final outcome of my work, this letter from the University of Toronto represented further academic recognition of psychic archaeology, since Dr. Emerson is the most influential man in archaeological circles in Canada. I discovered a reward for my ordeal in Arizona.

Along with his letter, Emerson sent me two papers he had written about his own research which had relied upon psychic aid. His psychic had been invaluable to him in his archaeological exploration. Emerson is not overly concerned with formal and protracted scientific proofs; the kinds of proof that critics and skeptics clamor for. Rather, his attitude is one of pragmatic action. He believes that it makes perfect sense to seize the unique opportunity provided by those who can tap the psychic sense. Both he and several of his colleagues have taken psychics right out into the field and have proven to themselves the tremendous help psychics can offer. So, asks Emerson, what is all the debate about? The system works; to ignore it out of emotional bias would be nothing short of derelict. The Canadian professor calls for the immediate and full-blown appreciation and incorporation of psychics in archaeological research as another weapon in its armory. Time itself will work out the details of the marriage.

Under Emerson's protective wing, graduate students in his department have conducted their own research employing the use of psychics. He chaired a seminar at the Canadian Archaeological Association on psychic archaeology where no less than eight separate papers were presented. Assuming the role of spokesman for the cause, he helped film a documentary about psychic archaeology which featured one of the psychics he uses. He has even "loaned" some of his psychic helpers to other Canadian archaeologists working to solve their own difficult problems.

It is no surprise that Emerson's foresight has spurred this mind revolution in Canadian archaeology. Over twenty-five years ago Emerson was one of the few professors of archaeology in Canada. Because of his influence, innovations, and guidance numerous departments of archaeology have been founded throughout Canada. But now that he has become the father of conventional archaeology in Canada, it seems that he wants to revolutionize his own brainchild with psychic archaeology. Rather than being a pharaoh who banishes any heretic propounding a new religion, this king is out there converting the people himself.

Emerson's own confrontation with psychic archaeology began in a fun-and-games atmosphere with a psychic truck driver friend named George McMullen. George could psychometrize artifacts; he could hold an object in his hand, concentrate upon it, and then relate details about the people who originally made and used the object. When Emerson realized that George was receiving accurate information, Emerson was encouraged to get down to serious business. The fun and games were over, it was now time to roll up their sleeves and prepare to work.

Emerson's specialty is the archaeology of the Iroquois Indians of east Canada and he has collected hundreds of their artifacts. Based on his expertise of the Iroquois and their culture, it was easy for him to tell whether the information George was giving was right. If his own knowledge failed him, he could always check excavation reports and historical documents to see if they supported George's statements. On one occasion, Emerson handed George a fragment from the Black Creek site in Toronto, an old Iroquois settlement. After meditating on it, George correctly reported that the fragment was a pipestem, gave its correct age (according to George, the colder the artifact feels, the older it is), and the location of the site from which it came. He told how the pipe had been manufactured, described its maker, and gave details about the community and its life-style. Grabbing pen and paper, he then sketched a picture of the pipe bowl from which he claimed the broken stem had come. Emerson, the world's foremost authority on Iroquois pottery, immediately recognized that the picture represented an Iroquois conical-ring bowl that was popular in that culture over a thousand years ago. George was similarly accurate when "reading" a fragment from an effigy bowl and an old coin of King George III vintage. As with Aron, there were many instances where George's ESP impressions could not be explained away as shrewd guesswork or the product of late-hour homework at the local museum.

Once it seemed that George was absolutely wrong. He was giving information about a particular village site in Ontario and said that the population *had not* cultivated corn, beans, or squash. This was hard for Emerson to accept. Emerson believed the site must have produced these traditional Iroquois crops since the archaeologists who excavated the site recovered abundant evidence of corn, beans, and squash, which all seemed to prove that George was wrong. But Emerson decided to give him a full hearing. After all, the Iroquois might have obtained these vegetables by trade rather than by direct farming. One archaeologist investigating the site admitted that a good case could be made that the Indians of this settlement bartered with stone. To resolve the problem, Emerson had soil samples taken and studied for pollen traces. If these vegetables were locally grown one would expect to find traces of them in the soil. Only *one* possible grain of corn pollen was found, camouflaged in the plentiful pollen grains of the local vegetation. This is a strong indication that George was right after all.

Besides his obvious psychometric ability, George becomes psychically sensitive to any site he visits. According to Emerson, who directly observed him, George would walk very rapidly over a site area to orient himself and would then give a reading about it. He would first give the age of the site, then describe the people, their dress, dwellings, general behavior, and even their economic system. Then he would really get fancy. He would "go back in time" and put himself right out on the limb by giving specific information as to where ruined structures could be excavated. These predictions could be easily checked by digging. George once walked around the perimeter of what he said was an Iroquois long house while Emerson followed behind him placing surveying pins in the ground. Six weeks later, the entire long house was excavated exactly where George said it would be.

On yet another occasion, Emerson took George north of Ontario to Parry Sound where an archaeological survey crew had been unsuccessfully working all summer. George quickly located Indian tools and carvings that were 7,000 years old. He also at one time helped Canadian archaeologist Patrick Reed who was digging up a tenth-century Indian village buried under a weed-choked field. Reed was pretty skeptical about George at first, but was soon convinced:

"I thought I'd ask him where the stockade wall of the village had been. I was pretty sure it had one, but I hadn't been able to find it. George told me, 'It's there,' and traced out a line forty feet long. Twelve inches under the ground, I found the stockade remains. It scared the hell out of me."

As if to emphasize his psychic talents to the skeptical scientist, George later located the remains of a buried house in the same village. According to Emerson, when George visits a possible excavation area, ". . . he almost quivers and comes alive like a sensitive bird dog scenting his prey," and adds, "He has given me enough advice on where to dig and what I will find to keep me busy for a decade."

It is very unlikely that George would know much about archaeology normally. He had to leave school in the eighth grade and go to work during the Great Depression. He has had little formal education and has done little reading on Indians or their folklore. Although George admits that he once visited the Royal Ontario Museum, he didn't find the experience pleasant because he was "disturbed" by the mummies. Instead, he feels that his impressions about the Canadian Indians come directly, ". . . from Indians who lived five hundred to six hundred years ago. I don't go into a trance. It's as if I'm looking down from above. I can see where a village is and how the Indians used to live. This power used to scare me at first, but now that I know what it is, I like to use it in areas where it can do some good."

Even though George's sources of information are not infallible, Emerson has found him to have a high degree of reliability and estimates that his accuracy over the past three years is about 80 percent. George is personally very interested in Indians, so it is not odd that his psychic perceptions have proven to be the most accurate when it is focused on them.

One of the most dramatic episodes highlighting Emerson's brand of psychic archaeology came during the annual banquet of the Canadian Archaeological Association in March 1973. A skeptic asked George to demonstrate his ability by psychometrizing a black argillite stone carving right on the spot. Very little was known about the artifact except that it came from Queen Charlotte Island in British Columbia and appeared to represent the head of an apelike creature. The owner thought the carving represented a sasquatch, the Canadian counterpart of what we call the Abominable Snowman or Bigfoot. As George held the artifact in his hand before the group assembled, he stated that it had been carved by a Negro from Port-au-Prince, Haiti. Emerson was appalled by this statement: the carving originated in British Columbia, and any suggestion that it was carved by a black man from the Caribbean seemed totally out of the question. Emerson tried to call off the impromptu experiment and told the owner that they would have to work with the object later.

This attempted dismissal didn't stop George from proceeding with his outlandish story even after he had returned home. He studied the object further and gave Emerson an even more fantastic tale. He said that the carver was a black man who was a native of West Africa who had been captured and taken as a slave to the Caribbean by the Spanish. Later he had been taken on an English ship sailing to British Columbia where he escaped and was sheltered by the native Indians. There he married an Indian, raised a family, and died.

Puzzled by this narrative, Emerson took the carving to some other psychics who acted as advisers. Each of seven psychics was independently asked to psychometrize the object, but none was told what the others had reported. Besides adding a wealth of new information about the figure, each psychic independently confirmed much of what the others had said. Here are just some of the statements Emerson recorded:

George was the first to catch onto the jungle theme and said, ". . . it was very heavy, very thick jungle . . ."

Sheila, another psychic, simply stated that, "Somebody who handled this at one time was a colored man . . . the jungle is behind me here . . ."

Two psychics picked up the slavery motif. George said, "Anyway, he ended up in slavery. He came over in a slave ship," while another psychic named Jim reported that, "they were raided by a renegade African and his cohorts who captured a few of his village . . . to sell them as slaves . . . He made the carving out of black rock from the mountains there nearby . . . Canada comes to mind . . ." This is very similar to George's story.

Sheila, too, got the impression that the man was a Negro and even pinpointed the origins of the carving, "Kind of looks like the kind of stuff that comes from the Queen Charlotte Islands—what is a black man doing in the Queen Charlotte Islands?"

Some of the new information given by the psychic team included the name of the ship that sailed to British Columbia, details about Russian sailing ships in the Canadian area at the time, a description of a native African dance, and an old

English sea chanty. Emerson obtained over 200 pages of transcripts of these readings but still wondered if the story might not be a telepathically leaked fantasy from either George's mind or his own. Nonetheless, at the next annual meeting of the Canadian Archaeological Association in March 1974, Dr. Emerson reported that three independently corroborated themes stood out in the analysis made by his team of psychics: (1) The carver of the artifact was born in Africa: (2) He was taken to the Americas as a slave; (3) He fled to British Columbia.

The psychics were certainly accurate enough about the artifact's coming from British Columbia. But what about the rest of the information? Was all this consistent intertwining information true or just the result of telepathy between them? It was Emerson's view that prodigious historical research efforts would be required to check out the reading. During this search, such items as the names and movements of slave ships in colonial times could be tracked down. Emerson's *tour de force*, though, was that information he had *already* received stood in striking confirmation of the psychic's story. Before his astonished colleagues Emerson reported how he obtained an analysis of the argillite artifact from the Royal Ontario Museum made by an expert in African art specimens. Point by point and in great detail, this expert explained to Emerson that the art style used on the carving was typical of West Africa and, to be more specific, from the upper regions of the Volta. Even another ceremony that one of the psychics envisioned was highly evidential. It was identified as the *potlatch*, a Northwest Coast Indian gift-giving ceremony. Emerson asked, "If the life of this black man is available, why not the life of all men?"

This might be a good motto for psychic archaeology.

After scrutinizing and analyzing Dr. Emerson's research, I felt reassured in my own efforts. But I decided not to dash up to Canada and enroll in the University of Canada that fall. My first commitment still remained to Flagstaff and the only partially completed dig there.

I was able to meet Dr. Emerson at the seventy-third annual meeting of the American Anthropological Association, in Mexico City. Both Emerson and I were there to give papers at the Rhine-Swanton Interdisciplinary Symposium on Parapsychology and Anthropology. The late Dr. Swanton was a former president of the American Anthropological Association who in 1953 sent a six-page letter to all his fellow anthropologists urging them to open their minds and look into the field of parapsychology. It took twenty-one years for Swanton's plea to be heard. The Rhine-Swanton Seminar was the first time anthropology had taken up the subject of parapsychology since Sir William Barrett read a paper on telepathy before the anthropology section of the British Association for the Advancement of Science in 1876.

I didn't know, nor would have ever believed, that such a seminar was being planned until I received an invitation from the seminar chairman, Dr. Joseph Long, to give a paper. Somehow Long, an anthropology professor from the University of New Hampshire, and Southern Methodist University, had found out about my work at Flagstaff. It was a golden opportunity for me since a number of important archaeologists would participate. These participants included several department heads, a number of distinguished professors, and a past president of the Parapsychological Association, the international organization of professional workers in parapsychology. (Full membership is restricted only to those who have made a substantial contribution to the field.)

When I finally met Dr. Emerson, I was immediately put at ease by his casualness, which was no better illustrated than by the big ankh he wore around his neck. I was disappointed to learn that because of a change in plans, George had not accompanied his patron to Mexico City. Emerson originally planned to bring him down and let him turn his psychic talents loose on the Pyramid of the Sun at Teotihuacan, a large prehistoric structure situated just outside of Mexico City. This pyramid has long puzzled archaeologists. A film crew from the University of Toronto was to have filmed George in action, but this would have to be rescheduled for later in the year.

During the next five days Emerson and I spent hour after hour comparing notes. Often our main focus was another strange Mexican structure—a fruit-salad pyramid at the nearby health-food restaurant. Emerson told me how George had first helped him with a personal problem long before they did any archaeological experimentation together. Edgar Cayce's readings were another factor that turned Emerson's interest to the possibility of using psychics as a research tool.

However, we really didn't have to sit around and swap after-the-fact stories, for there was a tremendous psychic talent right there with us in Mexico City. Before we would leave the convention, Emerson and I were to witness yet another breakthrough in psychic archaeology: this through the psychic genius of Fran Farley, who also helped at Flagstaff. Fran has already been acclaimed for her psychic skills. She was once studied by the famous author Aldous Huxley and was recently featured in *Psychic* magazine. Although she has had a long career using her psychic abilities in various fields, including medicine, where she has given clairvoyant diagnoses to seventy doctors, Fran wanted to try her hand (or ESP) at psychic archaeology. She came out to dinner at a local Japanese restaurant with some of us the evening before one of my meetings with Emerson. While the chef was preparing the meal at our table in true Japanese fashion, Fran psychometrized an artifact I just happened to have with me. When she psychometrizes something she rubs the fingers of her free hand lightly back and forth over a smooth surface. Her fingers "stick" when the right psychic impression comes along. It was quite a scene—Fran gently rubbing, the waiter flamboyantly cutting, and my friends talking in 78 rpm animation. All the commotion didn't affect her ability.

There was a lot of informal talk about psychic archaeology at the convention in addition to the formal papers being presented. A friend of mine told me of a talk he had with Dr. Margaret Mead, one of the foremost anthropologists in the United States, during which she said that we must learn to recognize that psychic ability may be a cultural development in those peoples who recognize and support its development and use. She said that in some cultures ESP is not considered unusual but rather to be expected in at least some members. She also informed him about a very good sensitive she had studied who was a friend of her father's. Dr. Mead's interest perked up considerably when asked about using psychics to discern the whereabouts of buried artifacts. It was Dr. Mead's impassioned plea at a meeting of the American Association for the Advancement of Science that played a key role in the acceptance of the Parapsychological Association's petition for election as a component science in 1969. (When the AAAS's publication *Science* rejected a paper on ESP, one wisecracking referee sent back the manuscript with a picture of Dr. Mead stapled to it captioned "Woman of the Year!")

Since psychic archaeology was such a burgeoning new

field, Emerson and I marveled about the fact that a third paper on archaeology and parapsychology would also be presented during the meeting. The author, Dr. William Wolkowski, was a professor from the Sorbonne in Paris.

Another morning during the convention, Dr. Robert Van de Castle stopped by my room. Dr. Van de Castle is a professor in the psychiatry department at the University of Virginia, where until recently he headed a dream laboratory. He is also a former president of the Parapsychological Association and was presenting a paper at the symposium. Dr. Emerson and Dr. Wolkowski soon joined us and a lively conversation began. The door was slightly ajar and to our surprise a very attractive young lady walked in. She excused herself for being so brazen but explained that she had passed by in the hallway outside our room and, overhearing what we were talking about just had to hear more. She said that she had her own English-language talk show on a CBS affiliate station, one of Mexico's largest, and asked if we would do a show for her. We all shuffled off to her studio to continue our conversation about psychics and archaeology over the airwaves.

All this talk about psychic archaeology became much more dramatic when Fran entered onto the scene. Later that day some colleagues joined us and we got right down to work, the work of psychic archaeology. Fran was ready to pick up where she left off at our last session in the restaurant. After offering me more information on Flagstaff and a little demonstration of map dowsing, the fireworks really started. Emerson had brought something special for her to psychometrize and handed her a gnarled piece of metal. We waited for Fran to speak. The room grew silent as she started to get in tune with the object. Fran broke the silence, complaining that our quietness was making her feel too self-conscious. She wanted us to continue our conversation as she worked. After a few moments she said she was ready for questioning.

Emerson began by asking her what she "saw." Fran reported seeing Indians and white men, but that the white men didn't speak English. She added, "They were exchanging something. . . ." Emerson then told her excitedly that she was right and confirmed that the psychic had picked up a meeting between the famed French explorer Samuel Champlain and the Iroquois Indians. The piece of metal she was holding was from one of the kettles Champlain offered in trade to the Indians for their help as guides. At this point a best-selling author who was in attendance jumped up in amazement. "You can really do this!" he said in wide-eyed disbelief. Fran was taken aback. Hadn't he believed her for the last twenty years they had known one another? It was rather an embarrassing moment.

Fran quickly turned back to reporting the psychic impressions she was getting from the piece of metal. She described the village and the activities that went on there. As she so vividly depicted the village, the people, and the era, we felt dramatically catapulted to Champlain's side. Emerson was able to confirm the accuracy of many of Fran's impressions because we still have a document written by one of the members of Champlain's expedition, which describes the famous meeting in much the same way as Fran had. Of course we were confronted with two possible interpretations: either Fran had tapped Emerson's mind, or she had actually gone back into time to recapture the incident. This very problem of interpretation is why I like psychics to give information which can lead to the discovery of new artifacts, or give predictions about what we will find upon digging in a certain locale. The dismal outcome of the predictions made by two archaeology professors in Arizona while trying to outguess Aron, aptly demonstrates that it is very difficult to predict with any certainty what a dig will unearth. This type of experiment rules out telepathy. And Fran had this type of information for Emerson as well for she told him where to dig to find the council area of the village, a site Emerson had been unable to find. Emerson was intrigued by Fran's instructions, and we could sense that he would be somewhat anxious to test them in the spring when he resumed digging.

As Emerson concluded his questions, one by one other archaeologists sought the chance to question the psychic. They were like kids with a new toy they just couldn't put down. Or perhaps it was all a psychic version of "Face the Nation." I tried to keep the session brief so as not to tire her, but minute after minute ticked on until two and a half hours had rolled by. Fran was exhausted but a good sport.

When the day of the symposium finally arrived, the presentations seemed almost dry in the light of the dramatic use of the psychic potential we had seen Fran exhibit. But we were nonetheless full of trepidations. This would be another acid test. Psychic archaeology was about to make its official debut. We were all very tense, and none of us could predict exactly what the reactions would be. A fiasco or a breakthrough was equally possible. Our seminar was being allowed three times the usual period allotted for a symposium, and we were given a rather large room because we didn't know how many people would attend. There were countless seminars being given during the week-long convention, and usually each meeting could boast about thirty to forty people in attendance. We were amazed when over three hundred anthropologists showed up at our early morning seminar! We were going to play to a standing-room-only audience. What was even more remarkable was that we were up against stiff "competition" since author Carlos Casteneda (of *Don Juan* fame) was scheduled for another meeting at the same time. A tinge of nervous excitement hung in the air as we began.

The papers Emerson, Wolkowski, and I presented went smoothly enough. Most people seemed interested in what we had to say. But the ordeal wasn't nearly over yet since the important question-answer period was still to come. And it began with a bang with a diatribe offered by Dr. Aghananda Bharati, the head of the anthropology department at Syracuse University. After criticizing another participant's experiences with psychics, he leveled his guns at me and my description of how Aron was able to identify bones in the controlled test sessions.

"I don't believe it," Bharati concluded.

"We are willing to set up any kind of controlled test and have you participate in it, if you're sincere about that," I responded while trying to keep cool.

Dr. Emerson jumped into the fracas and said that George was capable of a very similar feat and had demonstrated his psychic know-how before a team of physical anthropologists. He ended his response with simple but firm words; "These people have to be worked with, seen, experienced, to evaluate them before we can say, 'Sorry, I don't believe it!' "

After the symposium was over, Fran told me that she wanted to get her show together and demonstrate her abilities to Bharati right then and there. But she was afraid she would be counterbalanced by his negativity. Too bad. It would have made an amusing divertissement.

Things calmed down a bit as Emerson and I were asked about the possibility of using psychics to pinpoint likely excavation sites on maps instead of having them visit the actual locales. This would be similar to the phenomenon of map dowsing, in which a psychic indicates on a map where water can be found instead of traversing the area with a dowsing rod. Emerson responded by telling the audience how the day before we watched Fran in my room move her hand over an aerial photograph, "very accurately indicating what was what." Emerson went on to report how he used psychics to dowse maps and as a result located no less than thirty-two sites on the Montreal River. His results had chagrined those who had just spent five years surveying the area unsuccessfully. He said they credited him with a perfect batting average. I added some information about some informal map dowsing I once ran with Aron.

Belated critiques came from Dr. Kenneth Kensinger of Bennington College and Dr. Roger Wescott of Drew University. Kensinger was critical of the amount of "blind faith" Emerson and I were placing in our psychics and in our research, but on the other hand Dr. Wescott said, "Intuitive archaeology is a welcome if overdue addition to our armamentarian of prehistoric research." He envisions a flood of new excavations resulting from our use of psychics. Some of his words deserve quoting:

". . . if psychics can locate more buried artifacts in less time than can more orthodox theorists by more rational methods so much the better for them, and so much the worse for their counterproductive detractors. . . . Should scholars then deliberately deprive themselves of an exhumatory bonanza merely because they cannot yet explain the means by which they obtain it?"

The meeting went on and on and we finally had to vacate the room because people waiting for the next symposium were pounding on the door.

It was only during the months following the convention that we really began to see the impact our presentations had. I received a steady stream of requests for reprints of my paper from anthropologists who were not able to attend the meeting. There was even a request from a Notre Dame theology professor. Numerous requests came from graduate students. Now that we had broken the academic ice, term papers on psychic archaeology seemed to be the new fad in anthropology courses across the country.

In the early spring of 1975, several months after the conference, the stack of presentations on psychic archaeology nearly tripled at the annual Canadian Archaeology Conference. Instead of three papers offered, there were eight. I was happy to see that Dr. Emerson's propaganda for the cause was effective. He was made chairman for the seminar. The presentations had such titles as "Psychometrics and Settlement Patterns: Field Tests on Two Iroquois Sites, Woodridge, Ontario"; "Iroquois Long House Dowsing"; "Site Psychometry in the Parry Sound District, Ontario"; and "Archaeological Map Dowsing, a Beginning."

It seemed that Canadian archaeologists were drifting down from their ivory towers to personally investigate the application of psychic techniques to their work. For example, Dr. William Ross, a government archaeologist, used map dowsing to locate undiscovered ancient Indian sites in the Canadian wilds without even having to leave the comforts of his home. He reported a 75 percent success rate and said that he has saved thousands of dollars by eliminating fruitless searching. His method consisted of suspending an ancient flint arrowhead over a map of an unexplored site area and being guided by it. Dr. Ross warned his audience that he was not an occultist and explained that normal dowsing might be explained as the sensitivity of the subject to a type of electromagnetic field given off by buried objects or water. Map dowsing calls for a different explanation, and he feels that the subconscious mind of the dowser might "intuitively be telling the pendulum when to gyrate in a circle over a site."

In a telephone conversation, Dr. Ross told me that he taught another Canadian archaeologist, Dr. William Noble of McMasters University, how to map dowse. Dr. Ross said that Dr. Noble reported that he used his new skill with great success on a recent archaeological exploration trip to the Arctic.

Not only does conventional archaeology now have to contend with this body of data, concerning archaeological map dowsing, but today it is also being struck by an avalanche of reports by other investigators engaged in other fascinating disciplines of psychic archaeology. The idea that Emerson and I were pioneers in psychic archaeology was being quickly replaced by the thought that we were just catching onto it!

Chapter 8

Psychic Archaeology From the Soviet Union to Tennessee

> It is fairly easy to take isolated bits and pieces of the phenomena of life and sweep them under the rug year after year but they start to accumulate and the bumps get enormous . . . you can't ignore them anymore.
>
> —*Stanley Krippner*, in *Psychology Today*

Psychic archaeology can be approached from many different directions. While I have relied mainly on just one psychic for guidance, Professor Emerson has been aided by a team of sensitives. Such archaeologists as Dr. William Ross seem to have developed psychic ability themselves. The variants of psychic archaeology are endless. Overtly or covertly, many researchers are using psychic help in their daily activities, and each of them is a pioneer in his own right.

Count Pino Turolla is a South American archaeologist engaged in government-sponsored research in the thin mountain air of Ecuador. His main project is unearthing the remains of hitherto-undiscovered cultures in the Santiago River region. At one site he has uncovered small pieces of jade, a ceremonial platform, and small statues. One of his more unusual discoveries was a group of carvings of what appear to be mastodons, which were supposed to have become extinct in South America over 30,000 years ago. At face value there is nothing out of the ordinary about Turolla's work—except for the fact that he relies on map dowsing and his own psychic impressions to guide him radarlike to his finds!

Count Turolla's intuitive approach to archaeology is not unique, for he is but one enthusiast who has stumbled either accidentally or deliberately onto the roots of psychic archaeology.

J.M. Radford, a professor at Merrimack College in Illinois, has been making use of a group of psychics who call themselves, colorfully enough, the Psychic Rescue Squad. This group, which works out of St. Louis, consists of several psychics who feel that they can use their collective ability for humanitarian and practical purposes, and they have even purportedly aided police officials. When a friend brought the group to Radford's attention, the professor decided to give the squad a try at archaeology. Through an intermediary he gave the psychics a tooth to analyze, which unbeknownst to them had come from one of the many skulls uncovered from a burial site excavated by the Missouri Archaeological Survey project. The dramatic result of the experiment left Radford puzzled as to the source of the detailed information the group had supplied. During a phone conversation, Radford quite openly told me that the group discerned that the tooth had come from a mass burial site, that the site was close to a river, and that the ancient inhabitants cultivated crops and used clamshells as tools. (Radford's research first made headlines in the tabloid press which claimed that the psychic squad had been able to do everything but walk on water. Radford attempted to correct the media claims for, unfortunately, it is just this type of irresponsible fanfare which keeps readers from seriously considering the worthwhile reports which do get media coverage. Indeed, Radford is now very reluctant about allowing further press coverage of his research.)

In England, retired Major-General J. Scott Elliot, is employing dowsing to pinpoint new archaeological sites. Dowsing can be applied to more than just finding water or oil. Elliot, who is a former World War II British brigade commander, has made archaeology a second career. After intensive study of the subject and learning the manner in which orthodox excavations are conducted, he learned how to use the divining rod under the tutelage of a local water dowser. Quite naturally and reasonably, he felt that this psychic art might prove to be effective in his archaeological work. When news of General Elliot's interest in "archaeological dowsing" was eventually coupled with reports of his successes he was swamped with requests from friends, acquaintances and associates to dowse *their* property. If the properties were too distant from his own home, Elliot would ask for a map and, employing proper military efficiencies, of course, simply dowsed the maps with a pendulum. (Elliot's technique is quite similar to the one used by William Ross.) At the present writing, Elliot has a massive backlog of map-dowsing results to field-check and possibly excavate.

Some of the general's psychic pointers have already borne rich fruit. In 1965, while dowsing a plowed field covered with stubble, he discovered a Bronze Age fire pit which dated back to approximately 1,980 B.C. (It does not seem odd that a year later he became president of the British Society of Dowsers!) Discovered along with the pit were a number of artifacts including a stone pounder and stone axes. The account of this dig was reported in the transactions of the *Dumfriesshire & Galloway Natural History and Antiquarian Society*. Although Elliot believes that this complex pit site may have been used for human cremation, he could only conclude that it "as far as can be ascertained to date is not recognizable as a known form."

Another one of Elliot's successes came in 1968. Through map-dowsing, he predicted that a large habitation structure would be unearthed in the garden of a cottage in Swinebrook. Now a garden is not exactly the most likely spot for an excavation—especially at Swinebrook, where there was absolutely no surface evidence to indicate the presence of a buried site. But archaeologists can be stubborn people, and some months later (in 1969) a five-by-ten-foot trial cut was made at the spot Elliot had pinpointed. Digging quickly proved that a structure *did* lie several feet under the garden lawn and continued digging gradually revealed postholes, animal bones, and pottery. More extensive excavation carried out in 1970 uncovered, among other things, floors composed of pieces of sandstone cemented together, a hearth, a line of accurately spaced stake holes, and two highly polished pointed ivory tools dating back to the Bronze Age.

In 1972 Elliot dowsed the garden and orchard of a manor house in Chieveley. His psychic impressions were striking—he not only predicted that the remains of a continuous series of cultures lay under the ground, but in doing so detailed a new site area which had hitherto been totally unknown to archaeologists. Formal excavations in 1973 and 1974 not only indicated the remains of several cultures stacked one atop another all the way back to pre-Roman times, but also unearthed specific structures, ditches, and roads, the locations of which *had been plotted on maps by Elliot before the excavation began*. The structures were discovered almost exactly where Elliot had designated that they would be found.

General Elliot does not guard his psychic secret jealously and has actually been training a few selected students in the art and application of archaeological dowsing. You might recall that in a similar vein Dr. William Ross has taught some of his fellow archaeologists how to dowse.

It is not only in Western Europe that dowsing is becoming a great assistance to science. According to Dr. Alexander I. Pluzhnikov, a docent and candidate of technical sciences (a Soviet equivalent to our Ph.D.), training in dowsing for archaeological use is advancing at a rapid pace in the Soviet Union where it has been renamed the "biophysical method." Pluzhnikov and his colleagues are using it to "search for and describe the contours of subterranean architectural and historical objects, no traces of which show above the surface of the ground." The Soviet scientist has also reported that dowsing was used to pinpoint the outlines of former fortifications, towers, moats, cemeteries, pillars, and buildings below the ground at the Iosif Volokamsky Monastery near Moscow; at the Kruitsky Palace in Moscow; and at the Kremlins in the cities of Serpukhov and Mozhaisk. A study which employed dowsing the old estate of Czar Boris Godunov (1552-1605), who was made famous through Moussorgsky's great opera, helped resolve a major conflict among historians and came up with what Pluzhnikov could only call "startling results."

The dowsing survey which covered the entire estate took only eight hours, compared to the many weeks it would take to make a comparable study using customary archaeological procedures.

The phenomenon of map-dowsing is not mentioned in Pluzhnikov's report and it appears that intensive field techniques are more commonly used in the U.S.S.R. Soviet dowsers are a little more jet-age than the water witches who populate rural America. Soviet archaeological dowsers, Pluzhnikov says, cover an area at about 10 to 30 miles per hour using motor vehicles. When a dowser feels that he has detected a site, a further exploration is made on foot. This may sound a little farfetched at first, but it brings to mind a report on the use of the "biophysical method" for geological exploration which has been made by Professor Alexander Bakirov, a doctor of mineralogy at the Tomsk Polytechnical Institute in Siberia. This report divulges that Soviet dowsers have been flown over unexplored terrain in airplanes or helicopters flying at altitudes of 800-1,000 feet at speeds up to 200 miles per hour. Despite these rather formidable conditions, the dowsers have made interesting discoveries about the macrogeology below. Bakirov has gone so far as to recommend that actual courses on dowsing be introduced into the advanced curriculum at the departments of geology and geophysics at Moscow State University, The Leningrad Mining Institute, and at the Tomsk Polytechnical Institute.

The use of dowsing as an aid in mineral exploration has been taken seriously by the Soviets for some time. In 1967 Dr. A.A. Ogilvy, chairman of the geology department at prestigious Moscow State University, made several endorsements of dowsing and in 1971 the Central Administration of the Scientific-Technical Society for the Instrument and Appliance Industry in Russia sponsored a seminar on the biophysical effect. Attending the meeting were 124 specialists on the earth sciences and related fields from 40 different research institutions. The delegates were told how the use of dowsing permitted a 30 percent reduction in the amount of drilling needed to mine gold deposits in the Northern Caucasus. In Karelia, near Finland, drilling based on dowsing resulted in over 60 percent more indications of rare earth-bearing deposits than in those areas where dowsing had not been used. Similar success was reported from the Asian republic of Kazahkstan, S.S.R. where, "dowsing for various ores permitted the reduction of overall drilling by some 35 to 40 percent and greatly raised its effectiveness."

Even Alfred Wegener—the famed German geologist who formulated the monumental theory of continental drift—was a dowser. A geology professor I know told me how he once watched Wegener dowse a fault from the back of a yak at an International Geological Conference field trip to the Urals (U.S.S.R.).

It is pretty obvious that American archaeology has a lot of catching up to do with the sister-science of geology, and with Soviet researchers who have made magnificant strides in the use, methodology, and potential of dowsing. The benefits that can be derived may give rise to even greater advantages for mankind than the space race.

"Oh, ancient peoples now slumbering . . . guide my shovel to the truth and beauties in the old fields . . . that I might bear witness to your life and be your voice from the past."

This is the chant of a thirty-year-old Tennessee artist, Kenneth Pennington, as he searches for buried Indian artifacts in the Chattanooga countryside. Pennington, who is of Cherokee descent, is yet another amateur psychic who is directing his talents toward psychic archaeology. Before each artifact hunt he offers this prayer song, and once in the field he finds himself overcome by an overwhelming urge which indicates to him just where to dig to find his treasures. The psychic once admitted, "Once within minutes after singing my prayer, I uncovered the rims of eight beautiful pottery vessels." Pennington's other finds include ornaments, shells, tobacco pipes, bones, stone tools, and weapons.

"At first my associates laughed at my chanting and prayer," Pennington rather candidly admitted, "but I began to have better and better luck. Then they asked me to sing it over areas where they wanted to dig and sure enough their luck improved too." The first vice-president of the Tennessee Archaeological Society, E. Raymond Evans, stated publicly, "While many people might doubt the value of Pennington's ritual, his excellent results speak for themselves."

I first heard about Pennington when I read a rather sensational story about him in one of the tabloid papers. Since I wasn't satisfied with the report I phoned the psychic to get a firsthand account of his work. Although he admitted that the story had been "puffed up" a bit, he asserted that the basic features were correct. He went on to tell me how much he really loved digging and how he did have "the ability to locate things." He assured me that he was absolutely sincere in his belief that he could locate anything if he set his mind to it. Pennington also believes that the fruits of his digs are his rewards for his sincerity, and he hopes eventually to build a museum to depict the way southern Indians "truly" lived.

The most unusual thing about Pennington's success is the number of "rare" Indian objects he finds, objects which no orthodox archaeologists have ever seen before. One skull the psychic found dated back several thousand years and had peculiar diamond-shaped markings on the brow. No one has been able to explain the meaning of these baffling marks. If Pennington was just "lucky" at finding artifacts in the Chattanooga countryside, why does he have such a penchant for discovering unusual one-of-a-kind objects? It appears more likely to me that his finds represent some sort of psychic radar or guidance at work.

Unlike some psychic archaeologists, though, Pennington's recent career has a grievous twist to it. His plight illustrates that even in our "enlightened culture," society still isn't ready to confront claims of the paranormal. He has stopped digging. Although he once could be found nearly any weekend with shovel in hand, Pennington told me that the whole affair had gotten to be too much trouble. After being featured in a story which appeared in the *National Enquirer*, he received a lot of crank criticisms and ridicule about his offbeat prayer routine, and was even threatened by archaeologists for violating antiquity laws too successfully. He told me painfully that he didn't understand what he does or how his prayer works, just that he loved digging and missed his weekend hobby. He would, he admitted, take up the work again when society was a little more liberal.

Pennington's whole story is disturbing. Is society today still strait jacketed by the biases and preconceptions of nineteenth-century materialism? Instead of hassling Pennington, one might have thought that archaeologists would have extended a helping hand.

At the Stanford Research Institute in Menlo Park, California, two physicists, Russell Targ and Dr. Harold Puthoff, are investigating an ability which they feel is widespread among psychics and non-selected subjects alike that is proving useful to archaeology. What they have termed "remote viewing" is the ability of a subject to describe or give information about locations or target sites which they cannot physically see. These targets may be as close as the next room or several hundred miles away. In the good old days of psychical research, this phenomenon was called "traveling clairvoyance," and Targ and Puthoff have discovered that this psi ability, which they first detected while working with gifted psychics, was also inherent in a great many volunteer subjects they evaluated. Their initial research was published in the rigorously conservative and prestigious British science publication, *Nature*.

One of their first subjects was the late Pat Price, a former Burbank, California, police official who participated in a series of nine tests. The protocol for the experiments was usually as follows: the experimenters were closeted with Price at the SRI buildings in Menlo Park. An assistant would be given a location in the San Francisco Bay area from another person not otherwise associated with the research and which was determined by random means. Any location from a potential of hundreds could be chosen and each was clearly different from any other. All were within a thirty-minute drive from SRI. After the target was chosen, the assistant and his team drove to the location without communicating with either Price or the experimenters. Alloting the team ample time to reach their destination, the experimenters then asked Price to "remote view" the site and describe it in as much detail as possible. The descriptions were tape-recorded for future reference, and transcripts were then given to five other SRI scientists who had not otherwise been associated with the research for independent evaluation. These judges visited the nine locations involved in the tests and tried to match which transcript described which site. Price's descriptions were so clear that the panel correctly matched six of the nine transcripts to the proper locales, a percentage astronomically beyond chance.

In one typical experiment, the target area was an arts and crafts garden plaza. Around the perimeter of the site were craft shops, gardens, flowers, ceramic pots, fountains, and pathways. Overhead were vines and redwood arbors. Price's psychic viewing of this target went in part: I'm looking at something that looks like an arbor . . . I can see some grass. Looks like a fountain . . . a little outdoor park . . . Basically I'm getting a very strong feeling of flowers . . . and iris . . . some decorative walls . . . a garden pond . . . a little bridge . . . small buildings . . . they're painted white . . . a mild recreational area . . ."

In four of the trials Price was placed in a double-walled copper-screened Faraday cage which blocks out electromagnetic radiation, so the basis of Price's success was not some form of physical energy. Distance from the target didn't seem to be a factor either. Price's descriptions were often clear and accurate, and read as though he were actually viewing the locale with his physical eyes. (In fact, he even sketched remarkably clear and accurate diagrams of the sites.) Price felt that some element of his mind detached from his body and physically visited the targets. The minor inaccuracies of his descriptions did not misguide the judges at all. Commenting on these exploratory tests at the Parapsychology Foundation's 23rd International Conference on Quantum Physics and Parapsychology (August 1974), Targ and Puthoff stated that, "We are convinced that certain people can obtain accurate information from remote locations without being there bodily."

Encouraged by the results of the Price experiments, Targ and Puthoff replicated the remote viewing tests with two new subjects they had found while screening some 147 volunteer subjects. These were a Mr. D.E., a scientist at SRI, and Mrs. H.H., a Los Angeles photographer. The new series of tests were similar in design to those done with Price, but a new twist was added. The subjects were instructed to try to describe the *activities* of the experimental assistants who traveled to the target locations as well as the locale itself. For one trial the chosen target was a train station. At approximately 11:22 A.M., Mr. D.E. said he felt that one of the assistants at the target location was touching a smooth rectangular metal surface, and at 11:25 said that he no longer saw the assistant at all. The timing and descriptions were consistent with the actual activities of the assistants. At 11:22 one of the researchers at the site had been guiding his hand over a large metal train route map, and at exactly 11:25 both assistants left the station. In another test Mrs. H.H. was able to state correctly that the target was in far-off Central America and that the assistant was in a beach chair by a pool.

What has all of this to do with psychic archaeology? The answer to this query will become clearer when we look back over the remote viewing work and the role New York psychic, Ingo Swann, played in the development of the procedure, which began as a method of psychic geographical probing.

During their first forays into the world of the paranormal, Targ and Puthoff worked with New York artist Ingo Swann, who first opened the physicists' eyes to the potential of remote viewing. Ingo is a personality almost too dynamic and robust for staid physicists. Tall and hearty, almost stout, he makes no bones about his psychic talents. He is rather like his paintings: colorful, robust, bold, but also philosophical. Instead of using the scientifically neutral term "remote viewing,'' Ingo claims that he travels out-of-the-body to gain his information: a talent, he says, he taught himself.

At Swann's suggestion, Targ and Puthoff designed a test to verify his claim that he could travel and perceive remote locations if he were merely given the geographic latitude and longitude coordinate for a given area. For one test Ingo was given the points of 15° N. latitude and 120° E. longitude. Ingo relaxed, sent a portion of his mind out from his body, perceived the locale and reported: ''Land with jungles and mountains, mountains which resembled some sort of peninsula-type mountains.''

The target coordinates designated the west coast of the Zembalies Mountains, a peninsula formation in the Philippines. Swann's success was pretty spectacular. Nonetheless, some of his errors were just as spectacular! Coordinates designating the middle of Texas produced the response of ''ocean,'' and a set of points in the middle of the Indian Ocean produced the response, ''mountains.'' But Ingo's successes far outnumbered his failures. It also must be admitted that the researchers themselves precipitated a fair share of buffoonery. Swann reports in his autobiographical book, *To Kiss Earth Good-Bye*, that one experiment almost turned into a fiasco when the investigators were shaky about the location of the target. It all started as Swann was relaying his psychic viewing of a target locale:

''. . . I actually have a sensation of moving through space over a body of water and landing on what seems to be land. I'd say this coordinate refers to a piece of land to the east of a large body of water.''

''No, that would not be correct since the coordinate we actually gave you is in the middle of Lake Victoria,'' interrupted one of the experimenters.

''Goddamn it, I don't believe it. Where the hell is a good map,'' the piqued psychic responded.

After a map was found and consulted, everyone (except Ingo, we may assume) was amazed to discover that the exact coordinates given referred to a peninsula jutting out into Lake Victoria east of Ukerewe Island just as Ingo had seen.

This incident seems to be of more importance than a mere humorous anecdote. It brings home the fact that as archaeologists begin to test psychics they must either be quite sure of the correct answers to their queries, or have some way, such as excavation, of obtaining the correct answers. It is also interesting to note that Swann's remote viewing is similar to the process Aron used during my Flagstaff dig.

Ingo first demonstrated his ability to see concealed targets during controlled experiments conducted by the American Society for Psychical Research (ASPR). In these experiments he was able to describe and draw representations of targets placed on a shelf above him and hidden from his view. In one trial he accurately drew a sketch of a heart with a dagger placed across it. He even discerned the correct colors. In order to monitor his brainwaves, the ASPR researchers connected electrodes to Ingo's scalp so an electroencephlagram (EEG) could be taken. When Ingo reported that he had induced an out-of-the-body state and was psychically looking at the suspended targets, the EEG showed a 19 percent decrease of mean electrical amplitude in the right hemisphere of his brain, and a 16 percent decrease in the left hemisphere.

Targ and Puthoff conducted similar tests with Ingo and were repeatedly astounded by his success.

Often, though, it was the experimenters who fouled things up. For one experiment Ingo was supposed to "look" through an aperture at a target placed in a box suspended from the ceiling. He couldn't see anything. He kept trying to determine why everything looked so extraordinarily black, so the psychic "floated" right into the box itself.

"The goddamn light is out over the target," he shouted angrily to the experimenters.

The investigators were dumbfounded and also skeptical. Ingo stuck to his guns and turned out to be right. Indeed, when the apparatus was dismantled, the box-light *was* out. In another instance Ingo was told that he had flunked a trial since there was no printing in the box-apparatus as he described. Ingo bristled saying that he clearly saw printing. When the box was taken down and inspected, printing was found inside just as he had described. It seems that the person who constructed the target had inadvertently left some print bare inside the box.

These incidents illustrate the many pitfalls that can ruin a psychic's ability to aid the archaeologist. If these simple tests could be so confused by experimenter error, just think how hard it would be for a psychic to help an archaeologist find a buried site. During the SRI and ASPR tests, the targets were spatially remote from the psychic. In psychic archaeology, the target is remote in both space and time, which means double jeopardy. We might even ask: when a psychic in the United States gives accurate information about an ancient site in Egypt, are the same mechanisms involved as when he gives information about a target in the next room?

Targ and Puthoff are now extending their research into areas which may directly contribute to psychic archaeology. They hope to develop techniques to enhance the remote-viewing ability to help subjects discern targets remote in time. (They have already been successful with remote-viewing of precognitive targets.) The SRI research demonstrates that many psychics have the remote-viewing ability and this may be the perfect approach to psychic archaeology. Just as Aron and George can give details about distant points involving targets hidden under the ground, the techniques developed by Swann, Targ, and Puthoff may eventually enable us to screen and discover more psychic helpers.

I had the opportunity to meet Ingo Swann at the Association for Research and Enlightenment's Professional Conference on Parapsychology, held in the spring of 1975, where we both had been invited to speak. Ingo had no qualms about the fact that he was frustrated and fed up with the traditional types of parapsychological experiments in which he had participated. The errors on the part of the researchers, their paranoia in removing every opportunity for him to cheat, and the abstract aspect of many of the experiments thoroughly annoyed him. He said that he had enough of these "mini-phenomena" tests. Now he wanted to try his hand at "maxi-phenomena," something big on the order of what Aron and George have done and which would be immediately useful. Over the next few days we discussed archaeology as the ideal laboratory for pure parapsychological testing and a good place to develop and demonstrate what Ingo has called "maxi-phenomena." Mother Earth and the ravages of time provide a better shield for a hidden target than any lead-lined room. Beneath the ground at a new excavation site are potential targets hidden from subject and experimenter alike and just waiting to be dug up. How does one cheat when giving the exact positioning of buried artifacts where enormous boulders back their discovery? Ingo said he was ready, willing, and able to try his hand at archaeological work. He was not tied to SRI, he grumbled, and would participate in my next project.

By coincidence, at that very time, another division at SRI

was beginning to get interested in psychic archaeology and had already made preliminary plans to use Aron in some of their research projects which included a probe of the Great Pyramid of Giza in Egypt. Someday soon the cloak of secrecy will be lifted from this project.

By the spring of 1975, it seemed as if everybody was about to hop aboard the psychic archaeology bandwagon. Besides SRI's new projects, Ingo's interest in my own work, the seminar on psychic archaeology at the Canadian Archaeological Association meeting, and papers on the subject at the ARE Converence, I soon discovered that Dr. Carlos Treviño, the general director of the Mexican Parapsychological Society, was about to join our ranks. The society's research director was an anthropologist by training and the group was planning some archaeological experiments for the near future. Another Mexican archaeologist, Dr. Jorge Angullo, had invited me to return to Mexico with some psychic helpers. Also that spring the California Museum of Science and Industry, the second largest museum in the United States, opened Psi-Search, an elaborate exhibition on parapsychology, which included a special display on the use of psychics by archaeologists. The Smithsonian now sponsors this display.

Not only was psychic archaeology taking hold at museums and anthropological societies, but even our conservative and dignified universities and colleges were being won over to this new and exciting discipline. One young student pioneer was Constance Cameron, who was working in the Anthropology Museum at California State University, Fullerton. Miss Cameron was also a graduate student in archaeology and had just received clearance to do her M.A. thesis on a parapsychologically oriented archaeology project. The first phase of her project would involve testing ten psychics using artifacts for psychometric readings. The second phase would involve retrocognition readings (ESP impressions of past events) of archaeological sites.

Another first came that summer when Walden University (Naples, Florida) awarded a Ph.D. to Maxine Asher for a thesis on psychic archaeology entitled "Recent Theories of Intuitive Perception Applied to Ancient Anthropological Inquiry." In it she discussed the Great Age of archaeological discovery around the turn of the century and how it was characterized by reliance on intuition and myth. She noted the role intuition played in the great work and discoveries of

Heinrich Schliemann's at Troy and Mycenae; Arthur Evans on the isle of Crete and the discovery of Knossus; J.J. Winkleman at Pompeii; and Henry Layard's discovery of Nimrud in Assyria.

The tenuous and fleeting encounters of these men with the real substance and potential of psychic archaeology reminded me of the work of Hans Holzer and Joan Grant. In his book, *Windows to the Past*, Holzer recounts some intriguing tales about the past that he has collected from several self-styled psychics. In an entire series of books, Joan Grant relates stories about past incarnations she said she had in ancient civilizations: stories which contain a number of potential insights upon which archaeologists can draw. The success of these writers is proof that people are really yearning to know about their past. Psychic archaeology may gradually fulfill a spiritual and psychological need as well as a scientific one.

Early in the summer of 1975 I went to Dallas to lecture on archaeology and psychic archaeology at the Fourth International Festival of Yoga and Esoteric Sciences. This may sound like a rather offbeat get-together, and I'm afraid that from a scientific standpoint the festival left much to be desired. I had complained to the organizers that people who frequent this type of convention are usually willing to believe anything and that perhaps a more educational and meaningful project could be included on the agenda. The next thing I knew, I was put on the spot and asked to organize just such an exhibition for the festival. I figured that no matter how well I detailed the abilities of certain psychics to give useful archaeological information and no matter how extraordinary I said this was, my efforts would still seem pale against the wild claims of the many self-avowed psychic wizards who frequent such affairs. So I chose an audience participation project. I set up two simple tests at the festival where anyone who wanted to volunteer could try his hand at psychometrizing some artifacts. They could also try to locate artifacts buried in a roped-off test plot on the lawn of the hotel hosting the gathering. By participating, people would see how unique and difficult such work is. I could also directly challenge all the "superpsychics" to prove how great they really were. In other words, it was "put up or shut up."

In order to help us out, the mayor pro-tem of Dallas, George Allen, came to select and bury the artifacts which the volunteers would try to find. After they tried their hand at psychic dowsing, I would have to check with Mayor Allen to find out which of the nine partitioned squares in the test plot had the buried artifacts, and exactly which artifacts were buried in which segment.

Sixty people tried the test. I might add that the superpsychics were in conspicious absence. Instead, they stood on the sidelines telling everyone else how to do it! The volunteers who tried to discover where the artifacts were buried used a wide range of techniques from meditation to dowsing. No psychic stars appeared on the Dallas horizon, and the overall results were just as one might expect from pure and simple guessing. Two people showed some promise in the psychometry tests though. Both seemed to be clearly picking up fragments of the ancient history of the objects. But questions remained: Could these people, with practice and training, learn to follow the psychic threads they had latched onto and get back to the full body of information psychically impressed on the artifacts? Would they be successful with other artifacts as well?

The simple experiments in Dallas pointed out to me just how precious are the truly gifted people who can give accurate and detailed information. Reviewing the successful research that is presently going on around the world (in the United States, Canada, England, and in the U.S.S.R.), I wondered what new developments the future for psychic archaeology holds.

Chapter 9

Put Your Shovel Where Your Mouth Is!

I find no fault with those who do not take an interest in this subject or with those who are skeptical regarding it, but (I do find fault) with the fact that the present attitude towards it in the scientific world is *not* scientific. It (this attitude) is a standing refutation of the claim that science is interested in truth and only truth without regard to its source or the implications involved in the acceptance of it.

——Dr. John R. Swanton, former president of the American Anthropological Association, in a letter sent in 1952 to all listed anthropologists regarding parapsychology

If you don't believe in the potential of psychic archaeology, or if you harbor any doubts or reservations about the cases presented throughout this book—then I *challenge* you to meet me on the field! Leave your brass knuckles at home; they won't be needed in this duel. Instead, bring along a shovel. It's not a field of battle, but a field of discovery. I challenge you to put your shovel where your mouth is.

We'll go out and dig to see whose views our new discoveries will support—those of conventional archaeology or the revelations about the past offered through psychic archaeology. We could start by following up Bligh Bond's work at Glastonbury. The predicted positions and details of the monks' kitchen and the Loretto Chapel can still be checked out today. Unless, that is, you are too afraid to discover that men can communicate with the dead. Or we could trek to Poland along with a group of psychics and have them psychometrize the same artifacts Ossowiecki used to peek into the world of Paleolithic man. Quite possibly our psychics would confirm the insights made thirty years ago by the Polish seer.

Now, if you were really daring and not too afraid of having your beliefs about man's prehistory shattered, we could take our shovels and trowels and pack off to Egypt and Iran. There we might find the secrets of Atlantis, hidden chambers, lost records, and energy crystals. Can we be so blind as to ignore Cayce's leads? Leads offered by an entranced psychic who had no training in archaeology, but whose readings were startlingly accurate? Dr. Norman Emerson, the Canadian archaeologist, just journeyed to Egypt and Iran with his psychic superstar, George McMullen, in hopes of checking Cayce's information on the Sphinx, the Great Pyramid, and the "City of the Hills and Plains" in Persia (Iran). During this survey trip one of Iran's leading archaeologists, Dr. A. O. Negehban, was quickly won over to psychic archaeology and new excavations are being called for.

But even if a few archaeologists do have the guts to stick by our psychic informants, is conventional archaeology ready to allocate a small portion of money to psychic archaeology? It would only need be a trifling amount out of the large sums they unquestionably hand out to "more of the same" archaeological research . . . research that is not leading us toward any practical goal.

This is the challenge of psychic archaeology today.

The challenge is not merely an academic one, but also a personal one. Besides my Flagstaff project, I shall soon be out in the sun-baked deserts and mountains of the Southwest searching with the aid of several psychics for remnants of that ancient absurdity, the hairy mammoth. Would any of you like to come along for a little hard work, discovery, and revelation?

However, even beyond Flagstaff I can offer two more test cases which may ultimately prove the value of psychic archaeology:

The first test takes us to Chaco Canyon in New Mexico, one of the best site areas housing prehistoric artifacts in the Southwest. However, despite the abundance of prehistoric ruins which have been uncovered there, archaeologists have been frustrated by their inability to resolve several enigmas about the people who inhabited the site. During the first millennium, A.D., this twenty-mile-long canyon was a thriving center of Pueblo Indians, complete with roads and complex water control systems. Within the canyon were apparently thirteen towns and several hundred villages. The towns were characterized by primitive apartment-house-type dwellings constructed up to five stories high and built to a formal plan containing as many as 800 rooms. Even urban renewal was practiced. Experts estimate that at times a population of over 15,000 people lived at Chaco. Strangely, despite this very dense population, the primary burial sites have never been found! Dr. Gwinn Vivian, the head of the Arizona State Museum, had to admit, "Several extensive searches for town cemeteries have been made. None has been successful." Archaeologists have abandoned attempts to locate the burial areas of this primitive metropolis, yet we know that Pueblo Indians did not practice cremation. So where could the burial areas be?

In January 1972 I asked Aron for his ideas about these missing Chaco burial grounds. In the course of his psychic reading, he said that these Indians had originally come from Mexico and he gave their religious philosophies concerning death and burial. In his discourse *two specific locations* were mentioned where burials could be found.

One location lies between the Pueblo Bonito and Chettro Kettle town sites. Aron predicted that human skeletal material could be found in this area directly opposite and approximately forty feet from the petroglyphic markings on the north canyon wall. He added that this was once both a ceremonial and trading area and that artifactual remnants of these activities could also be found there. The other site is in the area of the present arroyo directly opposite the Pueblo Bonito site. One hundred feet to the east of the bridge that crosses the arroyo is a small north-trending side arroyo which comes off the north margin of the main one. On the east wall of this lateral arroyo, close to where it intersects the main one, Aron predicted human bones and implements could be found five to ten feet beneath the surface. Time will tell us how accurate he has been.

The second new test case is at the Olmec site of San Lorenzo in Mexico. The Olmec was Mexico's first full-fledged civilization. As I said in a previous chapter, this is the culture that Dr. Betty Meggers of the Smithsonian feels is directly related to the Shang dynasty of China. But the exact origins of the Olmec are still shrouded in mystery. As Dr. Muriel Weaver of Hunter College stated, "The Olmec have left us a heritage of puzzles." The site of San Lorenzo represents the oldest of the known Olmec sites. Huge stones were hauled over long distances to this site from which unprecedented carvings were rendered. The Olmec had a distinctive art style characterized by figures with snarling mouths, clefts in the middle of the head, flaming eyebrows, smashed noses, claws instead of hands, and thickened lips. Over sixty large stone sculptures have been found at this site. These consist mainly of colossal heads with Negroid features and which weigh five to ten tons each.

In the center of the San Lorenzo site lies a large mound 3,750 feet long and over 150 feet high. According to a reading given by Aron, deep within this mound rests the key to many Olmec mysteries. Aron believes there are artifacts and mummylike human burials just waiting to be found there. Even more remarkably, he says that instead of finding evidence which would set the origin date of the Olmec at 1,500 to 2,300 B.C., as is currently believed, new evidence will push back that date as far as 30,000 B.C. You see, Aron believes that San Lorenzo was one of the several outposts of the Mother Civilizations that he feels existed long before the Near Eastern area cultures developed (the so-called "cradle of civilization" from which we allegedly evolved). So at San Lorenzo we should expect to encounter evidence to support an entirely different version of man's prehistoric development.

The challenge has been made! You can either accept it or reject it. The choice is yours. But before concluding this book I would like to offer some thoughts about the future of psychic archaeology. These may sound like science-fiction fantasies, but then, science fiction does have an uncanny habit of coming true.

Could we see the production of a neurological version of H.G.Wells's mechanical Time Machine? Let's toy with the idea. We know that electrical impulses are produced by the functioning of the human brain. When the mind's eye pictures mental images, electrical vibrations are produced. The relationship between these electrical impulses and imagery has been demonstrated by recent research in which blind people have been able to "see" crude geometric shapes via electrical stimulation of their brains. Then imagine a device that could convert the electrical vibrations of these images into actual physical projections, images which could be seen by the human eye via the conversion of electrical vibrations into vibrations with wavelengths in the visual spectrum. When someone mentally pictures an apple, this image could be projected into an actual physical image which others could observe. Thus, when someone is thinking about scenes of—or traveling back to—Atlantis, the imagery going through his mind could be directly observed by others. Possibly a device such as a ruby laser could be used to make this energy conversion. Once such images were obtained, they could possibly be projected holographically. Holography, a rather recent technological development, is a lensless photographic technique that uses laser light to produce three-dimensional images.

If we could develop such a device, we would have the ultimate archaeological tool. As a psychic holds a prehistoric artifact in his hand, the ancient scenes brought to mind by the contact could be observed by countless others. The problem of our having to rely on the psychic's interpretation of what he sees would be eliminated, and archaeologists could make their own observations as they walked around the three-dimensional scenes being projected into the room. It would be as though the archaeologists were actually there walking among the ancient villages.

Admittedly, if such a technological breakthrough could be made, it will be many years from now. What can *you* do in the meantime?

The quickest way to confront the world of psychic archaeology is to get your own feet wet. It is a physiological fact that we all dream, and most of us produce other forms of mental imagery. Much research has and is being done to show that psychic influences contaminate a small percentage of our dreams. At Maimonides Medical Center in Brooklyn, several successful projects have been conducted which prove that a sleeping subject can dream about a picture being looked at by another person a few rooms away. So our dreams may be a window to the past. And what about déjà-vu, the feeling that you have seen or done something before? Many experts believe that déjà-vu is caused by the fleeting memory of a precognitive dream. You dream about seeing something or doing something but forget it, and when the event actually occurs all that is left is a vague memory of having been in the same situation before. For example, once I dreamt about going to a restaurant and eating a turkey sandwich accompanied by a tall dark girl. Well, several days later my wife's cousin visited, a tall dark girl, and indeed we went out to eat at a delicatessen. As I bit into my turkey sandwich I knew I had done all this before. A quick check back to the notebook where I record my dreams confirmed it. Could we not then go back in time in our dreams as well?

Each of us has a potential for psychic archaeology within the recesses of our minds.

Meditation can also be used as a personal springboard for traveling back in time. Many workers and visitors to our Flagstaff site began having dreams or had meditation images about what took place there in the past. An Air Force colonel, for example, who visited the site on several occasions dreamt about a reddish stone tool. The next day we found just such a tool in the same spot designated by the dream.

Another way in which to become personally involved in psychic archaeology is by joining both a local parapsychology group and an amateur archeological association. Within this milieu, you could very well come into direct contact with people who have more developed psychic ability. They could be tested by psychometry with ancient artifacts and possibly you may even progress to the point where you want to try a trial excavation.

But the greatest personal involvement in psychic archaeology will come when we recognize a different concept of reality. A new age in which every one of us takes the psychic world into account when we mold our philosophies of life, an age when we shall begin to develop spiritually. At that time the work of psychic archaeology will be made that much easier. Out-of-the-body travel, contact with the dead, reincarnation, a universal memory, the Akashic Records—these are all concepts which add nobility to man's heritage. The message behind these concepts reveals a different kind of evolution for mankind—the evolution of an ethic. Beyond biological and intellectual evolution, our psychic potentials herald a spiritual and ethical development in man. Man will develop morally as well as physically. Because all of our past acts have been recorded, nothing has been lost, and all is available for us to reflect upon and learn from.

These concepts indicate that there is some aspect of man that goes beyond flesh and bone. It would seem that while this psi-component or soullike aspect of man usually resides in the body, it can also leave it temporarily during physical life, and may carry on after physical death. The only barriers to human behavior and capability are those imposed by our own minds. In Einstein's world of relativity and the realm of quantum theory, the physical limits of time and space are thrown open. The data we have collected from psychic archaeology, as well as from parapsychology in general, illustrates that the mind is not subject to space-time limitations either. The mind has the capability to obtain any piece of information from the past or future, from any age or from any location. It makes little difference *where* the information comes from, whether it be through out-of-the-body travel or from spirits of the dead. Detailing the particular mechanism involved is not crucial at this stage. Patterns will eventually emerge in our data which will ultimately point the way to an explanation.

What *is* crucial is that we realize that our behavior and potentials are set by the theories we harbor about our own nature, theories which for so long have been accepted unquestioningly as fact. If we hold inaccurate or limited concepts about human behavior and potentials—concepts which ignore entire realms of human experience and psychic phenomena—we directly limit man's capabilities.

Even though two recent nationwide polls showed that over 50 percent of the American public believes in psychic phenomena, Congress has found little money to support research in this general field, let alone in so specialized an area as psychic archaeology.

Decades ago we drilled for oil only in areas where that commodity literally seeped from the ground. Then came seismography and geophysics and we were able to "see into" the ground. A whole new age of oil discovery was ushered in. Today we are still excavating archaeological sites where artifacts, like oil, seep from the ground. Psychic archaeology heralds a whole new age of discovery. It provokes man to take an even closer look at himself—and everything around him.

Bibliography

Chapter 1: Dead Monks Speak—
Bligh Bond and His Quest at Glastonbury

Adams, Robert McC. "Archaeological Research Strategies: Past and Present." *Science*. 160; 1187-92, June 14, 1968.

Ashe, Geoffrey. *King Arthur's Avalon—The Story of Glastonbury London*; Fontana Books, 1957.

Bond, Frederick Bligh. *The Gates of Remembrance*. Oxford; B.H. Blackwell, 1918.

Hogarth, A.C. "Common Sense in Archaeology." *Antiquity*, VXLVI: pp. 301-04, December 1972.

Jung, Carl G. *Man and His Symbols*. Garden City; Doubleday, 1964.

Kenawell, William W. *The Quest at Glastonbury*. New York; Garrett Publications, 1965.

Kuhn, Thomas S. *The Structure of Scientific Revolutions* 2d edition: Chicago; University of Chicago Press, 1970.

Morwood, M.J. "Analogy and the Acceptance of Theory in Archaeology," *American Antiquity*, 40; 111-16, January 1975.

Williams, Mary (editor). *Glastonbury-A study in Patterns*. London; Helois Book Service, 1970.

——. *Britain—A Study in Patterns*. London; Helois Book Service, 1970.

Chapter 2: The Polish Wizard

Bayard, Don T. "Scientific Theory and Reality in the New Archaeology." *American Antiquity*. 34: 376-82, 1969.

Birdsell, J.B. *Human Evolution*. Chicago; Rand-McNally, 1972.

Bordes, François. *The Old Stone Age*. New York; McGraw-Hill, 1968.

Borzmowski, Andrzej. "Experiments with Ossowiecki," *International Journal of Parapsychology*. 7; 259-80, Summer 1965.

——. "Parapsychology in Poland: A Historical Survey." *International Journal of Parapsychology*. 4; 59-74, Autumn 1962.

Clark, Glen. *The Man Who Talks With the Flowers*. St. Paul, Minnesota: Macalister Park Publishing, 1939.

Coon, Carlton S. *The Origin of Races*. New York; Alfred Knopf, 1969.

Eisenberg, Leon. "The Human Nature of Man." *Science*. 176; 123-28, April 14, 1972.

Flannery, Kent V. "Archaeology With a Capital S" in Redman, Charles L. (ed.). *Research and Theory in Current Archaeology*. New York: John Wiley & Son, 1973.

Fritz, and Plog. "The Nature of Archaeological Explanation." *American Antiquity*. 35; 405-12, 1972.

Hemple, Carl G. *Philosophy of Natural Science*. Englewood Cliffs: Prentice-Hall, 1966.

Johnson, LeRoy. "Problems in Avant-Garde Archaeology." *American Anthropologist*. 74; 366-77, June 1972.

Jung, Carl G. *Man and His Symbols*. Garden City, New York; Doubleday, 1964.

Kuhn, Thomas S. *The Structure of Scientific Revolutions*. 2d edition. Chicago; University of Chicago Press, 1970.

McGimsey, C.R. Letter to members of the Society for American Archaeology Subject: The Exploration of New Directions for the Society and the Profession of Archaeology, July 15, 1974.

Moorwood, M.J. "Analogy and the Acceptance of Theory in Archaeology." *American Antiquity*. 40; p. 111-16, January 1975.

Ossowiecki, Stephan. Unpublished manuscript on Archaeological Experiments in Possession of Ossoweicki's stepson M. Swida, 1939.

Reed, Charles A. "Animal Domestication in the Prehistoric Near East." *Science*. 130; 1629-39, 1959.

Tart, Charles T. "States of Consciousness and State Specific

Sciences." *Science*. 176; 1203-10, June 16, 1972.
Wolkowski, William. "Archaeological Model Testing: Parapsychological Experiments with Stefan Ossowiecki 1939-1941." Paper at 73rd Meeting of American Anthropological Association in Mexico City, 1974.

Chapter 3: Edgar Cayce

Anonymous. *Earth Changes*. Virginia Beach: ARE Press, 1959.
Beck, Pluma O. "The Search." *ARE Journal*. 9: 167-73, July 1974.
Benson, E. (editor). *Dumbarton Oaks Conference on the Olmec*. Trustees of Harvard University, Washington, D.C.; Dumbarton Oaks, 1968.
Berlitz, Charles. *The Mystery of Atlantis*. New York; Grosset & Dunlap, 1969.
Breasted, James H. *A History of Egypt*. New York; Charles Scribner Sons, 1909.
Bro, Harmon. Doctoral Thesis on Edgar Cayce, University of Chicago, 1954.
Budge, E.A. Wallis. *The Egyptian Book of the Dead*. New York; Dover Publications, 1967.
Carlson, Vada F. *The Great Migration*. Virginia Beach; ARE Press, 1970.
Cayce, Edgar Evans. *Edgar Cayce on Atlantis*. New York: Paperback Library, 1968.
—— and Cayce, Hugh Lynn. *The Outer Limits of Edgar Cayce's Power*. New York: Harper and Row, 1971.
Church, W.H. "The Chronicles of Issa." in the ARE Journal. V. 5, No. 6, 1970.
Coon, Carleton S. *The Origin of Races*. New York; Alfred Knopf, 1969.
——. *The Living Races of Man*. New York; Alfred Knopf, 1960.
Crichton, J.M. "A Multivariate Discriminant Analysis of Egyptian and African Negro Crania." Senior Honor Thesis Harvard University, Cambridge, Mass.: 1964.
Donnelly, Ignatius. *Atlantis—The Antediluvian World*. Edited by Edgarton Sykes, New York; Harper and Row, 1949.

Drucker, Philip. "La Venta, Tabasco: A Study of Olmec Ceramics and Art." Bulletin 153, *Smithsonian Bureau of American Ethnology*. Washington, D.C.; 1952.

——; Heizer, Robert and Squier, Robert. "Excavations at La Venta, Tabasco—1955." Bulletin 170, *Smithsonian Bureau of American Ethnology*. Washington, D.C., 1959.

Ferdon, Edwin N. "Mexican Southwest Parallels." *Monographs of American School of Research*, N. 21, Santa Fe, New Mexico, 1955.

Ford. J.A. (ed.) *A Comparison of Formative Cultures in the American: Diffusion of Psychic Unity of Mankind*. Smithsonian Institution Contributions to Anthropology. VII 1969.

Furst, Jeffrey. *Edgar Cayce's Story of Jesus*. New York; Coward-McCann, Geoghegan 1960.

Genoves, Santiago T. "Some Problems in the Physical Anthropological Study of the Peopling of America." *Current Anthropology*. V. 8, No. 4: 297-312, October 1967.

Hanson, Marjorie. "Preliminary Report on Possible Egyptological References that Might Tie in with Edgar Cayce" Unpublished data, 1961.

Hatt, C. *The Maya*. Virginia Beach; ARE Press, 1972.

de Heinzelin, J. and Paepe, R. "The Geologic History of the Nile Valley in Sudanese Nubia." *Southern Methodist University, Contributions to the Prehistory of Nubia*, Dallas, 1964.

Heyerdahl, Thor. *American Indians in the Pacific: The Theory Behind the Kon-Tiki Expedition*. London; George Allen & Unwin, 1952.

Kelley, David H. "Calendar Animals and Deities." *Southwest Journal of Anthropology*. 16: p. 317-37, Spring 1960.

——. "Culture Diffusion in Asia and America" in H.A. Moran and D.H. Kelley (eds.). *The Alphabet and the Ancient Calendar Signs*. Palo Alto; Daily Press, 1969.

Kitter, Glen D. *Edgar Cayce on the Dead Sea Scrolls*. New York; Paperback Library, 1970.

Lehner, Mark. *The Egyptian Heritage*. Virginia Beach: ARE Press, 1974.

Marshack, Alexander. *The Roots of Civilization*. New York; McGraw-Hill, 1972.

Meggers, Betty J. "The Transpacific Origin of Mesoamerican Civilization: A Preliminary Review of the Evidence and Its Theoretical Implications." *American Anthropologist*. 77; 1-28, March 1975.

——; Evans, C. and Estrada, E. "Early Formative Period of Coastal Ecuador: The Valdivia and Machalilla Phases" Smithsonian Contributions to Anthropology, I, Washington, D.C., 1965.

Mercer, Samuel. *The Pyramid Texts: In Translation and Commentary*. 2 vols. New York; Longmans and Green Co., 1952.

Newman, Marshal T. "Geographic and Micrographic Races." *Current Anthropology*. 4; 189-207, Spring 1963.

Norbu, Thubten J. and Turnbull, Colin M. *Tibet*. New York; Simon & Schuster, 1968.

Said, P. and Issawi, B. "Preliminary Results of a Geological Expedition to Lower Nubia and to Kurkin and Dungal Oases, Egypt." *Southern Methodist University Contributions to the Prehistory of Nubia*. Dallas, Texas, 1964.

Satterwaite, Linton. "Evolution of a Maya Temple." *Bulletin—University Museum*. Vol. 7 No. 4; 3-14, Fall 1939.

——. Personal communication, 1976.

Stecchini, Livio Catullo. "Notes on the Relation of Ancient Measure to the Great Pyramid" in Peter Tompkins. *Secrets of the Great Pyramid*. New York; Harper & Row, 1971.

Sugrue, Thomas. *There Is a River*, New York; Holt, Rinehart & Winston, 1942.

Weaver, Muriel Porter. *The Aztecs, Maya and Their Predecessors—Archaeology of Mesoamerica*. New York; Seminar Press, 1972.

Wiley, Gordon R. *An Introduction to American Archaeology. Vol. 1; North and South America*. Englewood Cliffs; Prentice-Hall, 1966.

Chapter 4: Flagstaff—The Discovery of the Earliest Evidence of Man in North America (Round 1)

Bordé, François. *The Old Stone Age*. New York; McGraw-Hill, 1968.

Bryson, Reid A. and Wendland, Wayne M. "Radiocarbon Isochrones of the Retreat of the Laurentide Ice Sheet." *Technical Report #35, Dept. of Meteorology*, Madison, Wisconsin; 1967.

Coon, Carleton S. *The Origin of Races*. New York; Alfred Knopf, 1969.

Fryxel, R.; Malde, H.E. and McIntyre, V. Paper presented to Geological Society of America. Dallas Meeting, November 1973.

Genoves, Santiago T. "Some Problems in the Physical Anthropological Study of the Peopling of America." *Current Anthropology*. 8; 297-312, October 1967.

Greenman, E.F. "The Upper Paleolithic and the New World." *Current Anthropology*. 4: 41-91, February 1963.

Haynes, C. Vance. "The Calico Site: Artifacts or Geofacts." *Science* 181; 305-10, July 27, 1973.

Kreiger, Alex D. "Early Man in the New World" in Jennings, J.D. and Norbeck, E. (eds.). *Prehistoric Man in the New World*. Chicago; University of Chicago Press, 1964.

Kuhn, Thomas S. *The Structure of Scientific Revolution. 2d edition*. Chicago; University of Chicago Press, 1970.

Leakey, L.S.B.; Simpson, R.D. and Clements, T. "Archeological Excavations at the Calico Mountains, California: A Preliminary Report." *Science*. 143; 10-22, February 1968.

Mangelsdorf, Paul C.; MacNeish, Richard S. and Galiant, Walton C. "Domestication of Corn." *Science* 143; 538-45, February 7, 1964.

Newman, M.T. "Geographic and Microgeographic Races." *Current Anthropology*. 4: 189-207, Spring 1963.

Pewe, Troy L. and Updike, Randall G. "Guidebook to the Geology of the San Francisco Peaks, Arizona." *Plateau*, The Quarterly of the Museum of Northern Arizona, Vol. 43, No. 2, Fall 1970.

Protsch, Reiner, and Berger, Rainer. "Earliest Radiocarbon Dates for Domesticated Animals." *Science*. 179; 235-39, January 19, 1973.

Robinson, H.H. *The San Francisco Volcanic Field, Arizona*. U.S. Geological Survey Professional Paper 76, 1913.

Waters, Frank. *Book of the Hopi*. New York; Viking Press, 1963.

Chapter 5: The Return to Flagstaff (Round 2)

Ascher, Robert. "Recognizing the Emergence of Man—Specific Courses of Action are Necessary for Utilizing the Early Traces of Man." in *Science*. 147; 243-50, January 15, 1965.

Barnes, Alfred S. "The Differences Between Natural and Human Flaking on Prehistoric Flint Instruments." *American Anthropologist*. 41; pp. 99-112, Spring 1939.

Bordé, François. *The Old Stone Age*. New York; McGraw-Hill, 1968.

Klein, R.G. *Man and Culture in the Late Pleistocene: A Case Study* (Kostieki & Borshew Sites). Scranton, Pennsylvania; Chandler Publishing, 1969.

Mangelsdorf, Paul C.; MacNeish, Richard S., and Galiant, Walton C. "Domestication of Corn." *Science*. 143; 538-45, February 7, 1964.

MacNeish, Richard S. "Early Man in the Andes." *Scientific American*. 224; 36-46, April 1971.

Protsch, Reiner and Berger, Rainer. "Earliest Radiocarbon Dates for Domesticated Animals." *Science*. 179; 235-39, January 19, 1973.

Chapter 6: On Using Psychics in Archaeological Research

Stewart, Kilton. "Dream Theory in Malaya" in C.T. Tart, *Altered States of Consciousness*. New York; Anchor Books, 1969.

Swann, Ingo. *To Kiss Earth Good-bye*. New York; Hawthorn, 1975.

Tart, Charles T. "Studies of Learning Theory Application 1964-1974." *Parapsychology Review*. Vol. 6 No. 5. New York; Parapsychology Foundation. 1975.

——. *The Application of Learning Theory to ESP Performance*. Parapsychological Monograph #15. New York; Parapsychology Foundation, 1976.

Chapter 7: Psychic Archaeology from Canada to Mexico

Emerson, J.N. "Archaeology and Parapsychology." November tape of lecture given to Florida Society for Psychical Research, St. Petersburg, Florida, April 1975.

——. "Intuitive Archaeology: A Developing Approach." Paper presented at 73rd Annual Meeting of American Anthropological Association Meeting, Mexico City, November 1974.

——. "Intuitive Archaeology: A Psychic Approach." New Horizons. 1; 14-18, January 1974.

——. "Intuitive Archaeology: A Psychic Approach." *The Midden*, Publication of the Archaeological Society of British Columbia, Vol. 5 No. 3, June 1973.

——. "Intuitive Archaeology: The Argellite Carving." *The Midden*, Publication of the Archaeological Society of British Columbia, Vol. 6 No. 2, April 1973.

James, William. "Final Impressions of a Psychic Researcher." in *Memories and Studies*. New York; Scholarly Reprints, 1971 (reprint).

Long, Joseph. Discussion at Rhine-Swanton Symposium at 73rd Annual Meeting of American Anthropological Association, Mexico City, Mexico, November 1974.

Reid, C.S. Interview with Michael Adler, 1974.

Ross, William. "Archaeological Map Dowsing, A Beginning." Paper presented at the Annual Canadian Archaeological Association Meeting, Thunder Bay, Canada, March 1975.

——. Personal Communication, 1976.

Van de Castle, Robert. "Overview: Parapsychology and Anthropology." Delivered at 73rd Annual Meeting of American Anthropological Association, Mexico City, Mexico, November 1974.

Wescott, Roger. "Para-anthropology: A Nativity Celebration and a Communion Commentary." 73rd Annual

Meeting of the American Anthropological Association, Mexico City, Mexico, November 1974.

Chapter 8: Psychic Archaeology from the Soviet Union to Tennessee

Asher, Maxine. "Theories of Intuitive Perception Applied to Ancient Anthropological Inquiry." Unpublished doctoral dissertation. Walden University, Naples, Florida, 1975.

Bakirov, A.G. "The Geological Possibilities of the Biophysical Method." *American Dowser*. 14; 110-12, August 1974.

Bird, Christopher. "Finding It by Dowsing." *Psychic Magazine*, 6; 23-25, September 1975.

——. "Dowsing in the U.S.S.R." *American Dowser*. 1; 110-20, August 1972.

Brackman, A. *The Dream of Troy*. New York; Mason & Lipscomb, 1974.

Casslin, E.B. "Man Who Digs Up Rare Indian Relics Claim Spirits Guide Him in His Search." *National Enquirer*, April 15, 1973.

Ceram, W.E. *Gods, Graves and Scholars*. New York; Alfred Knopf, 1952.

Chance, P. " Parapsychology as an Idea Whose Time Has Come." *Psychology Today*. October 1973.

Grant, Joan. *Far Memory*. New York; Avon Books, 1969.

——. *Eyes of Horus*. New York; Avon Books, 1969.

——. *Scarlet Feather*. New York; Avon Books, 1969.

Holzer, Hans. *Window to the Past*. New York; Doubleday, 1969.

Mitchell, Janet. "Out of the Body Vision." *Psychic Magazine*. 4; 44-47, April 1973.

McDonald, D. "Psychics Give Accurate Description of Primitive Man." *National Enquirer*, December 10, 1975.

Ostrander, Sheila and Schroeder, Lynn. *Psychic Discoveries Behind the Iron Curtain*. Englewood Cliffs, Prentice-Hall, 1970.

Panati, Charles. "Quantam Physics and Parapsychology."

Parapsychology Review. 5; 1-5. November-December 1974.

Pennington, Kenneth. Personal communication; 1976.

Pluzhnikov, A.I. "Possibilities for and Results of the Use of the Biophysical Method in Researching and Restoring Historical and Architectural Monuments." *American Dowser*. 4; 116-18, August 1974.

Radford, James. Personal communication; 1976.

Scott, E.J. "An Early Bronze Age Fire Pit at Townfoot Farm, by Gleneagle." in the *Transactions of the Dumfrieshire and Galloway Natural History and Antiquarian Society*. 3d series, Vol. XLIL; 23-30, 1972.

Swann, Ingo. *To Kiss Earth Good-Bye*. New York; Hawthorn, 1975.

Targ, Russel, and Puthoff, Harold. "Remote Viewing of Natural Targets." *Parapsychology Review*. 6; 1-4, January 1975.

——. News Release. Stanford Research Institute, October 1974.

Turolla, Pino. "Psychic Guidance in Archaeology" taped lecture at PSI International—Florida Society for Psychical Research, Akita Enterprises, 11136 Dwarfs Circle, Dallas, 1975.

Chapter 9: Put Your Shovel Where Your Mouth Is!

Benson, E. (ed.). *Dumbarton Oaks Conference on the Olmec-* Trustees of Harvard University, Washington D.C.—Dumbarton Oaks, 1968.

Coe, Michael D. *America's First Civilization: Discovering the Olmec*, New York; American Heritage, 1968.

Eisenberg, Leon "The Human Nature of Man." *Science*. 176; 123-28, April 14, 1972.

Emerson, J.N. "Intuitive Archaeology: Egypt and Iran." *ARE Journal*. 11; 55-65, March 1976.

—— *ARE News*. VII: 1, January 1976.

Swanton, John R. Letter sent to Listed Anthropologists at that time. Dr. Joseph Long, University of New Hampshire, Plymouth, 1952.

Ullman, Montague; Krippner, Stanley and Vaughan, Alan. *Dream Telepathy* New York; Macmillan, 1973.
Vivian, Gwinn. "An Inquiry into Prehistoric Social Organization in Chaco Canyon, New Mexico." W. Longacre, (ed.). *Reconstructing Prehistoric Pueblo Societies*. Albuquerque; University of New Mexico Press, 1970.
Willey, G. *An Introduction to American Archaeology. Vol. 1; North and South America*. Englewood Cliffs, Prentice-Hall, 1966.

Index